THE DARK SIDE OF THE SKY

THE DARK SIDE OF THE SKY

The Story of a Young Jewish Airman in Nazi Germany

by

Harry Levy

LEO COOPER
LONDON

First published in Great Britain in 1996
by
LEO COOPER
190 Shaftesbury Avenue, London WC2H 8JL
an imprint of
Pen & Sword Books Ltd,
47 Church Street,
Barnsley, South Yorkshire S70 2AS

A CIP record for this book is available from the British Library

ISBN 0 85052 4989

Printed in Great Britain by Redwood Books, Trowbridge, Wilts

In memory of the crew of "S" for Sugar
shot down over Belgium in the early hours
of the 1st August 1942

Sergeant Bill Hall (R.A.F.V.R) Pilot
Sergeant Wilf Clarke (R.C.A.F.V.R) Observer
Sergeant Al Martin (R.C.A.F.V.R) Front-gunner
Sergeant George Miller (R.A.F.V.R) Rear-gunner

CONTENTS

ACKNOWLEDGEMENTS

I should like to thank my wife Joan for her unstinting encouragement and her criticial appraisal of the book, and Tom Hartman for his excellent "winnowing of the chaff" for which I forgive him.

H.L.

AUTHOR'S NOTE

For the elderly seventy-year old that I have now become, the writing of this book has been a voyage into a familiar, yet at the same time, alien world, a glimpse into the heart and mind of myself as a young man.

The book, which began as a re-telling of those long-past events, became for me a voyage of discovery. As the story advanced I found myself more and more drawn to examine the thoughts, hopes, despair and the foolish naïveté of the young man who had plunged so eagerly into a promised world of adventure and heroism.

I felt the need to portray the quirks and characteristics of those with whom I had shared those eventful years, of those who had risked their lives to help me, and those who had in some other way become part of my life.

Although unable after so great a lapse of time to repeat conversations verbatim, I have attempted to bring back to life the individuals, the situations, and the conversations which ensued.

It has been my intention to tell the story of those years with concern for the truth and with as great a literary skill as I can muster. It is my belief that those who shared similar experiences will vouch for the reality and veracity of what I have had to say.

To avoid giving offence I have changed the names of the characters involved.

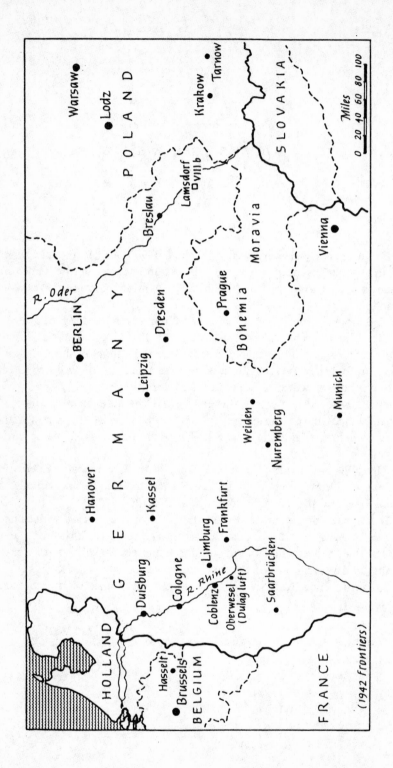

1

OPERATION DUISBURG

Friday, 31 July, 1942: Aircraft of R.A.F. Bomber Command attacked targets in the Ruhr. Duisburg attacked on three subsequent occasions

Tuesday, 4 August, 1942: Belgium: The first trainload of Jews is deported to Auschwitz.

I looked despondently around the large low-ceilinged room. Yet, all those weeks ago, when I first arrived at Honington, I had found the place exciting enough.

My eye had not then been offended by the plastic-covered tables littered with empty beer glasses. I noticed neither the greasy aprons of the middle-aged women serving behind the long counter nor was I bothered by the smoke-filled atmosphere, the clatter of crockery, or the strident chatter.

Squadron life was exciting and even this shabby building a place of enchantment, offering satisfactions I had never hoped to find in the working-class streets where I had been born.

There I had chafed at the drab reality of my everyday world, a prisoner as it were in a waiting-room full of locked doors.

On my eighteenth birthday, at the very earliest moment, I had volunteered as air-crew, hoping to be a pilot, but finally given the less glamorous role of wireless-operator/air-gunner, doubtless, and with reason, thought more suitable to my modest academic achievements. I suffered impatiently the long weeks and months of training, still waiting for that magic door to open.

At last I arrived at the squadron from the operational training unit where I had met and trained with my crew, sergeant's stripes and air-crew wing still shamefully, sparklingly new. Concealing eagerness behind an assumed nonchalance, intended to match the mien of the more experienced crews, I darkened my stripes and badge by running a lead pencil over their offending brightness.

Those early days on the squadron matched my expectations. Fear and excitement were there in equal measure. I enjoyed the hero's uniform, the routine of test flights low over the surrounding countryside and the dramatic briefings in the crew-filled room before a "trip".

However, the atmosphere of neatly ordered administration huts with flower-beds bordered by whitewashed stones hid a grimmer reality. The squadron kept from youngsters like myself the deadly nature of the game we were playing. Death and disfigurement were manifested not by screams, blood or horror, but by absence.

Death was discreet. When a crew failed to return, the station warrant-officer went quickly into action, removing all traces of personal property. Nothing was left to remind surviving crews of the loss suffered.

Those who failed to return had, in the laconic jargon of the day, "bought it". For the most part individuals hadn't time to become familiar figures, and their brief presence on the squadron quickly faded from memory.

For me, time, lived from moment to moment, day by day, seemed to stretch to infinity. Life was a bizarre mixture of naked peril and the banal. Nights were spent perched in a cage of metal struts covered with thin canvas, high over enemy territory, desperately hoping to avoid sudden death, and afternoons holding a girl-friend's hand in the back seat of a cinema.

I savoured those early raids as if they were amorous conquests. I would recite the list to myself boastfully, gleefully, as some of my friends would boast of the girls they claimed to have slept with.

I would mull over the list of names, a litany of towns and places: Emden, Dieppe, Borkum, Bremen. At first I remembered each flight in detail, then gradually images became confused and one raid would merge in my mind with another.

The raids, however, went on and on, two or three a week during that hot dry summer. My mind became tired and confused from loss of sleep, and the raids became more and more hazardous. We were now being frequently hit by flak, once belly-landing on returning, once overshooting and ending up in a potato field.

The last few weeks there had been no let up. Conditions had been perfect, moon full, not much cloud; bombing weather: Monday: Wilhemshaven; Tuesday: Duisburg; Thursday: Duisburg again; Sunday: Hamburg; Tuesday: Hamburg again.

I felt depressed. Fortunately we were now due to go on leave. On our return we were to go to Waddington to re-train on Lancasters. Then we were to return to help with the conversion of the squadron to the big four-engined bombers.

George and I were in the NAAFI waiting for the station bus, shoes polished, leave-passes and travel warrants tucked safely in the pockets of our best tunics.

I was bending down to pick up my haversack when Bill, our pilot, came through the swing-doors. I guessed something was wrong. He was not the most convivial of men and not likely to be joining us for a chat.

He made straight for our table. He didn't bother to sit down. Leave had been cancelled. We were on the battle-order for that night.

Friday, 31 July, 1942

The jeep took us out to the moonlit dispersal point where "S" for Sugar waited on its tarmac circle. We threw the parachutes from the jeep on to the grass and clambered down, heavy and clumsy in our flying kit.

Bill, and Wilf, the bomb-aimer/observer, climbed the ladder into the hatchway between the two engines to begin the pre-flight check. Al, the Canadian front-gunner, George and I, squatted on our haunches like miners, preferring to wait outside the plane in the cool night, delaying going aboard until the last possible moment.

"S" for Sugar climbed slowly upwards through the thousand-foot bank of clouds. Droplets of water, patterned by the slip-stream, sped over the engine nacelles, across the windscreen and down the curved surfaces of the gun-turrets. Ice was forming on the prop-shafts and ailerons.

Bill's voice came over the intercom: "Coast coming up."

I finished taking down the readings from the direction-finding loop, switched off the receiver and reached for my thermos.

Stowing the flask, I took off one of my leather outer gloves and reached with finger and thumb for the last remaining barley-sugar wedged under the transmitter. I folded the code-lists of stations and placed them in the log-book-housing between the pressed-steel cabinet of the receiver and the new Marconi transmitter.

Unplugging the intercom, I put on my glove and passed the loop-bearings to Wilf. He looked at the figures, nodded his head and raised his thumb in thanks.

I pushed against the table-top and levered myself upwards to a standing position. I felt the familiar sense of nausea as I stood balancing on my feet, adapting to the shifting motion of the plane. I bent down slowly and lifted my parachute by a strap, and, standing up straight, edged sideways past Wilf's position towards the astrodome and the oxygen bottles.

The cylinders were housed on a rack close to the roof of the plane. This was a chore I disliked, needing as it did all my strength to turn the wheel of each cylinder and open the valves. The effort, added to the movement of the plane, invariably increased my feeling of sickness.

Clambering slowly over the main spur, I stowed the parachute at my feet, checked the fastenings of the armour-plated door and took up my position amidships in the astrodome.

Beneath lay the thin curved silver band marking the Belgian coast. Soon we would be approaching the German frontier, the Ruhr, and our target, Duisburg.

We were carrying one of the new four-thousand-pound bombs, shaped like an elongated oil-drum; too big to allow the bomb-doors to be fully closed. Despite the load, Bill slowly urged the plane higher and higher, trying to reach bombing height.

As we neared Duisburg there wasn't the usual display of flak. The darkness of the target area was marked only by searchlights. In the distance the black shapes of fighters were, from time to time, momentarily silhouetted against the horizon.

This was our third trip to Duisburg. Little was said over the intercom. Occasionally Bill would confirm a compass heading. The atmosphere inside the plane was tense.

As we drew closer, I moved from the astrodome to my new position, kneeling at the flare-chute. My only view now was the small circle of sky seen through the bottom of the long metal tube.

On our first trip to Duisburg we'd been hit by flak. I'd been kneeling in exactly the same position by the side of the flare-chute. The floor of the plane heaved up with the force of a near-by exploding shell. A piece of glowing shrapnel pierced the wooden cat-walk, hitting wooden ammunition boxes used for the fixed scare-guns positioned either side of the plane.

Instinctively dodging down behind the flare-chute, I had struck my head. Momentary hopes of pretty nurses, invalid leave and a hero's welcome were soon dissipated. It was just a little bump.

Normally in my position at the flare-chute I would see, as if looking through a telescope, the coloured stars of bursting flak, and the heavier trace from anti-aircraft guns. Tonight there was nothing but the shafts of searchlight beams, crossing and recrossing in the net of light.

The run-up had begun. We were no longer free to weave from side to side to shake off German guns or fighters. We had begun the approach to the target. We waited in the darkened plane, jolted from time to time by flak exploding beneath us. With each lurch of the plane we waited for the words that would release us from this suicidal path; me, crouching at the flare-chute; George and Al, the gunners, alone, isolated in their turrets.

We waited for the words, the reprieve. We could then veer away from the line held and measured by Wilf's voice.

Stretched out flat on the floor of the plane he peered through his bomb-sight. His nasal Canadian drawl intoned, "Left, Left ... Right ... Steady!" keeping us tight on the line.

Then at last, the words, "Bombs gone!"

I pulled hard on the toggle-switch. The flare dropped away, bursting at its pre-selected height, the cameras automatically recording. The plane, released from its heavy load, soared up and banked to port as Bill pushed over the stick.

As we turned on to the first leg home the sky remained ominously empty of tracer and flak. The searchlights continued their careful play against the blackness of the night.

There was nothing now to bar our passage home, only the threat of those white fingers of light groping across the sky.

Once back in place in the astrodome, I pressed my body gratefully against the armour-plated shield. Bill's calm voice checked the crew and as they answered I could hear the relief and release from tension in their voices. I too, felt my own mood lighten as we banked away from the dangers of the target area.

Gradually Duisburg and the searchlights fell far behind us. Here in the astrodome I was an extra pair of eyes. From my position I searched the dark violet shadows. There are areas where vision is limited for both myself and the rear gunner. The greatest danger, however, the greatest threat, lies on the dark side of the sky, opposite the moon.

I needed to concentrate and not let my mind wander. I scanned the sky, first one side, then the other.

Suddenly a curve of luminous white tracer between tail and main plane! I yelled into the microphone, "Jerry! Jerry!"

Bill's voice, calm, steady. "Where?"

The gunners and I searched the shadows. We could see nothing. Where was the German? He must have attacked from beneath the starboard quarter, banking sharply away beneath us. We could see no sign of him.

As time passed, still with no sign or further attack, tension eased. Bill checked for injuries to the plane or to the crew and asked Wilf for a new heading. The plane veered on to its old course heading towards the North Sea and safety.

There was complete silence over the intercom as all our senses were directed towards the threatening danger. Then on the port quarter two white flickering points of light. The German was firing too early, well out of range. I, now prepared for and expecting attack, reported more calmly this time.

"Jerry ... port quarter ... two o'clock ... closing!" I tried to calculate the range, allowing the German to come in a bit closer, then yelled sharply, "Go!"

Bill threw the plane into a rolling, diving turn to port and George managed a short burst of his guns as the German shot past his turret.

We were again off course, had lost height and were now down to seven thousand feet.

It was clear that the Germans had us on their radar screens and were directing the fighters. Yet the coast couldn't be far now. Once we reached the sea, I comforted myself, we could drop down low, skimming the waves, safe at least from attack from below.

We again veered on to course and flew for some time without incident. Far above us to port I could see four gold rings floating in the air, the engines of one of our own bombers, probably a Lancaster flying a course parallel to our own.

The thought passed through my head that the crew would be eating sandwiches and sipping their coffee in debriefing whilst 'S' for Sugar was still droning homeward over the North Sea. I turned my head to starboard.

Almost in what seemed touching distance were the twin tail-fins of a Messerschmitt 110, the swastika clearly visible. I yelled into the microphone, "Jerry! Jerry! Starboard! Go! Go"

Bill's voice over the intercom was irritated, tired. "Don't be a bloody fool, it's one of ours!"

In a brief second, an eternity, I waited for the bullets to tear through the plane. No time for argument. No time.

As if in a dream I heard the German's guns, like the slow tapping of a typewriter. I felt a sharp blow on my chest and a pain in my left thigh, as if the flesh had been pinched.

When I became once more conscious of my surroundings the throbbing of the engines had stopped. There was a strange dream-like silence. I was slumped against the armour-plated shielding. At my feet oil was gushing from the pipes that ran the length of the fuselage.

I switched on the microphone: "Bill! Wilf!"

There was no answer. I thought that perhaps the microphone was dead; perhaps the cable was cut.

Slowly I unplugged my oxygen mask and pulled out the jack from the

6

microphone socket. I clambered over the main spar and held on to the oxygen-bottle rack. The plane was flying straight and level. I edged along to Wilf's position.

I stood looking down at him, at his dead profile, his pale face cradled sideways on the desk, eyes closed.

I moved forward to my own position behind the pilot. Bill was slumped over the controls, held by the straps of his harness. Through the port window behind him I could see the burning engine, a solid block of red and orange flame.

The extent of what had happened was now clear. We had reached the end. I was alone. The plane could explode at any moment. I had to jump.

My parachute was back in the astrodome where I had placed it at my feet. Inside my head there was a voice telling me what to do, making decisions, cool, clear, unaffected by fear.

I edged past the dead body of the navigator. The light from the burning engine cast flickering shadows within the darkened interior. I climbed once more over the main-spar and in the darkness felt for my parachute.

I clipped it onto the hooks of my harness and turned on hands and knees to crawl along the catwalk towards the rear of the gently swaying plane.

I couldn't move. The microphone lead trailing from my helmet was trapped in a pipe or girder. The tanks could explode at any moment!

I jerked my head back trying to free myself from whatever was holding me. I took hold of the lead and pulled with all my strength but couldn't break free.

With difficulty, mastering a mounting sense of panic, I stopped tugging at the lead and unfastening the straps of my helmet, wrenched it off.

In the tail-end of a plane there is little room to walk upright. I crawled on all fours along the narrow wooden catwalk, past the scare-guns, to the diamond-shaped escape hatch, a flimsy partition in the floor of the plane, located near the rear-turret. Holding on to both sides of the fuselage, I kicked out the panel.

I sat on the edge of the hole my feet dangling in the void. I looked forward along the fuselage towards the front of the plane lit by the flickering light from the burning engine.

The plane was still flying straight and level with only a slight oscillation from side to side. Bill must have had it on automatic pilot before the last attack, or had, perhaps, slipped it into automatic as he was hit.

I had only had one practice jump, and that was from the inside of a hangar. A long queue of air-crew trainees waited their turn to climb the ladders to the tiny platform high up in the roof of the hangar. I fastened a hook attached to a rope to my harness. Looking down below at the tiny figures on the stone floor of the hangar, I felt a tight ball of fear in my stomach, but with a long line of men behind me, there was no question of turning back. I stepped off the edge of the platform.

But this was for real. My fear now was far from being concerned with jumping, but with the possibility that the plane might explode before I could get clear. I took one last look along the flame-lit interior, saw George's turret swinging without control from side to side with the motion of the plane and slipped off the edge.

I caught a fleeting glimpse of the black shape of the fuselage slipping past. I counted slowly, one second, two seconds, three seconds. Then I felt a violent tug on my shoulders. I considered quite calmly that I might be about to die and hoped that it might not be long-drawn-out. I wondered, too, how long it would take to reach the ground. It seemed important. The plane had been at about seven thousand feet after the second attack. Why was it taking so long?

I could now hear the yelping and barking of dogs beneath me. Then, without warning, I landed, my knees forced suddenly and painfully into my stomach. I lay without movement, my face against the wet soil. As my head cleared I sat up carefully and looked around.

I had landed at the very edge of a cornfield. A distant line of trees was silhouetted against the sky.

I released my harness. The parachute lay spread out on the ground behind me. As I tried to stand, my legs felt weak and my stomach hurt.

2

EVASION

I sat for some time trying to take in the significance of what had happened. I was now completely alone, and in enemy territory. Soon the numbness I had felt in my chest changed to pain. I undid the buttons of my battledress blouse and put my hand on the dark stain on my white aircrew sweater. It felt wet and sticky. I had to get help. Peering into the shadowed darkness of the field, I could see near at hand the dark shape of trees, a line of poplars. There might be a road.

Once more I tried to stand, struggling first to my knees, then conscious of the pain in my right side, got to my feet. Now that I was standing, I could see within the shadows clustered in the far right-hand corner of the field, a denser, darker shadow. It might be a haystack, or perhaps a house. I stumbled step by step over the rough ground. Each step sent a sharp pain through the ache in my side. I had to get to a doctor.

I was, almost certainly, in occupied territory, Belgium or possibly Holland. I might be able to get help. There was no thought of escape in my mind. My one aim was to remain alive; it was this which urged me forward.

As I neared the corner of the field, the dark shadow resolved itself into the shape of a small cottage. My hopes rose. Whoever lived there would help me to find a doctor.

I had now reached a shallow ditch bordering a dusty path. In my present state it presented a problem. Fearing any sudden jolt, I lowered first one foot, then the other, into the ditch, and climbed up on to the path. Once on firm ground it was much easier to walk.

There was no front garden. The house stood a yard or two back from the road, seemingly isolated from any other. There were no lights to be seen. Neither the barking of the dogs nor the sound of machine-gun fire overhead had disturbed the sleep of the inhabitants.

Using my left hand, the one on my uninjured side, I hammered on the door. I waited, listening for a sound or for a light of some kind. There was no sound; no light.

Thinking perhaps, I hadn't knocked loudly enough, I remembered the torch tucked into my flying-boot. It was, surprisingly enough, still in place. I drew it out and hammered again on the door. I waited. There was still no sign of life. They must have heard. Perhaps there was no one living there. They might be afraid to answer at this time of the morning. I leant against the wooden post of the porch and closed my eyes. I was feeling quite dizzy. Then a gleam of light appeared in an upstairs window. After a while I heard movement. A moment later the soft gleam of a lamp shone through the cracks of the shutters shielding the front-room windows.

There was the sound of a bolt being drawn and the rattle of a chain. The door opened a few inches. I could make out the faint pale smudge of a face.

The man's voice was guttural, certainly not French, but could be Dutch or Flemish, or perhaps even German.

I spoke slowly, distinctly, as if addressing someone hard of hearing, "English! I'm English!"

The man opened the door a little wider. He was tall, elderly, with a drooping moustache like the picture of Kitchener in the First World War.

He stood looking at me without speaking, his face expressing neither surprise nor fear. Then, taking my hand in his, he shook it warmly. Without speaking he stepped back into the living room and beckoned me in.

The room was almost bare of furniture, containing only a couple of wooden high-backed chairs and a table on which stood an oil-lamp. There was no covering on the flagstone floor.

He pulled forward a chair and gestured to me to sit down. he stood over me nodding his head and smiling. Then, taking hold of my hand, shook it even more vigorously than before. It hurt. I winced with pain and murmured, not knowing whether he would understand, "Doctor!" I opened my jacket and showed him the blood-stained sweater.

He showed no emotion on seeing the blood, neither surprise, nor even concern, but continued to smile and nod. I again pointed to the blood-stain and repeated,

"Doctor!" and added, "I need a Doctor!"

The old man nodded, seeming to have understood, and leaving me slumped in the chair, slowly climbed the wooden staircase. For the first time I felt reassured. I found it difficult to sit upright, but held on grimly to both sides of the chair. I can't remember seeing him returning, but I gradually became aware, as if in a dream, of the old man marching to and fro in front of me across the kitchen floor, a spiked, decorated Belgian helmet of the 1914/18 war on his head. I realized that he was telling me that he too had been a soldier, stressing the bond between us. At the same time I felt alarmed. Perhaps he was a bit soft in the head. If I didn't get help I could end up dead in the chair with the old man strutting backwards and forwards in front of my corpse. I tried again, pointing to my chest. "Doctor! Doctor!"

He came to a halt, turned towards me, nodded his head gravely several times and sat down. As he sat there opposite me, I felt a little more reassured. He seemed so solid, so certain.

My memory of intervening events is vague as I floated between a conscious and unconscious state, but I remember sitting astride an old upright bicycle and being wheeled along a narrow country track between fields. The bicycle listing to one side, we progressed slowly along the lane. After some time we came to a stop. I thought the old chap was having a rest, but that wasn't so. he had sighted something gleaming white in the early morning light. Still supporting both myself and the cycle, he stopped, picked it up, folded it carefully, and put it in his jacket-pocket.

I recognized it immediately. It was a leaflet dropped by one of our bombers. I myself had dropped many thousands of them. They were designed to counter German propaganda. It occurred to me, with a certain feeling of pique, that the man wasn't really displaying the sense of urgency the occasion warranted.

The house at which we finally arrived was a large modern villa standing in its own grounds. Wrought-iron gates in a high hedge opened on to a wide gravelled carriage-way leading to the front of the house.

Once inside the gates and safely hidden from the road, the old man helped me get off the cycle and motioned me to wait. Leaving me and the cycle behind, he crunched his way up the gravelled drive towards the house.

Leaning my back against a tree, I began to take in for the first time the danger of my position. We had of course thought about and talked of the violent ends that awaited air-crew. George, like many tail-gunners, seemed to delight in descriptions of bits of bodies scraped out of gun turrets, but we rarely spoke of being taken prisoner.

Now I, who had never before set foot on foreign soil, found myself in enemy-occupied territory. The Germans, who in England had been frightening images on cinema newsreels, goose-stepping monsters, were all around me. Moreover, my position was unlike that of other air-crew. They would surely know from looking at me that I was a Jew. I had a large nose and this, for them, would be sufficient evidence.

From the direction of the house came the sound of approaching footsteps. My friend appeared and, with his help, I made my way painfully towards the house. As we drew near a small figure detached itself from the shadowed porch. It was a young girl, slight of build, about fourteen or fifteen. She came forward and, taking hold of my free arm, did her best to help the old man get me into the house.

Inside the large unlit hall I had the impression of polished wooden floors, a wide curved staircase and closed doors. The girl ushered myself and the old man into a long low room lit by a small lamp on a table.

As the three of us stood hesitantly waiting, a far door opened and the girl's mother came into the room. She was small and dark with high cheekbones. Her appearance seemed vaguely exotic, like Tahitian women seen on the cinema screen. She was not young but her hair was black, her figure slight, her movements quick and neat.

She immediately took command. Pushing forward an armchair, she said, "*Mets le ici!*"

Recognizing the sound as French, thanks to my limited study of that language, and knowing we were not in France, I assumed that this was Belgium. My two helpers lowered me into the chair.

The lady, waving the other two aside, leant over me. "You must not worry," she whispered, her English fluent, with little trace of accent. "You are with friends. We are going to look after you."

As I heard the comforting sounds of my own language, I relaxed and closed my eyes. I heard as if through cotton-wool the murmur of her voice as she spoke to her daughter and to my elderly Belgian friend. I asked no questions, content to submit entirely to the administrations of the lady and her daughter.

Some time must have elapsed before I woke from my torpid state. The old man had gone and the lady, helped by her daughter, had managed to take off my battle-dress blouse.

The rest of my clothing, blue air-force shirt and the special underwear designed to protect air-crew from the cold was, in the area near the wound, stiff with blood and difficult to remove.

"We must wait for my husband. He is a doctor, a very clever man. He will know how to help you."

The lady took my hand in hers and asked in whisper, "What is your religion? Are you Church of England?"

Fears I had chosen to ignore stirred and rose to the surface. Why did she want to know my religion?

"I'm Jewish," I murmured. She was about to say something when a door opened.

Her husband, a tall elderly man, white-haired, aristocratic in appearance, elegantly dressed in a silk dressing-gown, entered the room. His wife bent over me and whispered, "This is my husband, Dr Vekeman. He will help you."

Next morning I awoke in a strange room in a strange bed. I looked with interest around the attic with its sloping ceiling, skylight and dormer window. The space around my bed held an accumulation of a family's history: rocking-horse, baby's crib, bundles of magazines tied with string, precarious towers of books, a child's bicycle.

As I tried to sit up, a sharp pain in my chest gripped like a muscle in spasm. I had difficulty, too, in breathing. Gingerly I put my hand to my chest where the bullet had entered and realized that Dr Vekeman had swathed my chest tightly in bandages.

My head on the pillow, eyes closed, tired but relaxed, I felt as if I were recovering from a long illness. I stretched my legs between the cool sheets. Now that I was wounded I still felt as if I were playing a part. A wounded airman! Me! Hiding from the Germans in an attic in Belgium!

There was a good chance now, I mused, of getting back, through France, over the Pyrenees into Spain, and then ... home. They might, I reflected, put me back on 'ops'! This struck a sour note, but, I reassured myself, I'd heard that if you'd been shot down they took you off flying, or sent you to an OTU training new crews, or to some other Command.

There was the sound of footsteps on the stair and a light tap on the door. Madame Vekeman came into the room followed by her daughter Mérèse. The girl was carrying a bowl of some hot liquid. Mme Vekeman took the bowl and a spoon from her and crossed to the bed.

Mérèse, a pet-name, I understood, for Marie-Thérèse, had decided, out of vanity or coquetry, not to wear her glasses. She stood by the door and, from a safe distance, peered myopically towards the bed.

Mme Vekeman, bowl in hand, stood looking down at me. "How are you feeling?" she asked and, before I could reply, continued, "You're looking better. Oh yes! Much, much better!"

"I'm fine," I replied, "a lot better, thanks."

"And your wound?" she asked solicitously.

"It aches a bit. Doesn't really bother me," I said, and added, "But ..."

"But?"

"It's the bandage," I explained, "it seems ... I find it hard to breathe properly."

Mme Vekeman smiled. "Silly boy!" "That is nothing. It is to stop the bleeding, a pad to stop the blood ... a ... what do you say? ... a compress."

Mme Vekeman sat on one side of the bed, bowl in one hand, spoon in the other. "You must have some tisane. It will make you strong."

I felt quite capable of feeding myself and would have preferred to do so, but thought it more polite to do as I was told.

Mérèse was still standing silently by the door, unable to understand the flow of English and too shy to come any closer.

Her mother continued talking as she fed me. "You seem much better now. We thought you might die. There was so much blood. You looked terrible. My husband gave you an injection, for your heart, I think ... to make it stronger. Now you must rest. No more talking."

There was little chance of my talking as the spoon was making regular journeys from the bowl to my mouth. Every time I opened it to speak or breathe the spoon was firmly placed in the gap.

"We'll soon have you strong again and then you'll be leaving for England."

With my hand I stayed the travelling spoon. "England!" I managed to interject.

"Yes, Yes. England! I am making already all the arrangements. A friend is getting in touch with some people. They will phone. They will ask about a puppy I have for sale."

Turning to Mérèse, she said something in French. Mérèse smiled shyly, but said nothing.

"I am telling Mérèse that it is you who is the puppy," Mme Vekeman explained.

"Do you know how long it will be before they come?" I asked.

"You will have to be very patient," Mme Vekeman wagged an admonishing finger. "Very patient! There is much to be done and the journey will need all your strength. You have lost a lot of blood. The journey will be long and tiring." She stood up. "We must leave you now to rest."

Mérèse said something to her mother in French. Mme Vekeman turned to me and said, "Yes, Mérèse is right. There are seven children in the house. Mérèse is the eldest. The others are very young. They must not know you are here. We must be very quiet, very careful."

Surprised, I echoed, "Seven!"

Mme Vekeman smiled, "Yes, my husband is, how shall I say, a very amorous man. I brush my fingers on the back of his neck and, *voilà*, another baby!"

Mme Vekeman continued. "Yes, we must be very careful. Children cannot keep secrets, can they? Still, all the village must know by now that you are here. These village people are terrible, you cannot keep anything from them. They must have found your parachute. We looked for it but it was gone. Dr Vekeman says the women must have taken it. If the Germans had found it we would all have been shot by now."

"But," I asked, "what would they do with a parachute?"

"It's made of silk, isn't it?" she asked.

"Well, yes," I answered.

"There are many things a lady can do with a piece of silk," she explained.

During the next few days visits from Vekeman and her daughter became quite frequent.

Mérèse, making English homework her excuse, would mount the steps to the attic. On the first occasion I heard her footstep on the stair and, after a lengthy pause, a timid knock.

"May I come in please?"

She crossed the room, bearing in her hand a tiny French/English dictionary, which she placed on the bed. Drawing a chair close, the lesson began, interrupted by long pauses whilst Mérèse searched in her dictionary.

"Ow are you today?"

"Very well, thank you very much." I pronounced each word with great care, as Mérèse, gaze concentrated on my moving lips, moved her own silently in concert.

"'Ave you any brozzairs?"

"Yes, I have one brother."

"What eez ees name?"

"His name is Reg." Mérèse attempted the name with some difficulty.

"Rr . . . eg."

"Good!" I said encouragingly.

Holding the dictionary, her hands rested lightly on the counterpane, yet I felt their weight and warmth penetrate the covers.

She looked up and, meeting my eye, turned a delicate pink from her neck to the roots of her hair.

"You're blushing!" I said teasing her.

"Blushing? What eez blushing?" she asked, forehead and nose wrinkling.

"Red. Your face is red . . . rouge."

"No, no, my face eez not . . . red . . . not blushing." She covered her face with both hands. "You are, bad, naughty boy."

I laughed. She took my hand and lightly smacked it. "You are stupeed ... Engleesh boy."

Mme Vekeman also enjoyed a chat. From her I learnt quite a bit about the Vekeman family. Her husband, a middle-aged medical officer in the Belgian Congo, had married her, the daughter of a prosperous planter, after a lifetime in the colonial service and had brought her back to his native Limburg. He wanted to give his children the education necessary for their station in life, and wished to spend his old age in his own country.

Unfortunately the Vekemans had never been accepted in the rural backwater the doctor had chosen for his retirement. Their neighbours, peasants and middle-class families alike, eyed them askance. The signs that this was a mixed marriage was only too apparent in the mother's features and in some of the children's too. They saw what was for them tainted blood and kept their distance.

However, the doctor was shielded from covert animosity by his own self-assurance and his aristocratic contempt for those he considered his social inferiors, an extensive category, according to Mme Vekeman.

His wife, however, ashamed of her mixed ancestry, and wishing above all to be accepted, feared and resented the prejudice and provincial stupidity of her neighbours. My fortuitous arrival gave her the opportunity of showing them that she was at least as patriotic as they, as courageous and as good a Belgian. They could now no longer ignore or look down on her.

She was avid for news of the war and berated me, as a representative of the Allied Forces, for failing to start the Second Front.

"I hate the Boches," she would say as she plumped up the pillows, "but I sometimes think they are right when they say that the English left us to do their fighting for them. It was the same in the First World War. The English looked after themselves, with lots of crocodile tears about 'brave little Belgium'."

I felt constrained by a deep sense of obligation and an uneasy feeling that there was some truth in her accusations. I shrugged my shoulders, but for once sensibly said nothing. Sensibly, because it was in my nature to speak first and think afterwards. However, she reacted to my gesture as if I had put up a full-fledged defence.

"Of course you defend your country," she added. "It is only natural, but it is true. The English are a nation of ... shopkeepers!"

Provoked, I felt forced to reply. "I think I'd sooner have a shopkeeper than a lunatic like Hitler."

Mme Vekeman, surprised by my vehemence, flushed and started

again plumping up the pillows and straightening the covers with even greater energy.

"You don't understand! I love England. Belgians have always loved England. It is the land of democracy, of justice. We all know this. We learn it at school, at our mother's knee. If this were not true, would I be hiding you in my house with all my children here?"

I was annoyed at myself for not having held my tongue. In attacking the English as she had, she had only been voicing her own anxieties and frustrations; her fears too, perhaps. I took hold of her hand and held it for a moment. She responded by bending down and lightly kissing the top of my head.

"I talk too much," she said. "It has always been my weakness. Take no notice of a foolish old woman."

I had now been in hiding in the attic for three days, and, growing stronger, was beginning to chafe at the inactivity. Mme Vekeman, however, insisted I stay in bed, she was afraid I might make a noise and attract the children's attention.

Later that evening, however, she had news. Two men would be coming very soon to collect me. They would have a car. Before leaving the room she turned and added, "I want you to remember to do something for me. I have told you that I listen to the BBC, to the European News. After the News they always give a list of messages in code so that the Boche won't understand. When you get home, you must send me a message through the BBC. You must say, 'The bluebird is out of its cage ... the bluebird is out of its cage'. Then I shall know you are safe at home."

That night I had difficulty in getting to sleep, wondering when the men would come for me and the events that might follow. Would we be going through France to Spain? How would I get home from there? Would I be put on 'ops' again? Did my family know that I had been shot down?

I was suddenly awoken by a light shining in my eyes and Mme Vekeman shaking me and patting my cheek.

"I'm sorry," she said, "but you must hurry."

"What is it? What's wrong?" I asked.

"They are in the village looking for you."

"Who?" I asked. "What?"

"The Boche ... the Boche. Hurry! Hurry!" Mme Vekeman handed me my clothes as I swung my legs out from under the covers.

"Neighbours are here. They will help you. You must go with them. You must trust them!"

"What neighbours?" I asked. "Where are they taking me?"

"Hurry! Hurry!" she urged, as, still pulling on bits of my uniform, I stumbled across the room in her wake. My hand gripped by hers, she pulled me along without answering my questions. I followed her as quickly as I could down the darkened staircase into the hall.

There was a faint chink of light coming from a partly opened door. A tall thin man was standing by the table in the same room I had entered that very first day. His hands, clasping and twisting a beret, were held awkwardly in front of him. His face was long and gaunt, his eyes blue, his lower lip pendulous. His eyes glanced down nervously at the floor when he spoke or was spoken to.

He and Mme Vekeman spoke in what I gathered, from the hoarse guttural tones, to be Flemish. From a drawer at the side of the room she drew out a checkered duster and showed it to the man, who nodded his head in approval. She turned and, giving it to me, said, "Put this on. It will look like a neckerchief."

The man looked me up and down with a critical eye and again spoke. Mme Vekeman nodded her head in agreement and, turning to me, said, "Your flying boots, you must cover them up." I looked down at my boots. "Pull the legs of your trousers down over them."

I did as I was told and she added, "And the badges. I have some scissors somewhere." She turned to Mérèse who pointed to a drawer.

With the beret given to me by the Belgian, a checkered neckerchief, and minus my badges, I looked a reasonable facsimile, in the half-light at least, of a Belgian peasant off to work in the fields.

I smiled at Mérèse who looked small and frightened standing there beside me, and taking her hand, whispered, "Don't worry! Everything will be all right."

Mme Vekeman, who had been talking to the Belgian, looked around, glancing at the two of us. Feeling guilty, without understanding why, I let go of Mérèse's hand.

"Come," said her mother, "we mustn't waste time. You must go quickly. You will hide in the trees at the bottom of the garden! The gentleman and his friend will come soon. They have bicycles and will take you to a place of safety."

I nodded, wondering what had happened to the promised car.

The Belgian stared at the surface of the table. Mme Vekeman concluded, "Now follow monsieur! He will show you where you must hide."

I looked first at Mérèse, who turned her head away, then crossed the room to Mme Vekeman. As I looked down at her, wanting to thank her, but feeling awkward and clumsy, not quite sure whether I should kiss her or not, I felt gratitude and regret at leaving this house where I had found such ready affection and courage. She took the hand I offered and, raising herself on tiptoe, reached up and kissed me on the cheek.

"*Bonne chance!*" she whispered. "Remember, 'The bluebird is out of his cage'. Don't forget. We will listen every night."

From the trees where the Belgian had left me I could see the dark outline of the house and the movement of the bushes stirred by the breeze. Now that danger threatened, I felt once again the familiar mixture of fear and excitement. However, as time passed and there was no sign of the man, I began to feel uneasy. Perhaps he had been stopped by the Germans. German soldiers, already in the village, could be at this very minute approaching the house.

I could see no lights, hear no sound except for the rustle of leaves overhead in the branches and the occasional barking of a dog. As the minutes passed the cold night air brought back the familiar ache in my side.

Then faintly, some way off, I thought I could hear something; a metallic sound and the snapping of twigs. It could be the Germans! From out of the shadows two men emerged. One was clearly the tall thin Belgian. The other, his companion, was short and thickset. Seen together they reminded me of an illustration I had once seen of Don Quixote and his fat little squire, Sancho Panza. The source of the metallic noise; the two cycles they were wheeling.

Without a word being exchanged I followed the two men as they wheeled the cycles along the patch which skirted the house and led through a wicket-gate to the road. Don Quixote, as I now thought of him, not knowing his real name, motioned me to take one of the cycles. He mounted the other and Sancho Panza settled himself behind, sitting side-saddle on the carrier.

As I swung my leg over the saddle I felt the same spasm of pain I had felt before, as if a hand had reached inside my chest and twisted the flesh. I gasped, and, bending over double, let the cycle fall to the ground; I remained like that, afraid to straighten up or even draw a breath lest the pain return.

The little man hurried to my side and, taking off a broad leather belt, put it around my chest and pulled it tight. With the support of the belt I had confidence to relax slowly and stand up straight. He helped me get into the saddle and, giving the bike a mighty shove from behind, ran alongside until he was sure that I had the machine under control.

With Don Quixote leading the way, Sancho Panza riding side-saddle and myself laboriously trundling along behind, we formed a queer cavalcade, needing only a windmill ahead to complete the picture.

Cycling along narrow country tracks, through the fields, avoiding roads, we finally came to the outskirts of a village. The Belgians, now some way ahead, slowed and stopped. The little man jumped off and ran towards the village, leaving the tall Belgian and myself together, silently waiting. Now that he was away from the atmosphere of the Vekeman's house, my companion seemed to have grown in stature, more assured. He smiled encouragingly, when, not knowing whether he would understand, I summoned up from my limited store of French, with a no doubt execrable accent, "*Qu'est-ce qu'il ya?*"

He replied, "*Les Boches.*" From that I gathered that Sancho was reconnoitring, looking out for German patrols.

After a short time the little man returned and soon we were pedalling over the cobbles of the village, silent and deserted in the dawn light. Closed and shuttered windows gave the empty streets a cold and threatening air.

Suddenly the silence was shattered by a loud metallic clatter. We came to a stop and looked around at the darkened windows of the houses. No light appeared. Sancho dismounted and bent down to examine the rear wheel of the cycle upon which he had been riding. He quickly found the trouble, and triumphantly held the broken spoke aloft.

We passed through the streets, meeting nothing but a wraith-like cat, which darted across our path, disappearing into a narrow passage between two houses.

We had been cycling for some time since leaving the village, had left the track through the fields and were now travelling along a metalled country road. Rounding a bend we saw, some way ahead, the pointed silhouette of a church steeple. Without warning, the Belgians stopped, braking sharply, and it was as much as I could do to stop running into them.

Ahead of us, barring the road was a line of men, cudgels and pitchforks in their hands. Don Quixote and his friend dismounted, conferred in urgent whispers, gestured to me to stay where I was and went slowly forward to meet the menacing group.

I could hear their voices and the shuffle of heavy boots and clogs. Soon the men, Don Quixote and Sancho in their midst, advanced towards me. Clustering around, each tried to shake my hand. I was bemused, wondering who they might be. None were wearing uniform and they were carrying some ugly-looking weapons.

The shortage of food in the towns and the ration system imposed by the Germans had given rise to raids on the potato crops by enterprising citizens. This had led to the setting up by the villagers of vigilante groups such as this. It was in effect internecine warfare, of which the Germans were no doubt aware but chose to ignore.

After mutual expression of goodwill, a deal of pattings on the back, and a great deal of shaking hands all round, we were allowed to continue our journey.

Soon our path lay through dense woods, depressing in the murky light. I felt very tired and, although there was no recurrence of the sharp pain I had experienced earlier. I still found it hard to take a deep breath.

My Belgian friends seemed worried about me, having been told by the Vekemans of my wound. The journey too, of some forty kilometres over rough terrain on heavy-framed ancient cycles, was not ideal exercise for someone in my condition. They would stop from time to time and insist on my taking a sip of schnapps from a flask the small man carried. The effect was to make the whole exploit seem to me even more dream-like, floating, as it were, on a mist of alcoholic vapour.

Soon after daybreak we came to a clearing in the forest. Scattered among the trees, and far from any road, was a gathering of dilapidated thatched cottages. This tiny hamlet had no link with the distant market town except for a single-track branch line a few kilometres away, which wandered, through the countryside.

Although it was barely six in the morning, children played on the beaten square of earth between the cottages. Many of the infant faces were marred by sores and scabs, their small feet encased in heavy wooden clogs.

We had arrived at our destination.

Fatigue, and the effect of the schnapps, blurred subsequent events. I remember vaguely a room full of people. All the residents of the tiny hamlet seemed to have gathered in that one small room, all intent on seeing the English airman.

Faces from a Breughel painting peered from the shadowed corners of the room. Men approached me in turn and solemnly shook my hand. Children clinging to their mother's skirts eyed me gravely from a safe distance.

Don Quixote and Sancho Panza seemed to have faded into the background. I should liked to have thanked them but they slipped away without a word.

Thinking about them, I felt the sobriquets bestowed on them well deserved. Don Quixote, whose mission was to slay dragons and rescue fair maidens, was not one whit braver than my tall lugubrious Belgian, and Sancho Panza no more valiant a squire than the Belgian's companion.

I woke that evening and found myself, without remembering how I had got there, comfortable and refreshed. The bed was soft, the sheets clean and cool. I looked around the small room with its sloping ceiling and dormer window. The wall at the end of the bed was covered in shelves full of books, mostly old and tattered. The one title I did recognize was *Das Kapital*; the others, mostly French, were, as far as I could make out, also concerned with politics.

Sill feeling drowsy, I lay for some time, my tired limbs stretched in voluptuous comfort. Then, feeling more awake, I prepared to get out of bed and get dressed. I looked around for my clothes but there was no sign of them. I thought they might have been put in the huge mahogany wardrobe next to the bed, but as I swung my legs out from under the bedclothes, I heard a heavy creaking from the stairs leading up to the room. I quickly got back into bed.

The latch of the rough wooden door moved upwards and a stout woman backed into the room carrying a tray. The lady, dressed in black, her hair tied in a kerchief, stood smiling down at me. Her eyebrows were thick, black, and formed a straight almost continuous line above small brown eyes.

She placed a plate of stew on the tray in front of me and made signs for me to eat. I had been fed by Mme Vekeman on a diet of gruel and tisane; the stew of meat and potatoes smelt and tasted indescribably good. The lady, standing by the bed, seemed to enjoy seeing me eat with such appetite.

Having finished, I said in my newly acquired Flemish, "*Dank u, dank u,*" and, extemporizing from vaguely remembered German phrases, added, "*Viel gut, dank u.*"

The '*dank u*' must have convinced the lady I had some grasp of the language. She launched forth on a long exposé of her premonitions and apprehensions, her mobile features reflecting the emotions expressed. I, of course, understood not a word of all this, but felt obliged to nod, smile and look concerned, matching the tone of her voice, or the expression on her face. From time to time, with gathering confidence, I would throw in a little shrug of the shoulders as if to say with sympathetic disdain! What can you expect?

The mystery of the missing clothes was resolved when a young man entered the room carrying a bundle which he put on the bed. I could see that they were not my clothes and was about to risk further incursions into Flemish when the newcomer said in pedantic but admirable English, "We have disposed of your uniform. These are more suitable."

22

The young man, Gérard, the woman's son, was in his early twenties, only a few years older than I, but his studied manner belied his years.

"I removed this from the lining of your battledress," he explained and carefully placed a small flat tin, a little bigger than a cigarette-case, next to the bundle of clothes.

"Ah! Good!" I exclaimed. "My 'escape kit!' I'd forgotten about that."

I sorted through the contents of the box, which I had never before opened, nor, indeed, had ever before taken out of the lining of my battledress.

An 'escape kit' was carried by all air-crew and contained maps disguised as scarves, compasses made to look like buttons, currency of different kinds, a minuscule file embedded in rubber for cutting through iron-bars, concentrated food, chocolate, and tablets to stave off fatigue.

I offered the currency to Gérard who accepted it without demur, and I was about to stow the rest of the contents into the jacket of the shabby old suit which he had brought for me. However, Gérard firmly vetoed this. I might be stopped and searched by the Germans.

Dressed in the borrowed suit, I was sadly transformed, and far from matching the secret inner heroic image I had of myself. The trousers were too long and had to be hoisted at the waist and tied with string, while the jacket could have fitted my old friend Sancho Panza, drooping on the shoulders, but leaving several inches of wrist exposed. The shoes fitted, but the uppers, creased and worn, testified to the long service they had given the previous owner.

I was not at all happy with my new appearance, but was assured by Gérard that I would pass unnoticed as a Belgian peasant, to my mind a doubtful compliment. He went on to give me precise instructions as to how I should act and what I must or must not do, but only such information as he thought necessary.

"You must talk to no one on the journey. You ..."

"Why?" I interrupted, "Where are we going?"

Gérard ignored my question. "You must talk to no one on the journey. Pretend that you are not with me. Walk a little distance behind. If anyone should talk to you, turn away, or if necessary, pretend you are deaf and dumb."

When, a little later that morning, we left the cottage, there was no one about. The villagers, I supposed, were working in the fields. After the warmth of last night's gathering I felt a little hurt by the casualness of the leave-taking.

I walked behind Gérard along the track through the wood, dutifully keeping some distance between us. Ever since the night I had dropped so painfully on to Belgian soil the whole adventure appeared unreal, almost comic. It seemed as if all those I met were playing some kind of game.

Mme Vekeman's 'the bluebird is out of its cage', the tall, thin Don Quixote, and perched behind, side-saddle on the pillion, fat little Sancho Panza, and now this business of following behind Gérard, all seemed culled from a boy's book of adventures.

A few people were gathered at the tiny railway halt waiting for the train. Much to my surprise there was no platform and little indication that a train ever stopped there. This was my first taste of being abroad. Surely trains had to have platforms? It confirmed me in my inbred conviction of the superiority of being English.

I stood, following my instructions, a little way from Gérard, but it didn't look as if I were going to lack for company. Next to me stood a small shrivelled old woman dressed in inevitable peasant black and wearing a pair of men's boots, a kerchief over her grey hair, and carrying a basket covered with a cloth.

She smiled up at me, the difference in our heights obliging her to strain her head backwards. She said something in Flemish, and as she was peering into my face, it was difficult to follow Gérard's instructions and pretend she wasn't talking to me or that I couldn't see her.

As for pretending I was deaf and dumb...! I smiled down at her and nodded my head. That was all the encouragement she needed. The old lady clearly felt that in me she had found a kindred spirit.

When the train arrived she pointed with her ancient umbrella to the carriage in which she had decided we would travel. She pushed me along with energetic pokes of her basket, handing it to me whilst hauling herself up the steel steps into the compartment. Inside the carriage she indicated that I was to sit next to her on the wooden bench, poking her umbrella into the ribs of a cud-chewing labourer to get him to move along and make room.

I was relieved to see that Géard had chosen the same compartment. He was my lifeline. If we were to be separated...! It hardly bore thinking about.

The old lady was a great talker. Nobody and nothing in the carriage escaped her attention. She directed her remarks at each in turn and elicited from one a smile, from another a nod. I, however, was the unhappy focus of her attention. She would address a remark to me and then turn to her audience to receive their smiles or confirmatory nods. At one point she took hold of my hand and pointed to a rash on my wrist, exposed because of the shortness of the jacket sleeve. She seemed to be giving me a mock scolding for some misdemeanour, but ended her diatribe with a high-pitched cackle. I felt all eyes in the carriage to be upon me.

Gérard, in a corner furthest from myself and the old woman, was reading a book and remained completely aloof, despite the old lady's attempts to inveigle him into the conversation, if such one-sided verbal utterances as hers could be called conversation.

The train had now stopped its meandering course through village and field. Building up steam, it pushed vigorously past a jumble of houses which marked the outskirts of a town. It slowed as it crossed a series of points and came to a halt in front of a signal-box bearing the name-plate Hasselt-Sud. Passengers leaving the train busied themselves with bags and parcels.

The train emitted a few sharp puffs of steam as it released its brakes and, with a jerk and a jolt, pulled slowly into the station where we had to change for our destination, Brussels.

Gérard and I were standing some distance apart as we waited for the Brussels train, when, to my surprise and dismay, a young woman, slim and attractive, approached me.

"*Monsieur*," she said, raising arched eyebrows questioningly, "*Le train pour Bruxelles?*"

Now I could have dealt with this linguistic problem quite easily under normal circumstances. We had dealt with this very situation many times in school in our French lessons *à propos* a certain M. Duclos. However, glancing at Gérard and noting the worried expression, I remembered his injunction.

I smiled apologetically, shrugged my shoulders and shook my head slowly. Without saying a word, I felt I had been able to convey with a great deal of sensitivity that in the first place I was sorry I couldn't help her, secondly that I felt an idiot in not having the answer to so simple a question, and finally that I thought her very pretty indeed and was sorry we couldn't have met under different circumstances.

As she turned and flounced away, I wondered what she might be thinking about me.

The journey from Hasselt to Brussels was without incident. The passengers were as uncommunicative and as sad as any train-load of English commuters. The train finally pulled into the station and, keeping at a distance, I followed Gérard along the platform, surrounded by a throng of passengers.

I felt a pleasurable excitement, feeling that this was really being 'abroad'. My pleasure, however, was tempered at the sight of olive-green uniforms scattered among the crowd. I needed to remind myself that I was not a tourist but an enemy airman.

Tickets, so I understood, would be collected at the barrier, and mine, given to me by Gérard, was ready in my hand. There appeared, however, to be some delay. A growing cluster of men and women was forming at the end of the platform. There was a pause in the flow of passengers and the long queue edged slowly forward.

I could no longer see him but I knew that Gérard must be somewhere ahead. Perhaps he had passed through and was now waiting for me to appear. On the other hand the Germans might have stopped him and asked questions, even arrested him. The thought filled me with anxiety. If I were to lose contact with Gérard, I would have no address of anyone I might contact, no money, and no identity papers. I peered over the heads of those ahead of me, straining for some sign of Gérard's curly head. What I did see were German soldiers at the barrier checking passengers.

I now felt very nervous. Should I press forward with the other passengers and hope to pass through unchecked? Should I go ahead in the hope that the Germans were not checking identity papers?

Go ahead! How could I go ahead? If they asked me anything, I was done for. I could speak no German, knew hardly any French and certainly couldn't speak Flemish. There was nothing I could do, nowhere I could run.

I could still see no sign of Gérard, but as I approached the barrier I could see that the soldiers were not looking at tickets or identity-cards but searching bags and cases. I reached the barrier. The stout German soldier gestured to the man in front of me to pass through. He then turned to me. His expression seemed to harden. I could see suspicion in his small pig-like eyes. He could see who I was, knew I was no Flemish peasant, could tell that I was a Jew. I couldn't think, couldn't act. I felt like a small animal about to be swallowed by a snake.

Then he turned away, his attention shifting to the next passenger, and waved me on. I stood for a moment, my heart beating rapidly, and my hands sweating, trying to regain my composure. I looked round for Gérard. After an interminable moment I saw him standing on the stone steps leading out of the concourse. His head was turned, looking towards the barrier, his expression as impenetrable as ever, but his face, it seemed to me, was several shades paler. I forgot all caution and waved wildly in Gérard's direction. He made no sign of having seen me, but turned and continued up the steps leading to the exit.

The narrow streets through which we passed were busy with people and traffic. Germans were everywhere, chatting at corners, seated in large groups at café tables, striding boisterously along streets in jackbooted arrogance. I began to understand what it must be like to live in a city under occupation. It must have been a constant affront to be jostled off pavements by insolent Germans in olive-green uniforms, to see German officers chauffeur-driven in large expensive cars, and to accept the fact that the Belgians had become an under-class in their own streets.

There were few private cars, some horse-drawn vehicles and cycles, lots of cycles. Single-decker trams, two or three coupled together, ran down the centre of cobbled streets where groups of would-be passengers waited silently on island shelters. I hoped that we, too, would take a tram, partly for the novelty and partly because I was feeling tired. Gérard, however, ploughed purposefully ahead.

Soon we began to enter the quieter and cleaner suburbs. Here shops and cafes were replaced by apartment buildings three or four storeys high, their austere façades relieved only by dilapidated shutters and pierced at regular intervals by massive double-doors leading to enclosed courtyards. It seemed as if life in this big city was lived with its back to the street.

We walked along tree-lined avenues and across cobbled squares, I following some ten or twenty yards behind. We finally came to a junction intersected by a busy flow of traffic. Turning right at the inter-section we crossed a wide boulevard. We were now in the Avenue Wagram and had reached the next stage of the journey.

Gérard motioned me to wait. He mounted a short flight of steps leading to the front door of a house whose imposing façade was decorated with wrought-iron balconies.

He rang the bell and, after some delay, I saw him engage in conversation with a figure partially hidden by the half-open front door. He turned and beckoned me to join him. Inside the wide entrance hall stood a small attractive woman. She spoke in French and she appeared to be trying to persuade him to stay a while. He politely refused.

I realized that I had hardly even spoken to this strange, silent young man to whom I owed so much and should probably never see again. I tried to convey my thanks and admiration. Gérard smiled a prim, embarrassed little smile, and, turning to the lady, shook her hand, nodded to me, opened the door and left the house.

Madame Walters, as I later learned she was called, turned to me and said in English. "He is a brave young man."

"Yes," I said.

"I'm sorry," she added, "the lift is not working." Holding the long skirt of her housecoat with one hand, she began to mount the stairs.

"Nothing works nowadays," she added ruefully. I followed her without replying, conscious of the wide staircase, the hanging tapestry and the pictures on the stairway wall. The drawing room was furnished in ornate style, all gilt, curves and carving, appealing to the eye but not, I thought, very comfortable. Impossible to put your feet up, sprawl or lounge in those stiffly upholstered chairs, or lie comfortably on the damask and mahogany chaise-longue. In my shabby suit I felt very ill at ease.

"Please sit down." Mme Walters gestured towards a chair. "You will have some tea, won't you?" she asked. "I know you English love tea." She went on, "My husband and I drink nothing else in peacetime, but nowadays...". She shrugged her shoulders and added, "Of course you may have coffee if you prefer."

I said eagerly, "Tea will be fine." My expectations in relation to the tea were sadly disappointed. Mme Walters, at great expense no doubt, had got hold of an expensive brand of China tea, and this she served, two sachets in an elegant tea-pot. She poured the faintly coloured liquid into shell-like cups. I looked at the tray. There was no milk! There was no sugar! Mme Walters hovered over me while I sipped the tepid tasteless liquid.

The table was being laid for the evening meal. I had had a bath and a nap and felt much better. Still wearing the same bedraggled suit, I was sitting on the chaise-longue trying to think of something intelligent to say to Mme Walters as she passed to and fro from the kitchen to the dining-room.

When her husband returned home he showed no surprise at seeing me and, nodding affably in my direction, handed a small package to his wife. She seemed quite excited by the gift and tore open the paper wrapping. The package still in her hand she turned and kissed her husband on the cheek.

Turning to me she exclaimed, "Look what my clever husband has brought home!" and held out her husband's gift for me to admire. To my surprise it looked like a piece of meat. It *was* a piece of meat! I did my best to look impressed.

"Isn't he clever?" she asked. I assumed this to be a hypothetical question, but thought it better to make some response and smilingly nodded agreement.

"Do you like steak?" she asked.

"I don't mind. Anything will do," I replied.

I was incapable of appreciating what a piece of steak meant to these citizens of an occupied city, nor did they realize that air-crew in England were fed on the fat of the land. They probably judged my reaction to the rarity they were offering me as an example of English phlegmatism.

Next morning at breakfast I sat sipping the ersatz coffee Mme Walters had prepared. It tasted, if anything, worse than the tea of the day before.

I felt more at ease and Mme Walters and I talked freely to each other. She spoke of life under the Germans and I of life in England, giving an optimistic account of the progress of the war.

I learnt from her that not all Belgians were loyal to the Allies. Some, for the most part of Flemish origin, were openly hostile. They were known as 'les Belges noirs' and formed a 'fifth column' ready to work for the Germans and even betray their fellow countrymen. For those patriots resisting the German occupation 'les Belges noirs' were an added danger.

"You cannot trust anyone," Madame Walters explained. "My husband has worked with people in his office for many, many years. He is their employer and has always been kind to them, but he can never be sure that one of them will not one day betray him."

Later that morning Mme Walters was busy in the kitchen and I, in the other room, was attempting to decipher one of the magazines she had lent me. Suddenly there was the sound of a door closing, feet mounting the stairs, and a moment later we heard the key turn in the lock. Mme Walters came out of the kitchen and stood, a puzzled, worried expression on her face, looking towards the door. Her husband entered the room, closing the door behind him. He turned towards his wife and they looked at each other without saying a word. Then he crossed the room and, putting his arm around her shoulders, spoke gently, explaining, reassuring.

She sat down on the couch as if her legs were no longer able to support her. Walters sat down beside her and, holding her hand, continued to talk, his voice almost a whisper. I looked from one to the other, not understanding what was being said, but well aware that something had gone wrong.

"You musn't worry. It is nothing. A change of plan, that is all." She gestured for me to sit down beside her and continued, "My husband has been told that the Germans are suspicious. They are looking for you."

I said, "For me . . . looking for me?"

Walters nodded his head in confirmation as his wife continued, "My husband's contact, who has arranged for you to come here, thinks that they must suspect us, that they may come to the flat. We must hurry. My husband is going to take you to another flat straight away. You must not worry. It is all arranged."

They decided that my suit, which hadn't looked out of place in the country, would draw people's attention here in the town. Monsieur

Walters found a trilby hat and an old raincoat which, although not a very good fit, would make me look reasonably inconspicuous.

I was to follow behind him as I had followed behind Gérard, but this time we were taking a tram.

I stood on the platform at the rear of the crowded car, the money for the fare in my hand. I looked towards the front of the car where Monsieur Walters was standing. My borrowed raincoat gave me a respectability not afforded by the shabby suit it was hiding, but the trilby hat was quite special. With the brim pulled down over my eyes, I was Spencer Tracy. I was James Mason ... two cinematic heroes rolled into one.

This journey across Brussels to the next 'safe house', that of a Monsieur Kauffmann, was clearly hedged about with danger. The tram had a sprinkling of German soldiers and officers among the passengers and, according to Mme Walters, seemingly innocent civilians could well be 'Gestapo' or the infamous 'Belges noirs'.

Two peak-hatted German officers were standing at my side, yet their very presence intensified the perverse pleasure I derived from what was still for me an adventure. In my mind was a gleeful "If only they knew!"

My belief in my own invulnerability had been reinforced by events and left me still held by the youthful romanticism which had, in the first instance, urged me to volunteer for air-crew. Such an attitude, after the shooting down of the plane and the death of my crew, is, I suppose, difficult to understand. I could have been taught no harsher lesson on the fragility of life, the reality of death. I knew that I had escaped by the barest of chances. I knew, too, that I was still caught in a net of circumstances that could so easily end in capture or death, or even, had I dared to think about it, a concentration camp.

I was, however, still buoyantly optimistic, still in heroic mood, when we reached Woluwe St Lambert, a prosperous suburb to the east of Brussels. We got off the tram and soon reached Monsieur Kauffmann's flat.

A long narrow path between high brick walls led from the street to a small flight of stone steps flanked by a wrought-iron balustrade. At the top of the flight of steps we turned left and passed along a narrow verandah leading to the front door. We stood together waiting for Monsieur Kauffmann to answer the bell. After a few moments the door was opened sufficiently for a face to appear in the narrow gap.

Monsieur Kauffmann seemed to eye us with a great deal of suspicion. He was a short stout man in his late forties with dark eyes and a thin, carefully trimmed moustache. His black hair was brushed smoothly back. He looked at us for some seconds without speaking, until Monsieur Walters, seemingly embarrassed, felt forced to stutter a few words in French. I imagined it to be some kind of password, as the two men had never met before, had not even known of each other's existence.

There was no change of expression on Monsieur Kauffmann's unsmiling face. Walter's voice grew firmer, repeating what he had said. Kauffmann, seemingly relenting, nodded and, opening the door a little wider, stood aside and allowed us to squeeze past.

The small room exuded an air of domestic comfort and pride. Lace antimacassars adorned the back of each seat. The polished gleam from the wooden surfaces testified to the dedication of the housewife. His wife, wispy grey hair and pale gaunt face, was taller than her husband. She stood at the back of the room, a smile on her lips. It hardly merited being called a smile; it was, rather, a simper. Next to her, in a corner of the room, a youngish woman was seated, almost lost in the depths of one of the extravagantly upholstered armchairs.

Kauffman faced Walters across the table, "*Eh bien, monsieur?*" he said.

The tone of his voice indicated that he was waiting for Walters to say or do something. Walters seemed puzzled, appearing not to know what was expected of him. Then, as if suddenly remembering, he said, "*Ah, oui!*" and began searching feverishly through, first his overcoat, then the pockets of his jacket. At length he took out of an inside pocket half a torn playing card and placed it on the table. It was the Jack of Spades. Monsieur Kauffmann examined it closely without touching it, crossed to a small book-case, took out a book, opened it and drew from its pages the other half of the Jack of Spades. Crossing to the table, he carefully placed his half of the card next to that of Walters. The two halves fitted perfectly.

For the first time Kauffmann allowed himself a little smile and took hold of Walters' hand and shook it vigorously. After a final round of hand-shaking, and on the part of Monsieur Walters, hand-kissing, the latter went home to his wife, leaving me alone with my new hosts.

That evening Monsieur Kauffmann, myself and the small lady, a Mlle Vera, sat down to a delicious meal prepared and served by Mme Kauffmann. Fortunately Mlle Vera spoke English fluently.

As for Mlle Vera, I wondered who she was when first I saw this timid rather plain-looking little woman, with short straight hair, hooked nose and protruding teeth. She claimed to be English, but, although fluent, she had a very strong French accent. Monsieur Kauffmann, winking and nodding his head mysteriously, and indicating the lady, claimed, "She – eez weez Breeteesh Anntelleegance!"

British Intelligence! I was impressed. She was no beauty, no Mata Hari, but she was, so it seemed, practically a spy! The world of cinema and reality drew closer together.

I understood from Mlle Vera that the great fear for those who worked secretly against the Germans was the danger of having their organization penetrated by German counter-intelligence agents. Such men were frequently infiltrated into a 'line' as airmen who had been shot down. It was for this reason Monsieur Kauffmann had asked her to contact British Military Intelligence to check whether I was who I claimed to be.

After the meal had been cleared away Vera sat down at the table, a pencil in hand and a sheet of paper on the table in front of her. Kauffmann stood behind looking over her shoulder. The lady, her eyes lowered, looking hard at the table, explained. "You understand, we have to ask you a few questions?" I nodded my head.

Kauffmann bent down and whispered in her ear.

"We have to make sure you are an English airman," she continued, her eyes still fixed on the paper in front of her.

"Yes, I see," I answered, and pointed out that we had been told to give only our name, rank and number. She had a whispered conversation with Kauffmann. They insisted that there as no need to worry on that account. My instructions only applied to being captured by the enemy, but any information I gave to them would go directly to British Intelligence.

My answers, according to Vera, would be transmitted to London, verified, and she would then be notified. The explanation sounded reasonable and I reluctantly gave details of my squadron, the type of plane I flew in, the name of the Wing Commander, and in addition, my own name, number and rank.

I still had my identity discs. I drew them out from under my shirt and passed them to her. She assured me that although they both were quite certain that I was English, they had to check for the sake of the 'Organization'. She put the discs and the piece of paper on which she had written the details I had given her into her handbag.

Later that evening a doctor who worked for the 'Organization' arrived to see my wound. He assured me that the difficulty I was having with my breathing was due to the bandaging and not the wound. There was nothing now to be seen but a small scab over the point where the bullet had entered. He placed a small dressing over the scab and secured it with a piece of medical tape.

Next morning – it was Saturday, 8 August – I woke in the tidy bedroom of the Kauffmann's flat in pensive mood. A great deal had happened in the seven days since I had been shot down.

I lay in that comfortable bed staring at the ceiling and thinking of all the people I had met, all those courageous people who had risked so much in helping me: Mme Vekeman who had risked her life, the life of her children, of her husband, out of patriotism for a country she dearly wished to espouse; Monsieur Kauffmann, rather like myself, playing the role of a romantic hero, but in his case at so terrible a risk to himself and his wife; the old man in his cottage, wheeling a wounded airman along a country lane, stopping to pick up forbidden leaflets and carefully folding them and putting them away in his pocket; Don Quixote and Sancho Panza, and the quiet studious Gérard and the Walters.

I was in the bathroom drying my face when there was a loud rapping on the door. I called out, "Shan't be a minute."

The knocking on the door was repeated, louder this time. I hurried over and opened it.

Outside in the corridor, framed by the doorway, stood two uniformed Germans. One held a pistol in his hand. The other shouted a guttural stream of German at me. Without understanding what he had said, I raised my hands above my head, shocked and hardly able to grasp what was happening.

In front of me stood these two men. I looked at their faces, everyday human faces. What did it mean, the revolver, the shouting? These were not cartoon character, nor villains in a propaganda film. These were ordinary human beings. It was the human quality of the two men that seemed to minimize the threat they posed. The one holding the gun was middle-aged, bald and fat. Surely he wouldn't use the gun? I couldn't believe he would actually fire it. But I had no thought of trying to resist.

In answer to the man's continuous shouting, holding on desperately to what remained of my dignity, I stuttered nervously in a feeble attempt at defiance, "I'll speak to your superior officer, not to you." My bravado came from the rôle I had been handed, a rôle in a drama that someone else had written.

The German's reply to my nervous insolence was to prod me with his gun and, standing back, indicate with a jerk of his head for me to move out of the bathroom. I wasn't sure whether he intended me to keep my hands raised, but in the circumstances it seemed the safest thing to do.

I walked ahead of the two men, prodded occasionally by the one with the gun, my arms bent, my hands on a level with my shoulders.

In the corridor behind the two men Mme Kauffmann was standing, the same simpering smile on her face. She, too, seemed to have been given a part in the play.

Betrayed was too big, too self-conscious a word to use, but the first unspoken words that came into my head were, "She's given me away to the Germans!" Her white face and that simpering smile said so.

My hands in the air, I pushed past Mme Kauffmann, scowling accusingly at her. Yet, in truth, my indignation was feigned, I felt no sense of betrayal. My rôle demanded some sign.

As I passed through the living-room with the Germans behind me, Mle Vera was there standing by the tiled stove. She stared blankly in front of her. The two Germans behind me, we passed out on to the balcony, down the stone steps and along the narrow path to the front gate where a black saloon car was waiting.

I sat in the back seat between the two Germans, who ignored me. I had become an obstacle, a non-person, a thing. Reality had caught up with me. Events were now no longer part of an adventure, but even so I was not yet completely crushed. As daunting as the future promised to be, the dominant emotion was not fear. Certainly not the fear I had known flying in raids over Germany. There, fear had been a taut line, a tightrope on which I balanced precariously.

Here in the car, faced with the certain prospect of a prisoner-of-war camp, and other darker, more fearful possibilities, which I chose not to think about, the dominant emotion was anxiety.

There was, however, still coexistent with that emotion, the same passionate curiosity that I always had concerning what might be waiting around the corner, the curiosity which leads a reader to read a novel to the bitter or triumphant end. What would happen to me? How could I prove my identity? Having changed my uniform for a ragged suit, I had lost the protection offered under the Geneva Convention, and now that I had given my identity discs to Vera I had no means of proving who I was.

I pursued endlessly in my mind the possible dialogue between myself and my interrogator. Question and answer, answer and question, formed an intricate maze. If they should ask me this ... I shall say that ... but if I say that ... they will ask me this.

I was experiencing for the first time a dull weight of worry that would now rarely leave me. Yet here in the car, and later, the ordinariness of my captors tempered my fears. They were men. No better, no worse.

At the *Feldpolizei* headquarters we passed queues of men and women waiting for documents, passes, permits and all the other paraphernalia necessary for citizens living in an occupied city. As we entered the building, the two Germans on either side of me, people looked at us out of the corner of an eye, not turning their heads. Inside the building there were no screams, no frightening sounds. Soldiers and civilians went about their business.

The German officer seated on the other side of the desk took a long pink form and inserted it into his typewriter. Without looking up he asked me my name. I had no intention of antagonizing him by telling him I would only give my name, rank and number. I was in enough trouble as it was, dressed in a ridiculous outfit, without the slightest proof of identity.

He, in fact, began by asking me my name, rank and number. He appeared to check these against a slip of paper, similar to that which Vera had used to note down details about my squadron. Beside it on the desk were my red and green identity disks.

He raised his head and looked at me through rimless glasses. "This is a Jewish name, is it not?" he asked.

This was a question I should have expected. Yet when it came I was unprepared. The word JEW was deeply incised into the identity discs. There was no question of my attempting to deny it. I neither could nor would.

The officer repeated the question: "It is a Jewish name isn't it?" I nodded my head slowly in affirmation. There was a moment's silence in which we looked at each other. Then he asked, "Monsieur Kauffmann's flat ... what were you doing there? How did you get there? Who took you?"

These were the questions I had been expecting. How could I give an answer that would appear credible yet at the same time protect all those who had helped me? These were the questions that had been running through my mind during the journey.

How much did the Germans know? Had the Kauffmanns, in fact, betrayed me? The disks on the table were those I had given to Vera. That was the paper on which she had noted details about my squadron. Were the Germans playing a game with me? Did they know everything?

I became aware of the German's face, chin tilted forward, awaiting an answer. "Well?" he asked.

"It was just chance. I was er ... walking along..., I ... didn't know where I was ... just walking ... I hadn't any money, any food. ... I had to find somewhere. I just knocked ... on this door. I didn't know who lived there. I just thought I'd take a chance. ... I asked this man if he could give me a room for the night." I paused. To my mind the story sounded pathetically thin, obviously untrue, but, to my surprise, the German was typing rapidly, taking it all down.

"I see," he said, "You asked him if he would give you a bed for the

35

night?" He looked up at me. "And how did you get to Brussels? You didn't fly here in your aeroplane, did you?"

"No, no, by train. I came by train."

"Ah!" said the German, "You came by train. Tell me about the train. At what station did you arrive?"

"I ... er don't know the name of the station," I paused, "but if you take me there I would probably recognize it." I had this wild idea that, if they were to take me at my word, I might escape and get a train into the country. It was a vain hope and I knew it to be so. The German looked at me without expression. "Who brought you to Brussels? You didn't travel here alone, did you? Someone paid for your ticket?"

My heart was beating fast as I sought desperately to put together a coherent story. "I don't know his name. He wouldn't tell me his name." I paused, glancing at the German, trying to judge his reaction. "He was an old man. I think he was pretty old ... and er ... fat, ... and he had a reddish beard."

The German smiled as he typed out this nonsense I had conjured up. I realized that he wasn't at all concerned with what I said. His smile made me realize that he would type whatever I chose to tell him. He was a functionary doing a functionary's job. My statement would no doubt be examined by others and there would be more questions.

He paused in his typing and asked, "You were wounded, weren't you? Show me!" He glanced at the small pad the doctor had put on the previous night and, looking back at the interrogation form, asked, "Who looked after your wound? Was it a clinic here in Brussels?"

I was surprised at the question and relieved that I could answer truthfully. "No," I replied. "After I'd been shot down, I can remember nothing until I woke in some kind of barn."

The officer typed out the words, repeating them as he typed: "some kind of barn." "Yes?" he asked.

"Yes, it was the old man who brought me to Brussels. He looked after my wound and gave me these clothes."

"I see," said the German. "Is there anything else you would like to add?" I shook my head. He took the form out of the machine. "Sign the statement," he said, and pointed to the bottom of the sheet.

I signed it with a feeling of relief. It had been easier than expected. The man was quite pleasant and if he seemed amused at my collection of lies it didn't seem as if he cared very much either way.

Emboldened by the man's courteous manner, I asked, "When will I be sent to a prisoner-of-war camp?" He shrugged his shoulders. "There are many questions that have to be answered first. You are in civilian clothes. For all we know you may be a spy."

36

He turned and spoke to the waiting German who had arrested me. The man rose from his chair, barked out "*Komm!*" and jerked his head towards the door. I followed him out of the office into the yard.

The German officer by my side, I walked along the busy streets of the city. I had no idea of what was going to happen to me or where we were going. I had a faint hope that it might be a P.O.W. camp, but that was hardly likely. Prisoner-of-war camps are not usually found in the centre of cities. The German accommodated his pace to my slow gait. I still had some pain in my side, but, in any case, I felt it a good idea to exaggerate a little the effect of the wound.

Soon we reached a white stone building which occupied several blocks. The forecourt and approach roads were thronged with ambulances, soldiers and army trucks.

I followed my silent companion along lengthy hospital corridors filled with wounded soldiers, some with heads bandaged, many with stumps of legs or arms. The officer was clearly a stranger to the place, stopping several times to question hospital staff. At length he managed to attract the attention of a doctor who shrugged impatiently, but was eventually persuaded to look at my wound.

Surrounded as we were by gravely wounded men, I was conscious of the insignificance of my own injuries and began to see myself for the first time as a German must see me: an enemy, responsible for these bandaged heads, shattered faces and severed limbs.

The doctor pulled open my shirt, pulled off the plaster and poked his finger on the scab. He spoke to the German who had brought me, clearly dismissing the wound as trivial. The attitude of the officer escorting me changed. Until then he had made no attempt to communicate, but had shown no aggression. Now, as we retraced our steps to the *Feldpolizei* buildings, he pushed me along with angry little shoves in the back, deliberately treading on my heels. With images of those mutilated men fresh in my mind, I could understand the Germans' reaction. I could feel the man's hatred directed against me, intensifying my feelings of isolation and mounting despair.

3

BRUSSELS

Saturday 8 August, 1942: Command of the Eighth Army is given to Lieutenant-General Bernard Montgomery.

From the *Feldpolizei* building, with two soldiers as escort, I was taken by car through the city streets to the prison of Brussels St Gilles. We passed through the massive iron gates set in high brick walls, the car coming to a stop in the courtyard.

The prison, the largest in Brussels, was, before the city had been overrun by German troops, a civil prison of the Belgian State, staffed by Belgian police. It was now staffed by the *Wehrmacht*. Now, in addition to a prison's normal complement of murderers, thieves and other civilian offenders, it housed German soldiers, condemned by the military courts. The largest section of the prison community, however, now consisted of political prisoners, those Belgian citizens who were guilty of, or accused of, resisting the German occupation of the city.

There was a central hall from which identical wings radiated. The women were kept apart from the men and different categories of prisoners were similarly separated. I was not searched or given prison clothes, nor did I see any prisoner wearing any special prison garb.

Standing in the central hall I could see through the iron grilles into the different wings. The cells ran on two levels around a rectangle whose fourth side gave access, through heavy sliding steel grilles, to the central hall. The upper tier was reached by an iron staircase and a gallery running around the three sides of the rectangle.

There was, in addition, a similar gallery running, like a bridge, from one side of the rectangle to the other. I noticed a steel-mesh netting placed across the hall, beneath the second-floor galleries, doubtless to break the fall of any prisoner with suicidal intent.

The grille slid open and I passed through with the German escort into the wing where civilian prisoners were kept, that is men charged with criminal rather than political offences.

One of the two German escorts, papers in hand, stood a little way behind talking to the *Feldwebel* in charge of the wing. I looked at the iron staircases leading to tiered galleries which flanked the empty hall. Each gallery was punctuated at precise intervals by blank steel doors painted grey. Far above, steel girders curved away into the distance, framing the mesh-covered glass of the roof. Encased in this web of steel I felt apprehensive rather than afraid, and, despite the circumstances, intrigued.

The *Feldwebel* stood before me, his face badly scarred; no eyebrows, no eyelashes, his nose a parrot's beak, the thin skin drawn tightly over the bone. I'd seen the same face at home among burned air-crew.

He shouted at the soldier standing on the bridging gallery. The man sprang to attention and, clicking his heels, gave the Nazi salute, and yelled, gazing straight in front of him, "*Jawohl!*"

As the *Feldwebel* looked at me, there was a slight softening of his expression. "Come," he said, "you go to school now!" He pointed to a staircase.

My feet echoed on the iron steps as I mounted the staircase to the upper gallery. The guard waited by the open cell-door. The iron door slammed shut and the key turned in the lock. The cell was small, about eight feet long by six feet wide. I stood in the middle of it looking up at the heavily barred window set high up; impossible to see anything but sky. Against a wall stood a hinged bed-frame, folded over, its mattress and blankets sandwiched between the metal springs.

After the events of the past few days I felt exhausted, both emotionally and physically. I looked longingly at the bed, but the blankets seemed so strictly folded and the bed so firmly closed that I hesitated as to whether I should disturb it. The disciplined order, the authority which pervaded this huge prison carried a threat which I dared not challenge.

In any case I felt it hardly worth while stretching out on the bed. They would soon be coming for me. There was a wooden chair beside it. I decided to sit on that until they came. I looked around the small cell. The door was a plain sheet of grey metal riveted to the sub-frame with a spy-hole at eye-level and a cover on the outside of the door which could be pushed aside by the guard.

Except for the patch of sky there was no view of the outside world. The barred window was too high and the spy-hole remained closed, except when the duty guard, peering into each cell, made his round. The cell contained a bed, a chair, and, standing beneath a water-tap, with a small half-circular basin fixed to the wall, a rusty latrine bucket with a chipped metal lid.

The cream-painted walls were unmarked by the graffiti one might have expected. Writing on walls was strictly *verboten*, as were many other things. There was a typed list attached to the wall opposite the bed. It was in German, French and Flemish. Prisoners, apart from not writing on walls, were not allowed to sing, shout or smoke. Beds had to be folded in the morning and prisoners were forbidden to sit or lie on them during the day.

After all the events of the past seven days, I was now alone with my thoughts. My one hope was that my being brought to this prison was an administrative mistake, that, as soon as this had been realized, I would be taken from the prison and sent to a prisoner-of-war camp. There was nobody I could ask, nobody to whom I dare complain.

I stood close to the door waiting to hear my cell number called. Nothing moved in the ordered world which lay on the other side. I could feel the silence, soundless, bottomless, lifeless.

I knew they would call my number. I'd go down the stairs and be taken off to a P.O.W. camp. They had to do that because that was the Geneva Convention. They knew I was an airman. They had my identity disks.

During the morning the *Feldwebel* twice shouted a number. A cell door would open and there would be the sound of feet on the iron gallery passing in front of my door, and then fading as the prisoner descended the staircase.

The idea of being sent to a prisoner-of-war camp now entirely possessed me. I'd be among my own kind there, among other shot-down aircrew. We'd be in uniform, living together in barracks. I felt I could bear anything if I were not alone, if I had someone to talk to. Then, as the minutes and hours passed and silence imposed a stifling vigil, my despair grew.

Later that afternoon the silence was again broken. There was the sound of great activity; footsteps, commands, trundling and clanking sounds, cell-doors being opened and shut. The sounds came closer. I stood in the centre of the cell staring apprehensively at the door. The key turned in the lock. The door was pushed ajar. I timidly pushed it open a little wider and looked out. An unkempt, unshaven figure, wearing some kind of loose linen overall and a round cap, was standing behind a trolley which carried a large dustbin-like container. He said something to me in German. I made out the word "*Schnell!*" repeated over and over again, with increasing irritation. I looked at him in bewilderment and shrugged my shoulders.

A second man, similarly dressed, having locked the door of the neigh-bouring cell, turned to me and I again heard the words, "*Schnell!*
Schnell!" and something else I couldn't understand. Urged by his companion, he approached and put my two hands together. He dipped a scoop into the container and ladling a pile of small fish into my cupped hands, pushed me back into the cell and slammed the door shut.

I stood there for some time looking at the scaly mess, complete with eyes and tails. This was, I supposed, my dinner. I wasn't hungry, but even had I been, the sight of those stiff little bodies and dead staring eyes would have taken away any appetite I might have had. I knocked off the lid of the latrine bucket and threw in the fish.

Some time later the same men brought me a bowl and poured in what I later discovered to be mint tea, a scented liquid tasting like hot water. I drank a little, but most of it was poured into the sink.

The window cast a square of fading light on the wooden floor of the cell, marking the dying day. At dusk the light, a single naked bulb, high overhead, came on. They were not coming. Tomorrow. They were bound to come tomorrow. I unfolded the bed, put in place the three square cushions which formed the mattress and spread one of the blankets over them.

Later that evening more food was brought round: weak coffee, two slices of a dark brown, sour-tasting bread, a small slice of sausage and a round piece of cheese smelling like fish. This time, hunger sharpened by the day's abstinence, I wolfed it all down.

I took off my shoes and socks and, folding my jacket, put it in place as a pillow. I sat on the edge of the bed for some time, unable to think, elbows propped on knees, head resting on my hands. Finally I stretched out on the narrow bed and pulled the other blanket over me.

I lay there in the cell, my eyes closed to the glare from the naked bulb. Without warning the light was turned off. The absence of the crude, glaring light, which had thrown into relief the miserable harshness of my surroundings, was a comfort. In the gloom I saw neither the walls nor the heavy bars at the windows, but I still found it difficult to get to sleep.

The mattress was hard and I found it impossible to lie on my left-hand side, the side which had been wounded. Yet I normally slept on this side. My body turned and twisted, reflecting the painful lucidity of my thoughts. My mind seemed forced to pursue the same path, returning time and again to the same point.

Had the Kauffmann's betrayed me? Had the Walters been arrested? Would they send me to a P.O.W. camp or would they...? They'd come and get me tomorrow surely! Would they interrogate me again?

Towards morning, as the thin dawn light filtered into the cell, my tired body found relief. Gradually a comforting sensation of warmth possessed me and a sensuous ease filled my limbs. My mind lost its clarity as pictures and patterns formed behind my closed lids.

I was awoken by the loud trundling of trolley wheels on the iron gallery, and the sound of the cell-door next to mine being opened. I sat up and looked around at the cream-painted bricks, the barred window, and remembered. I pulled on my trousers and pushed my feet into my shoes. I assumed from the sound that some kind of breakfast was being brought round. I felt sufficiently hungry to eat anything.

The two prisoners whose job it was to bring around the food were not the same, but they were just as taciturn. I had my bowl ready in my hand and that was sufficient for them.

Their progress along the line was an obstacle race. While one was ladling the coffee into a waiting bowl, his companion ran ahead and unlocked the next door. Then he would run back and lock up the cell of the prisoner who had just received his ration, and then run on to the next unlocked door.

The man wearing his round convict's cap and striped suit ladled the ersatz brew – it certainly wasn't real coffee – into my bowl. I thanked him and smiled, seeking some answering warmth or flicker of response. The face could have been chiselled from stone.

Replacing the lid of the container, the man pushed the trolley on to the next cell. I stood looking after him, waiting for the rest of my breakfast, but the man who had opened the cell-door now returned and, pushing me back inside the cell, pulled the door to and turned the key in the lock.

Facing the closed door, I took a few steps back, was that all I was going to get! I supposed they'd be bringing the rest of it later. A bit of that sausage I'd been given yesterday would be fine, or at least a bit of bread.

I sipped the coffee. It was weak, but hot and comforting. After standing for a moment where I was, gazing blankly at the grey door, I sat down on the edge of the bed. There was really no need to stand there. I'd hear them coming with the sausage or the bread, if there was going to be any sausage or bread.

Time passed. I finished the coffee. It was clear they weren't coming. That was it then. That was breakfast, a bowl of coffee. I felt very hungry. I couldn't remember ever having felt so hungry.

I thought regretfully of yesterday's bread ration improvidently eaten the night before. If only I had managed to save a slice, or even half a slice. Half a slice would at least have taken the edge off my hunger. If I had to stay another day in this place I'd definitely save some bread for the morning.

I spent most of the day listening at the locked door, unwilling to move away lest I miss hearing the number of my cell called by the *Feldwebel*. Few sounds broke the ordered stillness which lay behind the door. At one time a number was called, but it wasn't mine.

Sunday morning passed in similar fashion. I sat down on the chair next to the bed, afraid of breaking any rules. I sat listening for any sound that might signal my release, that might take me to the prisoner-of-war camp, distracted only from my listening by the torment of an empty stomach.

When at last the sound of the trolley broke the silence, I felt all the excitement of a child waiting for a promised treat. I welcomed the prospect of food and human fellowship, even if it brought with it the same two unsmiling creatures.

Sunday passed and Monday too. My number wasn't called. I grew increasingly hungry, but not sufficiently so to eat anything that was put or slopped into my bowl. There was, for example, a carton of *ersatz* honey of such unpleasant sweetness that, later on in the day, I gave it back to the startled servers. It so surprised them that, for the first time, they actually looked at me. Later, when my system had begun to crave sugar, I bitterly regretted my generosity and wondered how I could have been so stupid.

Each of the long days that followed was marked by the same sensation of hunger, the same listenings at the door, the same restless nights, but occasionally, at no fixed interval, I was allowed out of my cell.

The first time this happened I was at my post by the door when my number was called. I could hardly believe it. My face flushed and I could feel the rapid beating of my heart. I heard the soldier's *"Jawohl"*, heard his key in the lock. The door opened and a guard stood framed in the doorway. *"Komm!"* he said, and stood back to allow me to pass in front of him and step on to the gallery. I followed him along the gallery to a small locked door which opened on to another staircase. At the bottom of this there was yet another locked door, which he opened, and with a nod of his head motioned me in.

I found myself in a large triangular iron cage with grass and gravel underfoot and open to the sky. I realized that I was being encouraged to take some exercise.

As I followed the much-trodden path around the enclosure I could see the high red-brick wall that encircled the prison. It seemed almost close enough to touch. If I were to stretch an arm through the bars I felt I could have touched it. If only I could get through the bars. If only I could climb the wall.

The gift of honey to the servers had brought about a change in their manner towards me. They now looked at me with some curiosity. One of them asked, as he ladled soup into my bowl, "*Engländer?*" assuming perhaps that, being English, I was more likely to understand German than French. I nodded, spread my arms out wide and made the rat-tat-tatting noise of a machine gun. The man emitted a high-pitched cackle. He thought that very funny. "*Ja, ja,*" he said, pointing at me, "*Flieger! Flieger! Du bist Flieger.*"

I nodded, admitting the fact. Taking advantage of our newly established relationship, I pointed first to a large, empty cardboard box on the bottom shelf of the trolley, and then to myself. The man glanced over his shoulder and gave me the box.

I was delighted. The box was made of thin card and by dint of careful folding, creasing, and tearing – I had no knife – it could be made into a pack of playing cards. I went back into my cell hugging my gift.

As the long, lonely days passed and there was no sign of the hoped-for release, my mind sought distraction. Songs helped. At first I sang quietly, lest the guard overhear, but then, as confidence grew, I sang louder. No one could hear me, or if they could, appeared not to bother. Finally I sang with full-throated confidence as if in the bath at home.

The cardboard box was heaven-sent. The bullet from the Messerschmitt had bitten a perfect half-circle out of the pencil which had been in the pocket of my battledress. It was broken, and half its original length, but it could still be used. I spent hours making the pack of cards, a beautiful round head for the figure two, a flat top for the figure three. And Jack the Knave, has he got a hat? Give him straight hair, easier to draw. The Queen of Hearts, voluptuous, draw the pencil slowly, lasciviously, round the curve of her breast; long eyelashes, full lips.

Cross-legged on the floor, I'd play games of Patience for hours on end; no cheating, the longer it takes to come out the better.

When I became bored, I built "houses", or a prison, with cells and a long corridor, a prison within a prison. I'd balance one card against another, securing the structure by roofing over the rooms and corridors.

Once the big gormless-looking guard, peering through the spy-hole, had been sufficiently intrigued to unlock the door. "*Was machst du?*" A slow smile spread over his dull features.

They had arrested me at the Kauffmann's flat on Saturday the 8th of August. It was now Wednesday the 12th. I had been locked in the cell for five days. That was the day I head the *Feldwebel* call my number. I heard the guard approach and the key turn in the lock. Would this, too, be a visit to the exercise yard?

Leaving my cell I turned right, went down the stairs to where the *Feldwebel* stood waiting. He was, as before, grimly jocular, a stern but kindly schoolmaster. "*Aha! Der Engländer!*" he said. "You are coming from school, yes?"

In the central hall of the prison a German soldier came up to me and asked diffidently, "Are you English?" He spoke almost without a trace of accent, his voice soft and pleasant. I said, "Yes, yes, I am."

"I often act as interpreter here," he explained. "I spent many years in England, in business, and, for a time, at a school in your country."

"You speak very well," I replied. I realized, perhaps for the first time, how much a common language means. We had only exchanged a few words, yet already there was no misunderstanding that couldn't be explained.

"I wish I could speak German," I said. "It's so difficult here to make myself understood. Everyone seems to shout all the time, as if they're angry, especially when they're talking to me." The German laughed.

"I mean," I continued, "they may only be telling me the time or what the weather is like, but it always sounds to me as if they'd like to knock my head off."

He smiled. "Yes," he said, "I understand, but, you know, soldiers are not always the most cultured of men, nor the most intelligent, and certainly not always the best representatives of their country. It is the same in England, wouldn't you say?"

"Oh, absolutely!" I agreed.

"Did you not learn German at school?" he asked.

"No," I said, "only French."

"Ah, French! A beautiful language. I spent a long time in France before the war. I got to know Paris quite well. I spent some time at the Sorbonne. I had a small flat in the Rue Vaugirard, overlooking the Luxembourg Gardens." He lowered his voice. "Everything has changed. I was there a few weeks ago. It has all changed. It's not the Paris I knew."

The *Feldwebel* turned towards me. "*Komm!* You go now. *Schnell!*" My new acquaintance clicked his heels and, turning towards me, gave a barely perceptible bow. They were not all Hitlers or Himmlers.

Grey was the dominant colour of life in prison: grey bars, grey men, and over all a pall of silence and stillness. I savoured my ride through the busy streets of the city, sensitive as never before to the joy of colour and movement.

The officer acting as escort was a fat German wearing gold-rimmed spectacles. Chauffeured by a young soldier, we sat together in the back seat of a black saloon.

Encouraged by the civilised exchange I had had with the German interpreter, I was encouraged to attempt a few anodyne remarks on the passing scene, but my lame observations were met with, "Zat I am not knowink".

At the headquarters of the *Feldpolizei*, the equivalent of our Military Police, I was confronted by the same interrogator who had questioned me on the day of my arrest. The same process of question and answer was again accompanied by the tapping of the German's typewriter as he noted my answers. This time, however, there was a greater insistence on detail. Was there really only one man who had helped me after I had been shot down? How had one man managed to carry me to the barn?

I admitted that there might have been others, but as I had been unconscious at the time I wasn't able to say. I added that all I knew was that, when I recovered consciousness, the man I had described before was there, old, fat and with reddish hair. I added a detail for verisimilitude: he was short and thick-set.

The German wanted to know the exact number of days I had stayed in the barn. I realized that they probably knew by now the precise day my plane had been shot down. I had to be careful to match the supposed time spent in the barn with my stay at Dr Vekeman's house and my eventual arrival in Brussels.

He again questioned me about the underground "clinic", the French word, I learnt later, for hospital, which was presumably located in Brussels. I could, with perfect honesty, deny all knowledge of it. However, it intrigued me to think that a clandestine hospital for wounded enemy airmen or resistance fighters could exist in a city under occupation.

The questioning went on. My statement concerning the accidental manner in which I had chanced on the Kauffman's flat – "I just knocked on this door" – was now dismissed as nonsense, which of course it was. Nevertheless I insisted on the truth of the statement.

The German stopped typing and looked at me without saying a word. There was a long silence. I could feel myself blushing and bit my lip nervously. I was tempted to speak, but something in his expression, a certain weariness and irritation that looked as if it might explode into violence, made me think better of it.

The man at length said, "You must not lie to me. I want you to tell me the truth, to tell me exactly what happened. You are in a dangerous position."

I was tempted to interrupt, but was again silenced by the threatening look on the German's face. He continued, "You must not think you are protected by the Geneva Convention. That does not apply to civilians, and you are in civilian clothes. We have no evidence that you are who you say you are. You may well be a spy. We would be acting quite correctly if we had you shot. Do you understand?"

I made no reply, and the German continued, "Why did you not tell us that you stayed with the Walters, and that it was the Walters who brought you to the Kauffmann's flat?" I could think of nothing to say.

The German went on, "We have arrested the Walters. They too are in prison at St Gilles. We know much more about this than you think. It is very silly of you to think you can deceive us. Do you really think you are the first prisoner we have interrogated? Where did the Walters hide you? You stayed there some time, didn't you?"

My feeling that I could outwit the Germans had been badly shaken, but I still attempted, whilst appearing cooperative, to deny them whatever information they were seeking. I answered with an attempted show of candour, "I'm not sure where it was, but I think I could recognize the house if you were to take me around the city."

I felt this to be a cunningly subtle offer, but the German ignored it, as he had ignored my previous proposition to identify the railway station. The interview ended at that point by my again signing the statement he had typed. I left the building escorted by the German who had brought me from the prison.

On the return by car to the prison I sat in my corner looking out of the window, making no attempt, this time, to communicate with the German escort. My mind was centred on the Walters. If the Germans knew about them, what else did they know? Who had given them the information? Vera? The Kauffmanns?

My thoughts were interrupted by the German who earlier that morning had been so uncommunicative.

"So!" he said, "You are coming from England. From what town are you coming?" I told him that I was a Londoner.

"Ah! You are coming from London."

He had, he informed me, studied at the Holborn College of English in London and was offended when I confessed that I'd never heard of it.

"You are coming from Oxford and Cambridge, I suppose?" he said.

I felt that the less I engaged this man in conversation the healthier it would be. I turned away and kept my eyes firmly fixed on the passing scene. Although I could feel the German's eyes fixed in my direction, I continued to stare resolutely through the window. Sitting bolt upright, his hands on his knees, he finally broke the silence. "So!" he said.

"Pardon?" I replied, turning my head towards him.

"How are things in England?" he asked. I looked at him blankly, not knowing how to answer.

"You are not liking the bombing, I am thinking."

I realized that I was under attack and replied hesitantly, "I don't know. People are used to it," and I added, "especially now that we're bombing German towns."

"Yes!" replied the German angrily. "That I am knowing. You are bombing German towns. You are killing innocent women and children."

I felt that the conversation was becoming dangerous and decided to hold my tongue. The German, however, after a reflective silence, continued, "It will do you no good, this bombing. No good at all. You are finished! *Kaput! Fertig!* Rommel has beaten your army, destroyed your tanks. Tobruk has fallen. *Alles ist kaput.* You have no food. Our submarines are sinking your ships. The people of England are starving. Soon this war will be over. *Fertig.* That will be good for you. You will go home. No more *Kriegsgefangener* for you." I shrugged my shoulders, but he wasn't satisfied. "Tell me how it is in England. Is it not true what I am telling you?"

I answered, in what I considered to be a reasonable and conciliatory tone, "No, not really. We've plenty of food. And even if we hadn't, it wouldn't matter. It's strange, but no one ever thinks that we'll lose. Some say it'll soon be over, now that the Americans are in; some think it might take years, but I've never heard anyone talk of the possibility of our losing."

I said this in as objective a manner as possible and was all the more surprised when the German, face purple, suddenly raised his hand and slapped me across the face.

After a moment or two he turned and touched my shoulder. "I am sorry," he said, "very sorry. I should not have done that."

During those first two weeks I was taken frequently to the *Feldpolizei* headquarters, and I looked forward to the interrogations as if to an outing. There was the journey by car through the streets of the city and, at the end of it, the game of cat and mouse with the interrogator. I would spend hours in the cell rehearsing in my head likely questions and possible answers. With the interrogator I was, of course, the mouse, but at times, having spent those long hours perfecting my fabrication of lies, I was dangerously self-confident, feeling sure I could outwit my questioner.

The methods used in the interrogations were repetitive but never violent and only mildly threatening, but even so stirred fears: "You are wearing civilian clothes. How can we be sure you aren't a spy? We would be within our rights to have you shot. You aren't protected by the Geneva Convention. That only applies to men in uniform."

I dismissed this as a threat. They knew I was an airman. They had my identity disks and I had seen the list giving details of my squadron on the desk, the list I had given to Vera.

Nevertheless I had a lurking suspicion that I might be mistaken, that those identity disks were not my identity disks, and that paper might not be the paper I had given to Vera.

My greatest underlying fear, I suppose, was that, being Jewish, I might be sent to a concentration camp. The possibility had never been voiced by the interrogation officer. I cannot remember ever being threatened in this way. However, the possibility existed.

Deep inside me was the conviction that such a fate couldn't be mine. The pictures I had seen of concentration camp victims were images drawn from a distant world, happening to a distant people. I hated what was being done to them and hated their persecutors, but I remained me, with an inalienable sense of my rights and privileges and a certain unwarranted arrogance.

Apart from the slap on the cheek I had met no physical violence, nor the threat of it, if one discounted the talk of shooting me as a spy. The interrogations were, in fact, a release from the dull misery of the cell.

Each session finished on the same note, "We only want to establish your identity, find out who you are. The more details you give us, the sooner you'll be released and sent to a prisoner-of-war camp."

The interrogator would enlarge on its delights: "You'll be free to go where you like – within the camp of course. They won't let you catch a train home, you know." And he would laugh a little, and I, sycophantic, would laugh too. I was ready to believe all he said. I wanted to believe it.

The interrogations were becoming a way of life when, at the end of the second week, they stopped. I would listen for hours at a time by the cell door, hoping in vain for my number to be called.

I now had to face the unrelieved rigours of solitary confinement, except for the rare occasional ten minutes' exercise in the triangular cage.

The setting August sun cast the shadow of the iron bars on the floor of the cell. My back to the window, I sat on the wooden chair facing the bed, the mattress a table for endless games of Patience. I carefully placed the blank letter-form, issued to all prisoners, beside the cards. There was a tick if the game came out, a cross if it didn't. I was working out "probabilities".

The administration allowed prisoners to send home one letter a month. I was a prisoner, but my category was not easy to define. I was not a political prisoner, nor a criminal, nor yet a German soldier convicted for some military offence. I dwelt in a prisoners' no-man's-land. Nevertheless, I was a prisoner, and as such was given one letter-form for a month. However, they were hardly likely to let me write home to England. The letter-form, a valuable concession to other prisoners, was of no use to me except for scribbling notes, doggerel verse, or, as now, noting "probabilities".

I laid out the cards in seven neat piles. The Ace of Spades I placed on its own above the seven piles of cards. I turned one over ... the Queen of Clubs ... red nine on the black ten ... the eight on the nine – A noise! I paused and listened. There it was again, that sound, low-pitched. I stopped playing. Nothing! I could hear nothing. Silence filled the cell. Must have imagined it. I played absent-mindedly, my mind no longer on the game, straining to hear. There it was again , a broken murmur, a rustle of leaves.

I had heard the same sound that first night, and again a few nights ago, a high-pitched sound this time. Laugher! Definitely someone laughing. I put down the cards, stood up and turned to face the barred opening high in the wall of the cell.

I looked at the chair and then at the window. It wouldn't work. I couldn't possibly reach the window standing on the chair. I picked it up and placed it, its back against the wall, directly under the window. I might possibly reach the bars if I could use the chair-back as a ladder.

I crossed to the cell-door and listened for a moment or two. There was no sound. I stepped up onto the seat with my face against the wall. The bars, high above my head, were quite out of reach. I raised my left foot and set it lightly on the top stile of the chair-back. The chair see-sawed, tilted a little, but held its position. Very slowly, with great care, I shifted my weight from the seat to the back of the chair, placing my right foot on the stile-back. Hands and crouching body pressed against the wall, the side of my face sliding up its surface, I gradually straightened up. My finger-tips could now reach the edge of the sloping window embrasure. Carefully, inch by inch, my fingers crept towards the bars. I stretched my body a shade more and finally held a bar firmly in my grasp. The rest was relatively easy. Holding on to two of the bars, my weight bore quite lightly on the chair-back. It gave me sufficient support, the bars firmly grasped, to straighten my body. My head now level with the window recess, I looked out.

It was as if I had escaped the four walls of the cell and the closed prison of my own thoughts. Outside, on the other side of the wall there was life, faces, voices, gestures. The wall of my cell had hidden all this from me.

In the prison wing opposite there were men's heads at nearly every window. There was the babble of conversation, and occasionally a laugh. The language was French.

The prisoners, several men to a cell, seemed seated comfortably, not clinging grimly to the bars as I was. They had an air of permanency, as if sitting at their own window at home enjoying the coolness of a summer evening. They must have had tables pushed under the window.

Sometimes a message or an object would be passed from one cell to another by means of a weighted string swung in larger and larger arcs until it reached the grasping hand. Sometimes the process had to be repeated several times, the object passing from one window to another until it reached its rightful recipient.

I watched and listened for a long time with great delight. They were clearly not ordinary prisoners. They wore their own clothes and seemed to share a strong bond of secret intimacy, a comradeship that closed them off from the dangers of the outside world. There were men of all ages: youths, old men with white hair, even boys.

Suddenly, I thought I heard my name. I turned my head in the direction of the sound. Then I heard clearly, "'Arry! 'Arry! *Par ici*! *Par ici*!" From one of the windows opposite I saw a hand gesticulating.

"'Arry! 'Arry! *C'est moi*! Kauffmann, Monsieur Kauffmann!"

I could make out in the fading light a pale face at the window: Monsieur Kauffmann!

Conversation was difficult. Finding my French for the most part incomprehensible, he enlisted the help of an English-speaking man in a neighbouring cell. I learned that both his wife and Vera had been arrested and were here in prison in the women's wing. They had arrested him at his office in the Town Hall, his colleagues unable to help, fearing to be implicated. I realized how wrong I had been, how unjust my earlier suspicions.

I, in turn, told of the series of interrogations I'd had, and of the Germans' claim to have arrested the Walters. I thought I had caught a glimpse of Monsieur Walters on my way back from interrogation.

Kauffman waved his finger from side to side. The interpreter said, "No, no, no! You must not believe the Boches ... all lies ... all lies ... never, never believe what they tell you." And, prompted by Monsieur

Kauffmann, added, "There is no question. The Walters have not been arrested. The Germans are lying."

The conversations at the other windows had gradually ceased as the prisoners realized the significance of the exchange with the lone face at the window opposite. Once they learned that I was an airman recently shot down their excitement was intense.

A voice in English shouted, "The Second Front? What about the Second Front?" This was the question that everyone asked me since the day I'd been shot down. However, for these people waiting to be transferred to concentration camps, it was literally a question of life and death.

I gave my usual optimistic answer, but one I believed to be true, an opinion garnered from the papers and the radio at home. It was, too, what my listeners wanted to hear. The Second Front, I assured them, would almost certainly begin by the end of that year, 1942, or at the latest by the beginning of next year. My answer was translated and repeated from cell to cell.

"What about Tobruk? The Germans say the British are surrounded." I explained that this was no defeat but tactics to engage and destroy Rommel's tanks. The fight-back had begun. The Germans would never take Cairo!

"The Russian Front? The Germans claim they are advancing everywhere."

This was, I told them, the historical 'scorched earth' policy that the Russians had always employed. The German lines of supply were overstretched. They would have to live off the land. Winter was coming. The Germans would never survive a Russian winter. The Russians would soon turn on Hitler as they had turned on Napoleon.

My listeners were clearly delighted, and the respectful silence with which they hung on my words and repeated them to each other urged me to greater efforts. I told them of the thousand-bomber raids on Cologne, Essen and Bremen, describing in some detail those I myself had taken part in. I talked of the huge thousand-pound bombs we now carried, too big to close the bomb doors. The bombing counter-offensive, I said, had only just started. The leaflet-dropping period was over. We were going to destroy Germany. They gave vent to their feelings with loud and unrestrained cheers.

Fearfully, I looked back into my cell, half-expecting the guard, hearing the noise, to come bursting in through the door. In any case the questions seemed endless and I was growing tired, my muscles aching from my efforts to stay balanced on the chair.

I promised to speak to them again the next day if it were possible. I waved to them all like some demagogue on a Town Hall balcony, and carefully climbed back down into the cell.

I looked with listless eye around the now depressingly familiar cell: the dripping tap above the sink, the rusty latrine-bucket, the grey bolt-studded door, the shallow metal locker recessed into the thickness of the wall, the list of prohibitions fixed with sellotape to the bricks, and the barred window, now a lifeline, an escape from isolation.

I had now been a prisoner in this cell for twenty-one days. Twenty-one days! Each day, each hour, an interminable unit of time, begrudgingly, wearily set against the misery of constantly disappointed hope. Compared with such pre-occupations, the bad food and the physical discomfort had mattered little, but as each day passed the squalor in which I had been forced to live became more and more intolerable.

That morning at the Kauffmann's flat, if only I had known, I could have taken what I needed. They would surely have let me take those basic objects on which human dignity rests; a clean shirt, a change of underwear, toothpaste, toothbrush. With the revolver pointing at my back, more pressing matters occupied my mind.

When the German had first waved his revolver, I had taken up my jacket mechanically, without thinking. It was just as well. It now acted as a pillow, a dressing-gown, or, supplementing the blanket the Germans had given me, a bed-cover.

I had walked out of the flat with nothing but a ragged old suit, a shirt, a vest, a pair of underpants and the battered shoes that had been exchanged for my flying-boots.

Lacking the protection of a prisoner-of-war camp and the status that conferred, I felt as if I were outside the laws of civilization. Nothing that the Germans might do would have surprised me. They had so far committed no wanton act of cruelty. Their attitude was marked by indifference, locking me up in a cell as if I were a letter to be opened later. After the first few days, I had been given a piece of ersatz soap which floated in water but produced no lather no matter how hard it was rubbed, and eventually, a bowl for my food, a spoon and toilet paper. My handkerchief I used as a towel and cleaned my teeth by dipping a finger in water and rubbing it over my teeth and gums.

I had few domestic skills when it came to looking after myself. My mother had washed for me, cooked for me, had in short seen to all my domestic needs. The RAF had taken over where my mother had left off. Eventually I was forced by the grubbiness of my shirt and underwear to make an attempt. I filled the basin with cold water and swirled each item around it. The soap produced not the slightest sign of lather. I rinsed the clothes in fresh water, wrung them as dry as I could and hung them on the cold "hot-water" pipes. They drooped there reproachfully, grey and wrinkled.

As I possessed neither shaving materials nor comb, my appearance now matched the bedraggled state of my clothes. After three weeks' imprisonment, the wild state of my unwashed, uncombed hair, my gaunt face with its few scattered hairs marking a nascent beard, and my skinny frame, seemed to confirm a status of concentration-camp victim rather than that of a prisoner-of-war.

The conditions under which I lived were, I supposed, the way the Germans treated all their prisoners. I bore the squalor with stoicism, but the hunger, that I couldn't ignore. I had always been extremely finicky about food. I would never as a child accept the bite of a friend's apple or a lick of somebody else's ice-cream. The prison food was both messy and smelly. I was hungry, but not yet sufficiently so to eat anything that was given me. I had lived for the last three weeks on a diet of water and a dark ersatz bread, which I at first found strange, but eventually enjoyed, liking its sour taste and finding its stodginess filling. Occasionally I would be given a piece of sausage or a small, evil-looking roundel of yellow cheese with a fish-like smell. These I found acceptable, but the mint tea which was served regularly I couldn't stomach, any more than I could the messy offerings of some kind of salad, and both would be emptied into the latrine bucket. As a result of this strange diet I grew paler and weaker. I too was now suffering from diarrhoea.

At the window, balancing on the back of the chair, I confided my difficulties to Kauffmann who urged me to complain to the guards. From my conversations with him, and those of his companions who spoke English, I began to see that the system was not as barbaric as I had assumed it to be.

Prisoners, it seemed, could complain without being beaten or shot. The freedom with which they spoke to each other at their windows, without seemingly having any fear of the guards, suggested that the prison authorities were not as oppressive or as ruthless as I had supposed.

The prison was run by the German Army, jealous of its authority, keeping the Gestapo at a distance and behaving with a military correctness that had its roots in a pre-Hitlerian era. I began to consider the possibility of complaining to the authorities.

My first timid efforts had little success. I was trying to explain that I wished to be placed on the sick list. My command of German was pitiful and I had to rely on a queer mixture of mime interspersed with

1. The author as an air-crew cadet.

2. 'The house at which we finally arrived was a large modern villa set in its own grounds' (p.11).

3. Mme Vekeman 'was small and dark with high cheekbones. Her appearance seemed vaguely exotic' (p.12).

4. Mérèse 'a young girl, slight of build, about fourteen or fifteen' (p.12).

5. 'There are seven children in the house. They must not know you are here' (p.14).

bits of French and German. I would place both hands on my stomach and murmur at intervals the word *"Arzt"*, the word I had been taught by my friends at the window; and when that failed I would try different versions in English and French, "Doctor" or *"Médécin"*. The guards brushed aside my mimes and my mumblings with a curt *"Verstehen nicht."*

The servers listened to me and nodded sympathetically, but always ended by shrugging their shoulders and pushing me back into my cell. Finally, exasperated by my failure to make anyone understand, I refused one evening to be pushed back into the cell. They looked at me, nonplussed. The guard, noticing the disturbance, shouted from below, *"Was ist los?"* and mounted the iron steps towards us. The servers explained.

The guard turned and looked me up and down with apparent distaste. *"Jude!"* he said. I well understood the word and the tone in which it was said. This was the first time since being shot down that I had heard it used as an invective. I felt my cheeks grow hot, but made an effort to control my emotion. I nodded agreement, deliberately acting as if the man were asking the politest of questions.

"Ja," I said, *"Ich bin Jude, Flieger, Engländer,"* and added, in English, "R.A.F."

The guard looked at me for a moment then said, "Moment!" and walked away, leaving the servers and myself waiting beside the open cell-door.

A few minutes later the guard returned bringing with him a small man, with thick wavy hair, heavy black eyebrows and blue eyes. He smiled at me and proferred his hand. I shook it.

"I understand you're English," the man said. "Can I help?"

The guard sent the servers about their business and, gesturing to myself and the interpreter to go into the cell, stood at the open door.

The relief at being able to talk English was so great I could have hugged the man. He was, he explained, a Belgian. He had been dropped by the RAF, but had been arrested almost immediately, his transmitter still packed in the suitcase he was carrying.

"Have you been here long?" I asked.

"Three months. Rather longer than you. I saw you arrive."

"Three months! That's awful!"

"I'm not complaining. As far as I'm concerned the longer the better."

"Why haven't they sent you to a prisoner-of-war camp? They have to. It's the Geneva Convention."

"A prisoner-of-war camp! Not in my case. I've been sentenced to be shot."

"But surely," I protested, "surely ... They...", I faltered, lost for words as I looked at him.

"They can, I'm afraid," he replied. He shrugged his shoulders. "I should have stayed a schoolmaster. I wasn't a good spy."

He looked towards the cell-door. "We'll have to hurry. Jerry'll be getting impatient. What's the trouble?"

I explained my lack of basic necessities, my inability to eat the food and that I was living almost entirely on bread and water. He listened sympathetically.

"You're an airman. You shouldn't be here. I can't understand why they're keeping you in solitary confinement."

I explained that I have been caught in civilian clothes.

"That shouldn't make any difference. They know you're an airman, don't they?"

"I think so," I said.

"You must write to the Commandant."

The guard opened the door and said something in German. The Belgian nodded and said, "*Zwei minuten, bitte*," and, turning to me, "We must hurry. This is what you must do. You must write a letter to the commandant. Tell him you're an airman. Give him your number in the RAF and insist that you be treated according to the Geneva Convention. Explain to him that you have no change of clothing and no toilet things. Perhaps you'd better not complain about the food. You'll get used to it and, if they transfer you to the military wing of the prison, the food there is much better."

The guard put his head round the door and growled, "*Schnell machen!*" The Belgian nodded to the guard, and then, turning to me, added, "Use the letter-form they give you. Address it to the Commandant. They'll have to give it to him. Anyway, don't lose heart. They'll send you to a prisoner-of-war camp. Don't worry, it'll all turn out all right."

He patted me on the shoulder and I thanked him warmly. As he turned to go he added, "By the way there's a compatriot of yours in the cell opposite, a soldier. He's been here a long time, longer than I have. His name is Dixey."

The Belgian had shown little sign of stress or fear. He spoke of his own execution as if it were a regrettable incident and he had turned from considering it to my own problems. How could a man endure such a burden? He had a courage whose source I found it difficult to penetrate and impossible to emulate.

Two days after I had written to the Commandant asking that I be

treated as a military prisoner I had a visitor when I heard the guard yell
"*Ein und zwanzig!*"

I jumped to my feet. It was my number. I could hear the clink of
keys as the guard approached. A key turned in the lock. The guard
stood in the doorway.

"*Komm! Schnell!*" I grabbed my jacket and passed in front of the
guard out on to the iron gallery. Could it be another interrogation?
Perhaps the Commandant had received the letter.

I followed the guard down the familiar iron stairs and on into the
central hall, but instead of the usual wait there the guard continued. I
followed him along unfamiliar corridors as my spirits rose. They must
be releasing me. If it wasn't an interrogation what else could it be? I
hadn't expected results so soon.

Half-way along a corridor the guard stopped at a glass-panelled door.
He knocked and a voice answered "*Herein!*" The guard opened the door
and motioned me to go in.

A middle-aged man, grey-haired and dressed in the uniform of an
officer of the Luftwaffe, was standing at a large desk which took up half
the available space. He dismissed the guard, telling him to wait outside,
then turned to me and pointed to a chair. He went to the other side of
the desk and sat with his back to the window.

His English was excellent and his manner kindly. "They haven't
given us much space, have they?" he said.

The office was very small indeed, with just room for the desk and the
chairs. I murmured agreement and waited for the officer to continue,
happy in the thought that this was part of the process of release.

"I'm afraid I don't know much about you. Let's see." He consulted a
sheet of paper on the desk in front of him.

"Yes, here's your name, your number." He peered at the sheet.
"1270422 ... er, yes, and you are a sergeant in the Royal Air Force. Is
that right?"

"Yes," I said, and hastily added "sir". This was a word I had some
difficulty in using, even with my own officers, but my spirits were high.
In any case he was a gentleman, and, in my understanding of the
expression, clearly worthy of respect, a man who, albeit German,
deserved the "sir".

"I understand that you have been here some time?" He smiled and
raised his eyebrows questioningly.

"Twenty-eight days," I replied.

"Twenty-eight days! Really!"

He continued, "I hadn't realized." He sat rubbing his chin reflec-
tively.

He stood up and looked out of the window. After a moment or two he sat down again. "When exactly were you shot down? Quite a time ago wasn't it? It's going to be difficult perhaps to trace your plane, if there's anything to. ... You see, I have to verify your story. I'll need to trace the plane. Check with our lists."

I realized that I was not to be released, not yet, and certainly not that day.

I answered the officer's remaining questions, which centred on the identification of the plane and crew. Finally the officer accompanied me to the door.

"It shouldn't be too long," he said, "As soon as we can confirm your identity you will be sent to a prisoner-of-war camp."

Emboldened by the man's kindly manner, I asked, "Can you tell me..." I paused,

"Yes?" the officer asked.

"How long will it be before...?"

"Before you get to a prisoner-of-war camp?" He hesitated, appreciating the anxiety behind the question. "Normally it would take only a few days, but you were shot down a month ago. A lot of planes have been shot down since then. It might take a few weeks."

Looking at the disappointment clearly visible on my face, he added after a pause, "or less with luck."

The guard at my heels, I followed the corridors leading back to the cells. I was disappointed and depressed, but even before I had reached the central hall my spirits began to lighten as I turned over in my mind the officer's final words, "a few weeks or less."

As I waited for the guard to unlock the door of my cell, I noticed that a small yellow card a little bigger than a visiting card had been fixed to the left-hand jamb of the door. On it had been roughly drawn in black ink the symbol identifying a Jew in Hitler's Europe, the Star of David.

That evening, in position at the window, I looked for Monsieur Kauffmann, eager to tell my news. There were ragged cries of "*Vive l'Anglais!*" "*Vive l'Angleterre!*" "*Vive le RAF!*" I genially acknowledged the salutations and Monsieur Kauffmann, hearing the noise, appeared at the window.

Conversation there was always difficult. I had to shout across the chasm and against a background of other shouted conversations. Added to the difficulty was that of language, of having to talk through an interpreter, whose expertise was questionable.

I gave Monsieur Kauffmann details of my interview with the Luftwaffe officer and learnt that he had no news of his wife or of Vera. He himself expected to be sent to Germany within a few days. My attempt at comfort – "The war will be over by the end of the year" – sounded meaningless.

The conversation turned to my meeting with the Belgian who had been arrested as a spy. Monsieur Kauffmann, that is to say Jules (we were now on first name terms) hadn't heard of him, but thought the idea of sending a letter to the Commandant excellent, though warning me not to be too hopeful.

Although he hadn't heard of the Belgian, when I mentioned the name of the English soldier, Dixey, there was an explosion of interest among the prisoners at the windows opposite. The sound of his name repeated a few times for the interpreter's benefit had been sufficient to stop all other conversations. They all apparently had some anecdote to relate concerning Dixey.

The man acting as interpreter explained that, when the British Expeditionary Force had retreated towards Dunkirk, Dixey had managed to find refuge in Brussels and had lived there, moving from one apartment to another, until caught some six months earlier.

As a result of his arrest forty-two Belgians had been taken by the Gestapo and the *Feldpolizei*. Each time a man or woman was arrested, Dixey was brought from the prison at St Gilles to identify them.

Although fully sympathizing with the indignation felt by those who had risked their lives to help the Englishman, only to be repaid by his act of betrayal, an unpleasant shadow touched my mind. How might I have reacted, placed in a similar position? How would I react in the face of any threat of death or torture?

Perched on the chair-back, listening to tale after tale of Dixey's perfidy, my attention was distracted by an onset of the same pains in my stomach that had been worrying me during the last few days. It was clearly related, to the drastic change of diet, and perhaps to the water. I said to Jules that I would like to get treatment but didn't know what the Germans' reaction might be. Not a favourable one I thought. Jules explained that there was a system of sick parades. Prisoners who wished to report sick had to give their name to the guard first thing in the morning. He added that if I were to tell the doctor that it would soon be my twentieth birthday, I might be able to wheedle a Red Cross parcel out of him.

Armed with the necessary German vocabulary given me by Jules – '*krank*'[sick] and '*Arzt*'[doctor], I determined to get myself on the sick parade the following morning.

As I turned from the window and began to climb down, I heard the key turn in the lock. I jumped and fell sprawling on the floor of the cell.

The German guards on duty in the cell-block would peer occasionally through a door's spy-hole. They wore rubber-soled shoes. The only warning I had had was the sound of the key turning in the lock. The guard was the same large, slow-moving German who had entered to have a closer look at the card-house I had been building on the floor. This time he had no smile on his face. From where I lay sprawled on the floor he looked at least ten feet tall. He lashed out with his foot as I scrambled to my feet and dodged out of reach. As he was wearing plimsolls, his aggression offered no serious threat. Nevertheless, I felt alarmed, not knowing how to deal with the situation. My instinctive reaction was to use words, to try to inject reason into the situation.

Unfortunately the German spoke no English, and I little German. This was one situation where any powers of persuasion I might have had were not likely to have effect. Despite this, I unleashed a torrent of expostulation and recrimination, as I dodged around the cell. What I asked, did he think he was doing? Was this the way a grown man should behave? Couldn't we be friends? During the whole of this monologue, oblivious to reasoned argument, the German sought clumsily to plant a kick on his moving, twisting, target.

Eventually out of breath, he came to a standstill, halted, as much as anything, by the surprising flow of sound from the prisoner hopping about in front of him. I took advantage of the apparent cessation of hostilities to seize the German's hand and shake it, trying to show that, on my side at least, all was forgiven. As I pumped his hand up and down, the German stood there with an expression of bewilderment on his face. Finally he disengaged his hand and, without a word, left the cell, shaking his head slowly from side to side.

Before the onset of my illness I was beginning to eat everything the servers slopped into my bowl: the evil-smelling cheese, the swede soup, the half-cooked potatoes, the mint tea and the heavy black bread.

My hunger reached its height between the coffee, which was all that I was given for breakfast, and the long wait for the midday meal. I had never managed to save from the daily ration a slice, or even half a slice, of bread to go with that coffee. Each day I determined to save something for the morning. Each day I failed to maintain my resolve.

At best I delayed the inevitable, sometimes managing to hold out long after the light had been turned off. After tossing and turning for an hour or so I would get up and, like a thief in the night, go to the little cupboard recessed into the wall, open the metal door, and take out the remaining half-slice.

It was always my intention not to eat all of it. I would hold it in my hand, bend my head down over it and smell its sour taste. I'd take the smallest of bites just to get the taste in my mouth, but once my palate had savoured the sour tartness of the dark bread I had grown to relish the battle was lost.

This happened, not once, but time and time again. My daily resolve not to eat that last slice mirrored the triumph of optimism over experience. And I saw, in the weakness of my resolve, a confirmation of the harsh judgement I had formulated concerning the intrinsic weakness of my own character. However, there was one benefit I drew from my present queasiness, and that was a complete loss of my former nagging hunger.

Whether from an excess of emotion engendered by my scuffle with the guard or simply because of the exercise involved, my stomach pains and the accompanying diarrhoea intensified, completely quelling all appetite. The misery of hunger had been replaced by that of diarrhoea, and I had reason to be grateful, having learnt that it was possible, even in that place, to get medical attention.

The usual difficulties of making myself understood were resolved by the advent of a young German guard who could speak English. The roster of guards changed every few weeks, a practice designed, I suppose, to stop familiarity developing between prisoner and guard.

The tall, slow-moving giant was replaced by a slender young man with blond hair and blue eyes, the Aryan of Hitler's Valhalla. The young German enjoyed speaking English and, despite his obvious fear of the *Feldwebel* seized every opportunity of having a few words with me. The first time we spoke he asked if there was anything he might to do help and, to my delight, promised to get me something to read.

We were never able to exchange more than a few brief sentences, but I learnt from whispered exchanges that, despite his uniform, he hated life in the army, and above all feared being sent to the Russian Front.

When I asked him whether he believed in the Nazis and their ideas, he shook his head, grimacing with disgust, and, looking quickly over his shoulder, mouthed the word, "Communist!" Then I asked him if I could see the doctor.

Some days later the *Feldwebel* shouted out a few cell numbers, of which mine was one. The cell-door opened and the young German put his head round the door. "Come along; you are to see the *Oberst*."

I stepped out on to the iron gallery and, looking over the rail to the floor beneath, I saw a group of prisoners standing in line. I smiled at the young German, thanked him in a whisper and, descending the iron steps, joined the others.

The young man next to me was about my own age. He was short and slight of build, his complexion pallid, black hair brushed straight back.

His appearance, clean-shaven and smartly dressed, contrasted strongly with my own dishevelled looks. He turned round to look at me, and said in a strong Cockney accent, " 'Ere, you're bloody English, ain't yer?" I looked at him in surprise. "I fawt yer was a fuckin' Jew-boy. You know, one o' them Poles."

I realized that this was Dixey.

The *Feldwebel* shouted to a guard who led us off to the medical room. As we waited, Dixey continued, "Yeah, when I saw yer in civvies, an' that, I fawt yer was a Pole. I didn't fink yer was English."

"I 'eard yer, didn'I, the other day with the guard? Fuckin' 'ell! I nearly died bloody laughin'. You talkin' to 'im in English. 'E didn' understand a fuckin' word. They don't understand nuffink, not English they don't. An' you goin' on at 'im. Tellin' 'im yer wanne be friends!"

I said, "Your name's Dixey, isn't it?"

His face changed from bland Cockney chirpiness to ferret-like suspicion. "What if it is?"

"The Belgian chap, the spy, told me. Said there was an Englishman in the cell opposite. A soldier."

"Oh 'im!" Dixey replied disparagingly. "Silly bugger! Caught wiv 'is parachute and everyfink. Bloody fool!"

"They caught you too, didn't they?"

"Caught me! They didn't catch me, mate. Nobody bloody catches me. I been on the run for nearly two fuckin' years. 'Ad a marvellous time, didn' I? Birds, booze, bags to eat, the lot. I can tell you mate, I 'ad the best of everyfink."

"But they caught you, didn't they? You wouldn't be in here if they hadn't caught you."

"Listen, chum," Dixey retorted, "you don't know nuffink about it. It was the bloody Belgians, see. Their bloody fault wasn' it?" After a pause he continued. "They was always on at me to escape. My bloody duty an' all that. Duty! did me fuckin' duty, didn' I?"

I said nothing. Dixey broke the silence. "Well, in the end I got cheesed off. They kept on at me all the bloody time. Couldn't go on 'iding me, too dangerous. In the end I'd 'ad enough. I reckoned I might as well 'ave a go."

"What happened?" I asked.

"I got nicked, that's what bloody 'appened. We got right to the French bloody frontier when they nicked me. I bin 'ere six bloody months. It don' look as if I'm ever gonna get out. I'd 'ave been all right if they'd 'ave let me alone. They'd never 'ave caught me."

I judged it prudent not to ask him about the forty-two Belgians who had been arrested because of him.

"Look, mate, you can do us a favour if you like."

"What's that?"

"It's me old lady."

"Your old lady?"

"Yeah, me mum. She ain't 'ad any news of me see, since I bin nicked. Those Belgians got it in for me. They won't lift a finger."

"Oh! Why's that?"

"They reckon I let'm in it. What the 'ell was I supposed to do? What could I do? Let the bastards shoot me? Not bloody likely, mate. You've only got one life, ain't yer? No, see, what I was thinkin' was, you're gonna get out before me. You could drop 'er a line. You know. tell 'er i'm safe an' all that."

"Of course," I assured him, "but why don't you write a note and give it to me to send? If she sees your handwriting, she'll know you're all right.'

Dixey answered briefly, "Can't write. Don't know 'ow."

"That's all right," I said, "just give me the address. I'll write as soon as I get to a P.O.W. camp."

The German doctor was tall, stout, with steel-rimmed spectacles.

"Ah, Mister Englishman! Take off shirt!"

He waited while I took off my shirt, and, wheezing asthmatically, sounded my chest using a short wooden tube quite unlike the familiar stethoscope.

"Good!" he said. "Is good." He took a step backwards and pointed to the small round scab on my chest. "What is?" he asked raising his chin enquiringly. I explained.

"A bullet, ja, ja. Is good ... is good," he said reassuringly.

"Open!" he continued, pressing my lower jaw down with one plump hand and introducing a wooden spatula into my mouth. "Is good ... is good ... all is good." He nodded his head several times in confirmation.

I said, "I've a pain here," and put my hand on my lower stomach.

"Ah, so!" replied the doctor not looking too impressed.

"I've diarrhoea, too." The doctor looked puzzled. I tried to think of some other way of describing my symptoms.

"*Viel scheissen!*" I said earnestly.

The doctor laughed.

"*Viel scheissen!* *Ja, ja* I give you something. No more *scheissen*." He spoke to the orderly who gave me a box of carbon tablets.

"Is good," said the doctor. "You are sick, you come back. *Verstehen?* You go now."

I hesitated and, encouraged by the doctor's kindly manner, said, "Doctor!"

"What is?"

I swallowed hard, feeling it was now or never. "Is it possible for me to have a Red Cross parcel?"

"A Red Cross parcel!" the doctor repeated, looking somewhat surprised.

I added, hoping it would give more weight to my request, "It's my birthday next week."

"Your birthday! Ach, so! How old?"

"I'll be twenty next Friday."

The doctor crossed to the sink and began to wash his hands, his back towards me.

"You come next week, on your birthday," and, after a pause, "is good! All is good!."

I went back to my cell pleased with my visit to the doctor, and the promise, vague as it was, of a Red Cross parcel.

When I got back to the cell-block the young German guard was on duty. He opened the cell-door and, as I stepped inside, followed me. Undoing a couple of buttons of his tunic, he took out a book and hurriedly thrust it into my hand.

The *Feldwebel*'s bellow cut short my attempt to thank him and he hurriedly withdrew, slamming the door shut and turning the key.

Although warmed by the guard's courage and kindness in getting me the book, I was disappointed to find that it was in French. Nevertheless, the very difficulty of teasing out the meaning with my meagre vocabulary absorbed my waking hours, reading and re-reading each line. I lived in a strange world people by characters with names like Lili, Firmin, and Milou.

The paper cover showed two men, one wearing a bowler with a curly brim, the other with long sideboards and a cigarette drooping from the corner of his mouth. In the background a man with a noose round his neck hung from a lamp-post.

The only detailed memory I have of the book is the title, *Le Pendu Rependu* (The man who was hanged twice). The book pictured the brutal life of the streets, fierce couplings in hotel bedrooms, drunkenness and petty crime. For me, however; it was not the cliché of Parisian life that one might have expected from the cover. In my reading of the book, the author's images became distorted, surrealistic, as I painfully picked my way through the labyrinth of vocabulary and syntax.

I had always been a gluttonous reader, swallowing books at breakneck speed. This avidity forced me on through the difficulty of the task

64

I had set myself. Nevertheless, I was grateful for such a task, enabling me to forget for hours at a time present hunger and apprehensions concerning the future.

Two days after my visit to he doctor I had an unexpected visitor. The *Feldwebel*, who had never before visited my cell, came, bringing with him the young guard as interpreter. The man showed no sign of his former friendliness. I assumed that the change in attitude was in some way related to the yellow piece of card pinned outside my cell. In the *Feldwebel*'s eyes I was no longer the young English airman, the "schoolboy" of our first encounter. I had changed into a "Jew".

I had met anti-semitism before. I had experienced it in my first love affair, at the age of ten.

I had seen the girl carrying a bundle of washing as she crossed the road at the top of the street where I lived. I thought her beautiful and the thought must have shown in my timid glance. She smiled and my heart leapt, but neither of us spoke.

I watched and waited for her to pass again, and some days later she did. This time she stopped and smiled.

"Hullo," I said.

"Hullo," she answered, looking down sideways at the pavement, and hugging her bundle tightly to her.

"I saw you last Tuesday," I ventured. She scraped the toe of her shoe in a shallow curve on the pavement.

"You don't live round here, do you?"

"No! Roman Road," she answered.

Roman Road was several streets away, a strange neighbourhood for me, full of poor houses with no railings in front of the house and a street-door opening directly into the living-room, but I knew it. I and my friends used to pass it on our way to Victoria Park to play football or cricket.

We smiled shyly at each other.

She said, shifting the weight of her bundle to the other hip, "Trrah! Got to go. Me Mum's waiting."

"Trrah!" I replied.

She passed on down the street. I stood looking after her. After a hundred yards or so she turned her head and, seeing me still there, gave a little wave. I waved back and stood waiting until she had disappeared round the bend in the road.

I felt a joy I had never known before. I was consumed with impatience until I could see her again, and when I did see her my heart missed a beat. When I left her side sure of her love, I skipped along the pavement lighter than air, and when I was away from her every small girl in the distance was, I felt sure, her, and when I found it wasn't I felt desolate and empty.

Our meetings proliferated. I went to her street to play. We would walk along together in silence, or engage in conversations where words counted for little.

"Me Mum's always on at me," she would murmur sadly. "Can't do nuffink without her being on at me."

"Yeah," I would sympathize, "I know what you mean."

The conversation was disjointed.

"Me aunt Flo's gotta lovely dress, all flowers 'an that."

"I'm going to have a bike soon, a real one, with dropped handlebars," I would counter.

"I'm gonna' 'ave one like 'ers, wiv flowers."

I would try to think of something to say.

The girl would continue, "She's got a necklace wiv real jewels, Aunt Flo. It's ever so nice. Gotta go now, Trrah!"

"Trrah! See you Tuesday," and we would part with the warm feeling that we loved and were loved.

I had never told her that I was Jewish. Even at that age I knew such things mattered. I could have said nothing, kept my secret, but being me, I felt the need for drama, the need to precipitate a crisis.

One afternoon as we sat talking on the doorstep in front of her house, I confessed that I had a secret and, after a reasonable amount of time, allowed her to persuade me to reveal it.

Having confessed that I was Jewish, we sat for some time in a thoughtful silence, a silence tinged for me with romantic melancholy. When I left we didn't exchange our usual farewells.

I waited that next Tuesday for her to pass. At length I saw her coming, but she crossed to the other side of the road. I couldn't bear to let her pass without forcing the issue, without playing out the drama to its conclusion. As she reached me, she looked away as if she hadn't seen me. I ran after her.

"Aren't you going to play?" I asked standing in front of her. She looked down at her feet, and I repeated, "Aren't you going to play?" and before she could answer, attempting to save the remnants of my pride, I added, "I can't anyway, I've got to go an errand."

She, however, wasn't going to let me off that lightly. "Me Mum says I musn't play with you," and after a pause, "Anyway, I don't like Jews."

I stood aside and watched her pass on down the street, watching until she disappeared round the bend hugging her bundle.

The guard stood to attention at the door while the *Feldwebel* wiped his finger on different surfaces. The German said haltingly, "The *Feldwebel* has said that the cell is not clean."

I guessed that the *Feldwebel*'s actual words had been considerably harsher. He continued his harangue and the guard translated: "Every inch of the cell has to be cleaned."

I nodded and replied, "I'll need something to clean with. I haven't anything ... brushes, soap."

The guard said, "Don't worry. I'll bring you everything you need."

Far from considering the *Feldwebel*'s orders as some kind of punishment, I was delighted to have another activity to add to my limited number of pastimes.

The water was cold and there was the usual bar of ersatz soap. I washed down everything in sight: walls, as far as I could reach, the floor, the door and even the iron bed-frame. As I scrubbed, the water sank into the joints in the floor-boards and little white insects appeared like tiny silver fish.

The next day there was an inspection by what seemed to me a high ranking officer, his uniform bedecked with gold braid. I wondered whether the cleaning of the cell and the visit were related, and whether either, or both, had anything to do with my letter to the Commandant.

The officer was accompanied by the *Feldwebel*, who muttered something to his superior. The officer said something in German. I couldn't understand the remark, but I was determined to take advantage of his visit and said slowly and carefully in English, "I'm an English airman. I have been in solitary confinement in this cell for six weeks. I should be treated as a military and not a political prisoner. This is against the Geneva Convention."

The *Feldwebel*, turning his back to me and lowering his voice, said something to the officer. I couldn't catch what it was he said, but I did hear the word "Jude" repeated several times. The officer nodded his head and walked out of the cell.

The *Feldwebel* paused at the door, and turning to me, said, "*Ja, ja, du verstehst. Alle Juden verstehen Deutsch.*"

There was some truth in what he said. Many first generation Jews coming to England from the ghettoes and Jewish *shtetls* [small Jewish villages] of Russia and Poland spoke Yiddish, a low form of German, and their children, whose first language was English, would be accustomed to hearing Yiddish spoken at home.

This was the case of my parents, who had been born in England, but I, as a third generation Jew, and having been brought up in a neighbourhood mostly peopled by non-Jews, knew hardly any Yiddish.

Nevertheless, I had managed during the six weeks in the St Gilles prison to understand a little German from listening to the guards and the servers.

The words of the *Feldwebel* echoed in my mind: *"Ja, ja, du verstehst. Alle Juden verstehen Deutsch"* There was a dangerous, unpleasant element in this latest meeting between myself and the *Feldwebel*, the feeling that I was somehow being accused of a cunningly concealed crime, that concerned, not my rôle as a prisoner of war, but one more hateful in the *Feldwebel*'s eyes, more heinous, that of being a Jew.

The day following the visit of the German officer I was given a haircut and shave, the first since my arrival at St Gilles. A chair was placed on the landing outside the cell. My sparse beard was scraped away with an open razor and my hair cropped.

The young German guard said in a whisper, "You are to see the Commandant this afternoon."

Freshly shaved, my hair a respectable length and my jacket brushed, I was escorted through a reception area and along corridors leading to the administration block.

The large room we entered was full of young men and women, some in civilian clothing, others in uniform. The guard left me in charge of two young men in uniform who were part of the office staff. I was to wait there until the Commandant was ready to see me. Both young men spoke English fluently. They were not much older than I and seemed delighted to have the opportunity of practising the language. They explained to their colleagues that I was an English airman who had been shot down. Interest was aroused and men and women gathered around asking questions through the self-appointed interpreters. Was I a pilot? How had I been shot down? Had any of the crew been killed? When they heard that I had been hit in the chest, they wanted me to show them my wound. Sheepishly, but with some pride, I undid the buttons of my shirt. They looked at the small pink circle that was all there was to see now that the scab had fallen off.

They were surprised that I couldn't speak German and asked about my school. They too, like the German who had slapped my face, spoke of Oxford and Cambridge. They seemed to assume that all educated Englishmen went to one of these two universities. I explained that I had joined the RAF on my eighteenth birthday, otherwise I might well have gone to Oxford or Cambridge – a fact that would have greatly surprised my teachers.

At last, the Commandant was ready to see me. The room and everything in it, including the Commandant, looked like a Hollywood film-set. The room was long and wide and furnished with heavy chairs and glass-fronted bookcases. At the far end of the room behind an enormous desk sat the Commandant.

His head emerged from the stiff collar of his uniform without the apparent intervention of a neck. The skin covering it was the colour and texture of parchment, with heavy furrows marking the forehead and deep fleshy creases descending vertically between faintly discernible eyebrows. The tiny button nose was almost lost in the declivities of the fat pock-marked cheeks, his thick lips set in a permanent moue of disgust. He wore a monocle. I could hardly believe it. A monocle!. Here, I thought, was a case of nature imitating art. Nobody at home would ever believe me!

The young interpreter had been given a small upright chair at some distance from the desk. He sat bolt upright, at attention, as it were, whilst sitting down.

I stood at some distance from the desk. I wasn't at all clear as to what military etiquette required. I was dressed in civilian clothes and this seemed to rule out the question of saluting, or standing either to attention or at ease. I compromised and stood with my hands lightly clenched in front of me.

The Commandant was not pleased and let out a succession of guttural screams. These sounds were translated into English by the interpreter;

"The Herr Commandant would like you to stand up straight."

I stood up as straight as I could.

"The Herr Commandant wishes for you to push out your chest."

I pushed out my chest as far as it would go.

"The Herr Commandant says for you to hold up your head like a soldier."

Of all the airmen in the Royal Air Force few had less soldierly qualities than myself. My long skinny frame just didn't fit in with the neat movements demanded by my mentors, and my attitude of mind failed to conform to their expectations. This reaction was inevitably interpreted by the corporal as dumb insolence. He rated me a thoroughly bad lot and the Commandant seemed to share the corporal's opinion, judging from the sounds issuing from his distorted features.

His temper was not improved by having to wait for the interpreter to translate his explosion into English, and further pauses for the translation of my nervous, almost incomprehensible, answers. The young interpreter was in almost as fearful a state as I.

However, I persevered in attempting to make the points I had outlined in my letter; that I should be treated as an airman and not as a political prisoner, that the Red Cross should be informed that I was a prisoner and that I should be allowed a change of clothes and the wherewithal to keep myself clean.

The Commandant appeared to have no intention of discussing the points I had made in the letter and when I falteringly mentioned the Geneva Convention, I thought that he was about to reach for his gun and bring the interview to a rapid conclusion.

Fortunately he was only reaching for a cigar, which he puffed nervously for some time without saying a word. I felt that writing the letter hadn't been such a good idea after all. The Commandant put down his cigar, pressed a buzzer and ordered the guard to take me back to my cell.

That night I didn't sleep well. The visit to the Commandant, instead of solving problems, seemed to have ruined my chances of ever getting released. The only reaction I had aroused had been one of anger. I'd be lucky if I escaped punishment. When I did get to sleep it was full of disturbing dreams. It was still dark when suddenly I awoke to find myself sitting bolt upright, my forehead wet with perspiration. My heart was beating fast. I tried to calm myself. It was only a nightmare, nothing to worry about. I looked slowly around the cold, dark cell.

Nothing! No! There is something! Voices! I could hear voices! I looked towards the barred window set high in the wall. The sound was not coming from there. It was coming from outside the cell door.

I threw aside the blanket and crossed to the door. The voices were coming from the cells on the ground floor.

There was the sound of whispering, of shuffling feet. Then a voice, loud and authoritative, called out a list of names.

"Roggermann!"

"Sancerre!"

"Sondheim!"

"Steiner!"

"Strauss!"

Each name was again followed by a low rustling murmur of men's voices.

"Tardeau!"

"Weil!"

"Weitz!"

the loud commanding voice stopped and the whispering rose.

Then that voice again – German – cutting through the murmur of prisoners' voices. The man now spoke calmly. I continued to listen, shivering with cold, but drawn by a fearful fascination.

The voice stopped. Then a clatter of feet on the tiled floor. The iron grilles of the central hall slid open as the group passed out into the hall. There was the sound of the heavy iron grilles closing.

Back in bed, I pondered the significance of the rollcall. What were they doing with the prisoners at this time of night? I thought of the Belgian schoolmaster condemned to be shot.

According to Jules, the Germans removed belts, braces, ties and shoelaces, anything that might help a man to commit suicide. Could they have been taking men out to be shot? I found it hard to believe. The condemned men, too, perhaps, found it hard to believe, right up until the last moment, when, tied to posts, or backs against a wall, the squad of German soldiers in front of them levelled their rifles.

I hurriedly dismissed the thought. I was exaggerating, dramatizing! A group of prisoners were being sent to work camps in Germany; that's what it was. The Kauffmanns and Vera might be in a similar group. I would find out in the morning.

However, I was not to find out whether my friends had been sent to Germany, or what the meaning of that rollcall had been. At about ten o'clock that morning my cell was opened by a guard I had never seen before. There had been another change of roster. I wondered what had happened to the fair-headed German guard. I hoped he hadn't been sent to the Russian Front.

His replacement was now standing in the cell. I couldn't understand what he was saying and had no idea what he wanted. Irritated by my inaction and apparent stupidity, he began to thrust into my arms whatever was movable. I realized that I was to take what few possessions I had with me. Was I to be released? Had the letter to the Commandant borne fruit, despite the man's apparent fury?

In my reception hall we passed the *Feldwebel*, his surly face full of hate. The guard and I passed through the gates leading to the next wing of cells. I followed the guard as he mounted an iron staircase. He unlocked the door of a cell, the twin of the one from which I had been ejected. I looked at the barred window high in the wall. This window, however, unlike the one I had left behind, overlooked the boundary wall of the prison.

I was not going to be released. In answer to my request to be treated as an airman and not as a political prisoner I had been transferred to the military wing.

An immediate advantage of being in this part of the prison became apparent when the daily meal was served. It was excellent, well cooked and varied. The doctor's carbon tablets had worked well; but because of the improvement in my health, hunger, like an aching tooth, was again with me. My hopes centred on the promised Red Cross parcel. The

71

doctor had said I should come and see him on my birthday. Next Friday, the twenty-fifth of September, I would be twenty.

The week passed even more slowly than usual, but at least I had something to look forward to. I imagined the possible contents of the Red Cross parcel. I considered tins of Spam, boxes of soft triangular cheese wrapped in silver paper, and jars of honey and jam, but the delight for which my heart, or rather my stomach, yearned was for sweets.

On Thursday, the day before my birthday, I explained to the guard that I was '*krank*' and showed him the box of carbon tablets I had been given. I repeated over and over again, as if to a half-witted child. "*Morgen ... krank ... Oberarzt.*"

The man looked at me dully, then as comprehension dawned, nodded his head and grinned. "*Ja, ja, verstehe! Du bist krank. Ja, ja! Gut! ... Morgenfrüh!*"

The doctor peered at me over the top of a pair of metal-framed glasses.

"*Aha! Der Flieger! Viel scheissen, nicht wahr?* What can I do for you? You are sick?"

"You said I should come back."

"Come back?"

"On my birthday."

"Aha! You are coming for your birthday present, *nicht wahr!*"

I nodded. "You said I could have a Red Cross parcel."

I returned to the central hall hugging my parcel, followed by the guard. The *Feldwebel* was standing at the open door of his little office. We waited for him to open the grille leading to the cells. He looked me up and down, then, noting the parcel clutched to my chest asked, "*Was ist das?*"

The guard explained. The *Feldwebel* seemed to explode. He strode over to where I was standing and pulled the parcel out of my hands and took it into his office. The guard and I waited outside.

It was some time before the man emerged. When he did he was smiling. I could see that the sealed parcel had been opened. When I reached the cell and opened the box, I saw the reason for the Feldwebel's good humour. Whatever could be opened had been opened and the contents poured or scattered into the bottom of the box. Jam was poured over cubes of sugar; honey, coffee and chocolate formed a sticky mess, impossible to salvage.

The following day I had a second visit from the Luftwaffe officer. This time the interview took place in a small stockroom in the cell-block itself. Books, brooms, pails and chairs were stored here. A space

72

had been cleared in the centre of the room to accommodate a desk and two chairs.

The officer, still wearing his greatcoat, looked ill at ease. He gestured to me to sit down as he took the other chair.

On the floor, at my feet, were a stack of French bibles. I imagined the wealth of reading they contained. Plenty there to keep me occupied! The officer, noticing my interest, asked if I could read French. I explained that I was not at all fluent, but enjoyed trying to make out the meaning. It was, I told him, like working on a crossword puzzle. He laughed and, encouraged, I said hesitantly.

"Do you think it possible for me to borrow one?"

"I'm afraid not. I have no authority here. None at all. These may have been confiscated. Bibles are considered by some people to be dangerous literature, you know."

He drew a packet wrapped in brown paper from one of the deep pockets of his overcoat.

"Here is something for you ... a little less nourishing than the Bible, but it will do you good."

Surprised, I turned the flat little packet over in my hands, thanked him and raised my head questioningly.

In answer the officer smiled. "Sausage", he said. "Germany is famous for its sausage. I thought you might like to taste some."

I was as much affected by the kindness of the officer's act as by the gift itself; more so, in fact. I stumbled out a few words of thanks.

The officer continued. "Eat it later in your cell. Put it away now, in your pocket."

He leant back in his chair and looking directly at me, said, "I'm afraid I have some sad news for you. I told you that I would need to find your plane in order to establish your identity." I nodded. The officer continued, "We have found the plane." He paused.

"We have found, too, your comrades, their bodies. The plane was almost completely destroyed by fire, but we have identified three of the four men." He drew a slip of paper from his breast pocket.

"William Hall, Alan Martin, George Miller. We were not able to identify the fourth body."

I listened in silence as the officer announced their deaths. I had seen for myself the dead bodies of Wilf, our Canadian navigator and Bill, the pilot, and was quite certain that neither Al Martin, the Canadian front-gunner, nor George, the rear-gunner, had escaped from their turrets. I knew they were all dead, but knew, without 'knowing'.

I had always spoken freely when questioned about the fate of the crew, but had felt nothing inside, no emotion. It was as if I too, or

73

some part of me, was dead. When telling the tale of our being shot down, it was as if I were telling the story of a film I had seen or a book I had read.

I had felt since being shot down that there must be something wrong with me that I could accept their death so easily. Now, hearing their names read out, the men neatly reduced to a list, their deaths officially confirmed, something happened inside me. I searched in my pocket for my ragged handkerchief, wiped my eyes and blew my nose. I avoided the German's eye, not knowing how he might take this unmilitary display. His expression unchanged, he said, "You will soon be leaving for a prisoner-of-war camp. Two or three days, I should think, no longer."

Although the officer had said three or four days, I was certain that he was just being cautious. Now that they had checked my identity, there could be no possible reason why I shouldn't be released immediately. The order might have already arrived at the prison. That would mean that they would come for me tomorrow or even that very night.

When night came and I hadn't been released my hopes shifted to the following morning, and then to the following day. And so the days spun out, accumulated one upon the other, listening at the cell door, listening for the number to be called, for the step on the iron gallery, the key turning in the lock. Disappointment grew into despair, and despair deepened as the days stretched into weeks.

The German's words, then, had been lies. His gift, his kindness, part of some softening up process, to what end I couldn't imagine. My hair and beard grew, and I became once more, with my pallid gaunt face, to resemble those others, the thousands, the millions of Jews trapped in Hitler's prisons and concentration camps.

Drained of energy, tired of inventing ways of killing time, too distracted to continue my laboured reading of the French book, I would pace the cell from one side of the bed to the other – eleven strides, past the door, along the wall with the cupboard and the notices, along under the window, and back to the other side of the bed.

In my perambulations around the cell, muttering to myself, the other voice inside my head, condemnatory as ever, would, as it so often did, comment on my behaviour: "You're play-acting, exaggerating. You're always doing it." Nevertheless, something was happening to me.

I longed for the night so that I could stretch out on the bed and escape into dreams, but when night came that voice inside my brain continued its monotonous monologue until my head felt as if it were splitting and I longed for the light of morning.

The October days were damp and cold and the hours of daylight growing short. The naked bulb would only come on when darkness had almost completely invaded the cell. I sat for hours in cold, cheerless gloom.

In the cell I struggled with fear and depression. it was now three weeks since my interview with the Luftwaffe officer. I had had absolute confidence in the man, in his kindness, his quiet dignity and undemonstrative compassion. He echoed for me the human values I had taken so much for granted back home in England. Surely such a man wouldn't have deliberately lied to me? He had said two or three days. Twenty-one days had now passed.

Of course the Luftwaffe officer might be powerless to effect my transfer to a prisoner-of-war camp. The Gestapo or the *Feldpolizei* might have brushed aside all requests to let me go. Perhaps my being Jewish introduced an element which made it impossible for the Luftwaffe to help me.

My letter to the Commandant might have been a mistake, might have made the Gestapo aware of my presence. I might now be completely at the mercy of these people and the hatred that possessed them, a hatred symbolized by the yellow card on my cell door.

It was now ten weeks, seventy days, since I had first been arrested. On Saturday evening, the seventeenth of October, as the shadows gathered in the cold, silent cell, I knelt beside my bed. My hands placed together, my eyes closed, feeling a little foolish, I prayed. My loneliness, my desire to be free, if only for a few moments, had pushed me to this exaggerated, most uncharacteristic of actions. The very act of closing my eyes allowed me in some measure to escape the confines of the cell. The closing of my eyes banished the sight of the cell walls, the grey bolt-studded door, the rusty latrine bucket, the barred windows.

I entered my inner world. There I struggled to push away the thick strands of my fears., The opening words of the Lord's Prayer echoed in my mind, words which I had, as a small boy, repeated in school-assemblies day after day and year after year, "Our Father which art in heaven...", but I could not bring myself to utter them.

The words were a statement of unquestioning faith, of unequivocal belief; they were instilled on my agnostic tongue. I could only whisper, "Dear God! Dear God!" over and over again. I could commit myself no further than this appeal for help.

Gradually there arose within me a deep pool of calm and peace, as, when a small child, recovering from an illness, I had lain weak but safe and warm in the comfort of my mother's large bed. I knelt now beside the prison bed, my heart and mind soothed by a deep silence.

That night I went to bed and, contrary to my usual tossing and turning, I slept.

I was awoken next morning by the sounds of the servers' trolley. I had slept well and felt strangely refreshed and at peace, as if recovered from a long wasting sickness. I lay still, listening to the sound of the trolley drawing nearer, of cell doors being opened and slammed shut.

The calm engendered by my attempt at prayer seemed to be with me still. No longer feeling like a bewildered victim flinching before each threatened blow, I accepted my condition, closing my mind to futile conjecture.

At ten o'clock that morning the *Feldwebel* called the number of my cell. I remained calm. There had been so many disappointments. However, as the sound of the guard's approach came nearer, it was impossible to contain a feeling of mounting excitement. The cell door was pushed open. The same tired-looking, middle-aged guard who had brought me to the new cell stood in the doorway.

"*Komm! Schnell machen!*" He pointed to my few belongings.

"*Alles! Komm!*" My mood of quiet calm burst like a bubble. I could hardly breathe for excitement as I hastily gathered together my few possessions.

The *Feldwebel* was waiting for me at the foot of the iron staircase. I followed him into his office. A young man in the uniform of the Luftwaffe was standing in a corner. The *Feldwebel* indicated curtly that I was to put my possessions on the desk.

He examined each object in turn: spare shirt, vest, toothbrush, my ragged pack of playing-cards, my book *Le Pendu Rependu*, and, after examining them, threw them, one by one, onto the floor.

He came finally to the letter-forms which I had used for scribbling down 'probabilities', for sundry attempts at poems, and for making a rough copy of my letter to the Commandant. He looked at them for some time, his scarred face growing red with anger. Crumpling the paper into balls, he threw those, too, onto the floor, his voice rising to a now familiar pitch of screaming invective.

Kneeling on the floor at his feet, picking up each of the articles he had thrown to the ground, I stopped what I was doing, raised my head and looked at the man. For the first time I confronted the hateful mask of a face, staring into the red-rimmed eyes, my expression registering an answering hate.

The ugly stream of sound from the *Feldwebel* stopped. I, my courage fuelled by anger, continued to hold his gaze. I said in English, "I'm glad I'll never see your ugly face again!"

The German, not understanding what I had said, but recognizing, no doubt, my sense of outrage, remained silent. The young Luftwaffe airman, who had been a silent witness, touched my arm and indicated that I should follow him.

In the cobbled courtyard of the prison there was a small newspaper van. A civilian driver, seated at the wheel, was waiting. I looked around for a military vehicle but there was none. The German airman nodded his head in the direction of the van. The authorities were clearly not worried about any attempt of mine to escape. I knew it was my duty to do so and I told myself that, given the chance, I would, but knew that if I were really honest with myself, the ten weeks passed in solitary confinement had weakened me physically and frightened me out of all former heroic aspirations.

The possibility of recapture in civilian clothes, without identification, and the unthinkable prospect of weeks or months once again in solitary confinement, with perhaps a concentration camp at the end, made it unlikely that I would ever attempt to escape.

Moreover, I had looked forward for so long to this transfer from the loneliness of my cell to the life of a prisoner-of-war camp that I couldn't bear the thought of putting that in jeopardy.

4

DULAG LUFT

Sunday, 18 October, 1942: Hitler orders execution of all British Commandos taken prisoner

We threaded our way along the platform between knots of soldiers in ill-fitting uniforms. The little Luftwaffe officer led the way, smart in leather belt, holster and polished jackboots. I and the American pilot followed, and, bringing up the rear, the young German soldier, a youngster, little more than a boy, having trouble with his forage cap and heavy rifle.

I glanced at my reflection as we passed a glass-fronted poster. The tall, thin, lugubrious image looked back at me, shadowy, ghost-like. Yet today I felt as happy and excited as any child off on a school treat. The prospect of life in a prisoner-of-war camp, among other air-crew, filled me with pleasurable anticipation.

As we passed a notice '*Herren – Messieurs*' in gothic script, black on white, I nudged the American and pointed to the sign. He grunted and shrugged his shoulders. Despite this lack of encouragement, I caught up with the officer, tapped him on the shoulder, and, pointing to the notice, said "*Pissen?*"

The officer looked up at me, and then glanced at his watch and replied, "*Ja, Ja! Aber...*" He tapped with his gloved hand the revolver housed in its leather holster and nodded his head.

The young guard was sent with us. The three of us stood silently in line facing the wall. For me there was freedom in the familiar ritual, despite the guard and the rifle. I turned and looked at the American and whispered, "What d'you think?"

He was, as usual, unresponsive, recognizing no kinship in our common plight. He muttered an unintelligible reply.

"With all these people we could get away, make a break for it," I said. "They wouldn't shoot. Not with all these crowds."

The German guard had stepped down from the urinal and was waiting for us to finish. The American just stood there making no attempt to reply or even deigning to turn his head.

"What d'you think?" I insisted.

He remained morosely silent, his refusal to react to my suggestion making me feel foolish and naive.

Then, still staring at the wall, the American muttered, "Forget it. I ain't playing soldiers."

He was, of course, right. I bit my lip and felt the blood rush to my cheeks. "Playing soldiers?"

I said, "Yeah, you're right. It's too risky."

The officer unfastened his belt with its holster and heavy pistol and placed them on the luggage net above the seat. He peered at his reflection in the glass of the framed advertisement and smoothed back his thinning hair.

The American took the corner seat opposite the officer, folded his arms and closed his eyes. The little guard sat down next to him, rifle between his knees. One hand holding the rifle steady, with the other he unbuttoned the flap of his tunic pocket and managed to pull out a small bag of sweets. He glanced across at the officer and put the bag on his lap.

I sat down next to the officer, opposite the German lad and looked at his bag of sweets with covetous eyes. After ten weeks of prison diet my body craved sugar as if a drug. My mouth filled with saliva as I watched him choose a sweet and put it in his mouth.

I looked across at the American. He had been a disappointment. The Luftwaffe corporal who had collected me from the prison had told me there was another prisoner, "*ein Amerikanischer Kamerad*".

I had looked forward eagerly to the sight of this "*Kamerad*", but was bemused to see in the small guard hut at the Luftwaffe air base an unshaven, miserable-looking individual, wearing greenish-brown khaki shirt and shorts; not a uniform I had ever seen. I wondered if the man was a German "plant". The American, looking up through steel-rimmed glasses at me in my shabby pinstripe suit, had grunted and looked away. And that was how it had been ever since.

I thought of the remark "I ain't playing soldiers". He's right, I reflected. I've no more intention of escaping than he has. I'm just less honest, still trying to play the hero.

Finding this self-examination uncomfortable., I let the thought go and smiled at the young guard sitting opposite, who, ignoring my gaze clearly fixed on his paper bag, continued stolidly sucking his sweet.

Leaning forward, I peered through the carriage window as the train rattled along through the flat Flemish countryside.

Where were we going? The officer spoke no English and I only fragments of German. Would it be directly to a prisoner-of-war camp or to the Dulag Luft?

Back on the squadron we had been warned about Dulag Luft, an interrogation camp near Frankfurt for shot-down air-crew brought to it from all over Germany and the occupied territories.

"Remember chaps, only your rank, name and number. Jerry's a cunning blighter. Even a bus ticket in your pocket'll give him information. Could cost the life of a crew, of some of your own chaps. He'll try to wheedle all kinds of gen out of you. Even have chaps dressed up in RAF uniform.

They never kept prisoners long at Dulag Luft. They'd try and get as much information out of you as they could, and after a day or so send you on to a prisoner-of-war camp.

Thanks to the list I'd given to Vera they already had any information they might have extracted from me. However, the nagging thought arose that they would also know I was Jewish. Would I be treated differently?

The young German was looking at me out of the corner of his eye. Partly joking, I pointed first to the sweets and then to myself. The boy seemed startled. His hand went slowly, not to the bag of sweets on his knee, but to his mouth. Taking out the wet sticky object, a shining yellow gob-stopper, he looked at it, bit it in two and offered half to me, the fastidious me who as a child would never accept the lick of another child's ice-cream. I accepted the saliva-covered gift and, with feigned pleasure, put it in my mouth.

Tuesday, 20 October: Allied aircraft begin a four-day operation to establish air-superiority over El Alamein; a preliminary to new ground offensive. German forces, after a massive attack on Stalingrad, are repulsed.

On arrival at Dulag Luft I was locked in a cell-like room in one of a group of long wooden barracks which made up the interrogation centre. The room was furnished with a bed, a table, two chairs and a wash-basin. There were heavy bars at the window.

I waited nervously all that first day to be interrogated, once again prey to the endless cycle of nagging doubt. Would I have to submit to the same questions I had faced in Brussels? Would I have to repeat the same fabrications? Would I be treated as a prisoner of war? Did they know I was Jewish?

The information about me must have been sent on from Brussels. They would know about my capture in civilian clothes and have all the information I had given to Vera.

I found it difficult to understand why I'd been brought here. What more could they hope to get from me?

I slept badly that night and was relieved when, through the barred window, dawn strengthened into day. I washed, dressed and straightened the covers on the bed and then sat waiting.

Soon I heard footsteps in the corridor, doors opening and a murmur of voices from the adjoining room. I tried to hear what was being said but could only hear an indistinct pattern of sound.

At last I heard the door of the next room close and footsteps approach. The door opened and a young Luftwaffe officer entered. I stood hurriedly to attention. He sat down at the table and motioned me to take the other chair.

The interrogation was not what I had expected. He made no reference to my arrest in Brussels nor to any of the questions which I had been asked by the *Feldpolizei*.

The interrogation consisted of answering questions from a form which the officer claimed was an official Red Cross document. It was needed, he claimed, so that my parents could be informed, but I had been warned about such forms. Nevertheless, I answered all the questions, being quite sure that in my case they already knew the answers.

When the form-filling came to an end and the officer rose to leave I nervously asked him if the fact that I was Jewish would affect my being sent to a prisoner-of-war camp. The officer looked surprised.

"I know nothing about that," he said, shrugged his shoulders and left the room.

As I entered the hut airmen at the table nearest the door glanced up with some surprise, then, for the most part, without a word, turned their backs and continued their conversation. Some, it was true, gave a perfunctory nod, but quickly turned away. No eager crowd clustered round to hear my story. Not quite the welcome I had expected.

The confidence engendered by my release from the St Gilles prison quickly ebbed away. An exaggerated awareness of my appearance overcame me: my lack of a uniform, my shabby suit. I felt loath to cross the room. I stood awkwardly by the nearest table, feeling like a gate-crasher at a party.

They all seemed to know each other. Yet they could only have been here a few days. There was a proliferation of "Taffs", of "Jocks", of "Chalkies". Most seemed to have been shot down with at least one other member of their crew.

I sat down at the extreme end of the bench and looked at the others, watching the play of facial expression that added, as they listened to the speaker, a silent commentary. The man holding their attention was Jock Graham, a fair-headed giant, with a sparse blond moustache and the neat features of a tailor's dummy. His prissy Scottish vowels, like those of a well-brought-up young lady, accorded strangely with his use of language.

"Ye ken what it's like back there, black as a nigger's arse. Well, he puts a leg over the fuckin' spar, to get his chute, ye ken. Puts his leg over an falls oot the fuckin' plane. Falls oot! There wassne anythin' there. Just a fuckin' great hole."

Sammy, a rosy-cheeked rear-gunner sitting next to me, gave me a solemn wink and inched along the bench, giving me a bit more room.

Palmer, a thin-lipped Cockney, hollow-cheeked, hollow-chested, attempted to introduce his own tale. "Talk about fall out of a pline..." Graham, indignant, thrust his face close to the interruptor. "Stop yer yap, yer Cockney git. I'm no finished yet!"

The door of the hut was suddenly kicked open and there was a cry of "Brew up!" Two men, prisoners like the rest, entered, staggering under the weight of a heavy dustbin-like container, hooked, sedan fashion, between two carrying poles.

"Quick! Grab the mug!" Sammy pointed to an unclaimed enamelled mug on the table, and, as I hesitated, insisted. "Go on, before some lying bugger says it's his!" I followed him, joining the queue, which formed with amazing speed. "You've got to be quick," Sammy explained. "Some of these gannets 'll be up for seconds before you've had your first."

The queue formed in a reasonably orderly fashion, the men shuffling slowly forward to where one of the servers ladled tea into each proferred mug.

"Real tea! Great!" I enthused.

"Pinched out the ruddy parcels, mite, pinched out the ruddy parcels!", said Palmer, behind us in the queue.

Sammy explained. "We're supposed to get Red Cross parcels. We're entitled to a parcel, see, a parcel each; Geneva Convention and all that. The nearest we've got to one so far is a brew of tea."

"Eh! You! Lofty!" Jock Graham's bellicose roar sounded from somewhere near the back of the queue. "You with all the fuckin' mugs!" He pushed his way unchallenged through the line of men until he stood near the front of the queue. I had some difficulty in seeing the object of his wrath, but, despite my interrupted view, I was almost certain I recognized the small man now faced by the angry Scotsman. The small figure, his pale boy's face blandly innocent, looked up at Graham. "Me?" he asked.

"Ay, Lofty, you!" said Graham, standing threateningly over him. The men around were silent. He was a very large man. The small man grinned, an appealing wide-mouthed grin, showing not the slightest perturbation. "My name's David."

"I dinna care if your name's Jesus bloody Christ. It's one man, one cup, see!" He poked his large finger into David's chest. "Ay, an' it should be only half a mug in your case, a wee manniken like you." He looked around to see the effect of his witticism.

David gestured towards three men, cards in hand, at a distant table. "I'm dummy," he explained. "I get the tea, see."

Graham eyed the three bridge players who seemed highly amused at their small friend's predicament.

Graham's tone became less bellicose. "All right!" he threatened. "You watch it!"

"I will. I will! Shan't take my eye off it," David murmured.

Graham, now at the head of the queue, served out of turn, went back, sipping his tea, to his domain, the table near the door.

As David followed carrying his four cups, I stretched out my hand and tapped him on the shoulder. David turned, half-expecting further trouble.

"How's it going, David?" I asked. David, an embarrassed smile on his face, eyed my civilian suit, my unshaven face, looking more like a refugee than a POW. Recognition began to dawn. The face was familiar. Seeing that my erstwhile instructor seemed to have forgotten me, I added, "Banbury, 12 O.T.U.!"

David screwed up his eyes, "Jesus!" he exclaimed. "What the hell you doing in that get-up?"

Thursday, 22 October: U.S. General Mark Clark arrived in Algiers by submarine for secret meeting with pro-Allied French officers to facilitate forthcoming North African invasion

At the station halt the engine loomed over us. We waited in small isolated groups, eyeing with some misgiving the train which was to take us to a prisoner-of-war camp somewhere in Germany.

One whole carriage had been reserved for the Dulag Luft prisoners and another for the twelve or so guards acting as escort. As they lined up behind us we scrambled into our designated carriage.

The seats were of wood and ranged on either side of a long central corridor. The antediluvian appearance of the train in general, and the carriage in particular, pointed to the First World War rather than the present one.

I had been adopted by David's small group of friends, partly, I suppose, on the strength of my former association with him. When I first met him I had just arrived at the O.T.U. with the rest of my crew to complete the last stage of our training before being sent to an operational squadron. He had already completed one tour of operations, about thirty trips, and was now serving a stint as wireless instructor.

He had always claimed that his one ambition was to get back on ops, which the cynical among us claimed to be a line-shoot. His presence here on the train, however, confirmed that his enthusiasm for active service was real.

An armed guard stood at either end of the carriage watching as we milled around in a noisy struggle for favoured seats near windows or with room for our friends.

A small bespectacled German got into the carriage and stood with the guard, looking on at the mêlée. After a few moments, with some difficulty, he called for attention. As the noise and bustle died down, he asked us apologetically, in strongly accented English, to remove our flying boots and place them in a pile next to the guard. "It is orders I am having to give," he explained. "It is," he laughed, "so that you are not running away."

Despite the loss of boots and the guards with rifle at each end of the carriage, an atmosphere of excitement reigned in the carriage. Some immediately started on the rations we had been given for the day's journey.

Philip, the doyen of our group, older than the rest of us and stamped with an air of authority both by his years and his sober presence, suggested we eat as little as possible until we could see how things were going. When, after several hours, the train had not yet begun to move his pessimism seemed justified.

Otto, the interpreter, his English hesitant, his manner kindly, had to bear the brunt of the prisoners' witticisms.

"What's up, Otto?"

"D'you want us to get out and push?"

"Got no coal left for the engine?"

"That's what they want our boots for."

"'ere's a match, put a light under the boiler."

"Put it under the driver."

"Put it under the bloody Führer."

Otto's smile was as kindly and as propitiatory as ever. "There is nothing to be worrying about. We are waiting for a new engine to be coming."

There were whoops of delight.

"They haven't got an engine."

"Old Goering's pawned it."

"Yeah! 'es gone to buy an aeroplane."

Otto retained his good humour. "The engine will be coming soon," he assured us.

"So will Christmas, mate, so will bloody Christmas!" Palmer's Cockney voice jeered.

"Ay, mon, you wanna take your finger oot! Dedigitate, Chum! Dedigitate!" Jock Graham's voice cut through the buzz of conversation.

I felt uncomfortable at what was, I suppose, a light-hearted attack on the mild-mannered German interpreter. My first reaction was compounded of distaste and surprise at this xenophobic attack, even if the victim was a German. It mirrored too closely the hoodlum action of a crowd confronting a defenceless victim.

I felt surprise, too, that my fellow airmen should seem unaware or uncaring of the strength that could be arrayed against them. They acted as if they were in a school playground engaged in some harmless game of cowboys and Indians.

In St Gilles, unlike my compatriots, I had had occasion to feel the dark force that lay behind the surface of the Third Reich. I had seen the cells filled with Belgian patriots. I had heard read out in the middle of the night, in front of a line of prisoners, the names of those who were to be sent to work as slave labour or condemned to be shot.

Listening to the hoots of laughter, I felt, what was for me the familiar cold isolation of an observer; unattached, distant, disapproving.

As the hours passed and the train still didn't move the prisoners' high spirits gradually abated. It became clear, even to the most optimistic, that we wouldn't arrive at our destination that day. Many had already finished the rations provided.

It was not until late that afternoon that the train moved slowly away from the station. There were a few weak cheers, but Otto's attempts to cheer us up – "That is more like. Now we are soon being there" – met with derision or morose silence.

For a time the train rattled along at a good pace and our spirits rose correspondingly. We agreed that at this speed it wouldn't take all that long.

Having been given a day's supply of rations, we assumed, reasonably enough, that the camp was at the most a day's journey from Frankfurt. We confidently assured each other that, even allowing for the delay, we would arrive, at the latest, by morning. It was clear, some pointed out, from the speed we were going, that the engine-driver had been given instructions to make up for lost time, but after half an hour or so the train slowed down and finally came to a stop. All that day we advanced by similar stops and starts. It was clear that, as cargo, prisoners had low priority. At times our carriage would be uncoupled from the train and left in a siding. On occasion we would be shunted back for miles in the direction from which we had just come.

Men grew hungry. Those who had eaten all their food eyed with envy those who still had something left. On the other hand, men who had husbanded their rations felt uncomfortable eating under the hungry gaze of the improvident.

When night came that first day it was difficult to sleep. Many of us were hungry and all of us tired. There was no heating in the carriage, and our stockinged feet without boots, were numb with cold.

Although there was sufficient space during the day for each man to sit, at night there was insufficient room to stretch out on the wooden seats. Some tried sleeping on the floor, leaving more space for the others. Even so, it was a constant struggle for those on the benches to guard their own space from the encroachment of restless neighbours.

The train rattled and swayed through the night, sometimes coming to a stop as brakes were applied with a hissing of steam and a clash of buffers. Those asleep would be jolted into startled wakefulness.

On those occasions when the train did come to rest, there would be peace and silence and a gentle background hissing from the engine. We would rearrange our limbs in more comfortable positions and again close our eyes.

Seemingly minutes later we would be jerked into stupefied wakefulness by the sudden clash of buffers as the carriages were coupled to a new engine and the train shunted to a remote corner of a marshalling yard.

We awoke on the second day, red-eyed, hungry and longing for a hot drink, but there was nothing to eat and nothing to drink; indeed water became our most pressing need.

6. Monsieur Kauffmann 'was a short stout man in his late forties' (p.30). This photograph was taken on his return from Dachau in 1945.

7. Mme Kauffmann 'wispy grey hair and pale gaunt face, was taller than her husband' (p.31). Seen together after their release from concentration camps.

8. The author with Mlle Vera, 'a timid, rather plain-looking little woman' who 'claimed to be English' (p.31). With the author in 1947.

9. The author with Mlle Vera and Mme Kauffmann in 1947.

Complaints to Otto became more and more bitter and he found it harder and harder to pacify us with promises of warm food and hot drinks awaiting us on arrival.

On the afternoon of the second day we drew into a station. Young women were standing at militarily precise intervals along the edge of the platform. They wore nurse-like uniforms with a red cross emblazoned on white aprons. The sight of attractive young girls would normally have aroused the usual undercurrent of sexual excitement. However, hungry and thirsty, we were less interested in the women than in the bowls of soup being passed through the windows of other carriages into the eager hands of the heroes of the Fatherland. There was no soup for this group of dirty, unshaven heroes. We were wearing the wrong uniforms, were prisoners, and, what is more, Royal Air Force prisoners.

The RAF were no longer the 'gentlemen' Goering had once named us. Now that we were dropping bombs rather than leaflets, we had become 'luftgangsters'. Many, so we heard, were hanged from lampposts.

It was almost midnight on the third day after leaving Dulag Luft that we arrived in the tiny village of Lamsdorf in Upper Silesia, close to the Polish border.

Prompted by Otto's "We are here! We are here! What have I been telling, and you not believing?", each of us found his own boots among those piled at the feet of the guard and then clustered at the carriage windows, peering into the darkness. The train slowed and finally stopped.

From the adjoining carriage the squad of guards descended and formed a line, waiting for us as we climbed down from the train. Thirty or so tired and hungry prisoners were quickly marshalled into ragged lines by harsh German voices.

Despite our tiredness, we were in better spirits. We had convinced ourselves that, now the nightmare journey was at last over, we would be embraced by the comfort of order and organization, looking forward to the promised meal, a hot drink and a warm bed.

The narrow road from the railway led through a forest of fir and pine. There was no moon. A light flurry of snow had begun to fall. The frost-covered surface of the road scrunched beneath our feet. I could feel the damp night air penetrate my miserably thin suit and the cold strike through the worn soles of my shoes. We trudged along between the two files of guards not knowing what to expect. We walked in silence. The road through the wood seemed never-ending.

Ahead, from the point of the column, a ripple of excitement.

* "What is it?" Paddy asked.

"Must be there," said Sammy.

I could see a scatter of lights shining through the trees on our right.

"This is it!" said Andy. "Hold on to your hats!"

We came to a halt some ten yards from the heavy wooden gates. A beam of light directed at the gate came from one of the wooden towers guarding the forecourt. The double gates swung open and we entered the camp.

More searchlights were switched on, holding us in a cage of light. We could see nothing in the blackness beyond. Voices shouted commands and there was a clatter of boots as soldiers ran to form up on either side of us. A command was given; another command and a ripple of sound as rifle-bolts were worked.

David whispered out of the side of his mouth, "Bloody hell, Paddy! They're going to shoot us!"

"They wouldn't do that, would they?" asked Paddy.

"Only joking, Paddy," David assured him. "course they won't. We haven't had supper yet."

"Not so bloody sure, mate," said Palmer.

The inner gates leading to the compounds were opened. Otto stepped from the shadows, his glasses sparkling with reflected light.

"Well," he said, "I must be leaving you now. I go back, now. I am wishing you all of the best. For you now the war is over. We are meeting again after the war perhaps. You must be doing now what the officer is telling you. Goodbye! *Auf wiedersehen!*"

As he stepped back into the shadows, we felt for the first time that we were now really prisoners of war. The excitement was over. The long dreary months, years perhaps, of privation stretched ahead.

We followed the officer along narrow paths powdered with snow, past shadowy huts behind high barbed-wire fences, and finally entered one of the compounds through wooden gates festooned with yet more barbed wire. The German pushed open the door of the first hut we came to, and, standing aside, gestured for us to go in.

Fixed three-tiered wooden bunks, placed close together along one side of the hut, filled half the available space. The rest of the hut, normally taken up with tables and benches, was empty. The broken cement floor was thick with dust, the cobwebbed windows frosted over and many of the panes of glass cracked or missing.

In the centre of the hut a long black pipe ascended to the roof from an unlit tiled stove.

Seeking reassurance, I turned to Phil. "This can't be it, can it?" He shrugged his shoulders.

Paddy pointed to the far end of the hut. "Look! There's a door. We probably have to go through there."

"Sure!" said Andy. "This's only a reception-area." Then, in a muttered aside, "The hotel's through that door."

The officer held up his hand for silence. "You sleep here: *Bleiben hier. Verstehen?*" There was silence, then indignant whispers.

"What's he say? Sleep here! What's he mean?"

The cold dampness of an October night filled the desolate hut.

The officer waited, frowning, then, turning to Philip, he asked, "*Sprechen Sie Deutsch?*"

"Go on, Phil," those nearest urged him. "Go on! Tell 'im!"

"What d'you mean 'tell him?" Phil protested. "I can't speak the damned language."

Reluctantly he took a step forward and faced the officer. "Sleep here?" he asked. "In this hut?"

"*Ja, Ja!*" The German nodded his head.

"But there aren't any mattresses, any blankets."

The German smiled grimly.

"What about the grub?"

"Where's that bloody hot meal?"

The officer again nodded his head. "*Ja, ja! Essen. Verstehe. Verstehe. Morgenfrüh!* Tomorrow!"

The men clustered around Phil. "What's he say?"

"Food tomorrow," Phil answered. "Nothing tonight."

"That can't be right. We were promised."

"What about the bloody Geneva Convention?"

"Where's our Red Cross parcels?"

The officer smiled. "No food. *Nicht essen. Essen, morgenfrüh.*"

Philip tried again. "We've been travelling for three days," he explained and held up three fingers. "*Drei Tage!*" and added, "No food. *Nicht essen.* We're cold. We need blankets."

The German listened, his face expressionless. Philip turned to the others. "Look," he protested, "isn't there anyone who can speak German. Make him understand?"

The officer smiled. "*Verstehe. Verstehe.*" he said. "Food, *Essen, ja, ja. Verstehe. Morgenfrüh!* Tomorrow!"

As he turned to go Philip put his hand on the German's arm. "Can you let us have some blankets?" he asked. The German nodded his head.

"*Ja, ja.*" he said and left the hut.

5

STALAG VIIIb

Sunday, 25 October, 1942: German counter-attacks at El Alamein are turned back as Montgomery presses his own local attacks; Rommel returns from sick leave to resume command. Germans capture two more streets in Stalingrad, but suffer heavy losses.

"I could weep," David complained. "It took me months to wheedle those flying boots out of stores. Months! Not canvas, real leather!" He looked miserably at his small feet now encased in huge, roughly shaped wooden clogs.

Sammy watched as Phil threaded string, taken from palliasses, through holes made in the leather tops of what were in effect wooden sabots.

"You don't need string," Sammy said. "What d'you want string for?"

"To stop the things falling off," Philip reasoned patiently. Sammy shook his head, his face registering a weary disgust. "My grandad," he said, "always wore wooden clogs – stuffed 'em with straw."

"There's an idea," said Philip, "Plenty of straw in the palliasses."

I stood for a moment thinking of Gérard; the thatched cottage in the clearing; the flaxen-haired kids running around in little clogs.

I'd arrived here in Lamsdorf still wearing the old shabby pinstripe suit and the thin worn shoes that Gérard had given me in place of my uniform and flying boots. I looked a sight then and looked no better now, dressed as I as in an old Polish cavalryman's uniform which came down to just below the knee and was sartorially finished off with a pair of clogs.

When are those rations coming?" Sammy asked anxiously. "They've been gone an hour at least."

"*Morgenfrüh, morgenfrüh!*" said Andy. "I keep telling you."

"We know you do," said David irritably.

The morning after our three days' journey and the gruesome night of our arrival at Lamsdorf, we experienced what was, in the circumstances, a strange euphoria. The sun was shining and fellow-prisoners, eager for the latest news, gathered at the wire of our compound.

We were inundated with offers of razors, toothbrushes and advice. The secret forebodings we had about prisoner-of-war life were dissipated by the warmth of the sun and even more so by the warmth of our reception.

However, now installed in a barrack that was likely to be our permanent home for the rest of the war, the reality of our state tended at times to break down barriers that we struggled to erect against an inevitable sense of depression.

Lamsdorf, Stalag VIIIb, near the town of Breslau in Silesia, on the former German–Polish border, now part of the Third Reich, held about ten thousand prisoners of war.

One of the compounds held RAF prisoners, the others soldiers. The history of the war could be garnered from the adventures of these men captured in one battle zone after another as Hitler's blitzkrieg rolled across Europe and Africa.

The men, all below officer-rank, being friends or coming from the same regiments, tended to keep together in their own huts. The RAF was an exception. Isolated by the Germans in one compound, they tended to form a little world apart.

Many of the soldiers captured early in the war, and apt by their experiences to weather hardships, fitted prisoner-of-war life like an oyster in its shell.

On our entry into the camp one such soldier, no doubt recognizing innocence and vulnerability when he saw it, befriended me.

"Most of us were taken at Dunkirk. We marched most of the way from Dunkirk to the Polish border. Went through France, Belgium, through Germany – right here to Lamsdorf. Thousands of us. Don't know how many. My unit was near a canal. A lot of us cut off, wandering about. Didn't know where we were, or what was happening."

Sergeant Steve Fletcher, long-serving infantryman, had spent most of that service in India. He talked, lying on his side, ensconced pasha-like on a top bunk, his head resting on a hand. I studied the sad face in front of me without embarrassment as if I were looking at a portrait. With the years his thin brown hair had retreated like the tide, leaving a high domed forehead, brown-blotched and furrowed. The thin face, long nose, small mouth and round receding chin were given life by the hooded gleam of warm brown eyes shining through unexpectedly long lashes. He talked and, perched on the side of his bunk, I listened.

He spoke as if in a dream, not looking at me, making no claim for my attention, asking for no response, his eyes fixed somewhere over my shoulder. "The French weren't very friendly, far from it! They'd lost most of their officers. Woke up one morning. Officers gone. Scarpered. They reckoned everyone had let them down: officers, Government, the British, especially the British; just like the last time, they said. No, they didn't think much of us, and we didn't think much of them, come to think of it."

A heavy pall of smoke from improvised cooking stoves hung close to the ceiling. Khaki-clad figures could be seen through the smoke-filled air. Men sat at the tables playing cards or lay on their bunks reading or sleeping.

"There wasn't much food. Too many of us; even if Jerry'd wanted. Gave us bread though. Lorry'd come along and a Jerry'd chuck out loaves over the side as if he was feeding ducks. We'd push and shove and curse.

"There wasn't much else; just the bread. Course, we'd pinch potatoes, turnips and that from the fields; anything that was going. Must've been like a load of locusts passing!

"Slept where we could; ditches, barns, anywhere. The French and Belgian civvies wouldn't give us the time of day. We'd left 'em in the lurch. That's what they reckoned.

"Some of our lot couldn't make it. Sat down by the side of the road and wouldn't get up; wouldn't budge. Don't know what happened to 'em. Didn't want to know really. Every man for himself it was. There were rumours, talk of Jerries shooting. I don't know about that. I didn't see anything."

He turned his head and looked across to an adjacent table where a young soldier was sitting engrossed in a book. "Alec!" Steve's voice rose a couple of tones, "Put a brew on lad. Two mugs!"

Alec marked his place in the book, slowly rose and said, "Get it yourself, you lazy old bugger," but went to a shelf and took down two tin mugs made from empty cans from Red Cross parcels.

"Been here two years now. Two years in this same hut. Never been out of the camp. If you're a sergeant or above they don't make you go. I could've gone out. Could've volunteered, gone out on some cushy working party, but no."

The long-drawled-out negative wearily rejected the idea. "Sit tight! That's my motto. Make yourself comfortable! That's the way! Take my word for it! You won't have to work, not aircrew. They wouldn't let

you even if you wanted. Anyway, mark my words. Sit tight! Make
yourself comfortable! Take my word for it."

*Thursday, 5 November, 1942: Montgomery announces that British forces
have won a complete and absolute victory in Egypt and that the German
Afrika Corps is in full retreat.*

The snow-covered, hedgeless fields surrounding the camp sparkled
beneath a full moon. They reached away to a horizon faintly marked by
the dark green of a distant forest. The snow lay in deep drifts at the
perimeter fences and clung to the coils of barbed-wire strung between
them; against that pervading whiteness the dark heavy beams of the
watch-towers formed stark, angular patterns.

Within the confines of the camp a canopy of snow covered roofs,
compounds and paths, and lay unsullied, waiting for life to stir in the
crowded interiors of the huts.

"*Alles raus! Fünf Appel!*" The familiar call invaded the dreams of
sleeping men. Unwillingly they stirred and twisted, waking to the
depressing reality of another day.

David, chirpy and cheerful, was already out of his lower bunk and
busily folding a blanket.

"Hands off Cocks! Put on socks!" he uttered his now familiar and, for
some, irritating morning cry.

Guiltily, I took my hand away from the warm comfort between my
thighs, stretched my legs and arched my body.

Palmer's head appeared above the cardboard partition he had erected
between the head of his bed and my feet.

"Look what you're doing, silly bugger!"

"Sorry!"

"Yeah! Sorry! Sorry! You will be sorry one of these bloody days." he
case me a viperish look as, sheepishly, I swung my offending feet over the
side of the bed and dressed hurriedly in the dark alley between the bunks.

"Crissakes!" exclaimed Andy, his pyjama jacket pulled well up, his
head down looking at the red weal that now encircled his waist. "What
is it, for crissakes?" he asked.

"Pox," said David.

"You should know," replied Andy, his head bent down even closer.

Philip, already dressed, glanced across. "Fleas," he said. "It's your
pyjama cord. They get stuck at the pyjama cord."

93

"Ach! They'll no kill you, you soft Sassenach!" Graham scowled contemptuously from a neighbouring bunk.

"Sassenach!" exclaimed Andy. "I'm a Methodist!"

"Fleas," said Sammy, standing fully dressed by the table.

"Pardon me!" said Andy.

"No trouble, fleas!" Sammy insisted enigmatically. Then, seeing he had aroused our interest, he expanded, giving us as always an improving little lecture. "Slide 'em under your thumbnail, see! They can't move. Slide in your fingernail and, Pop, that's it! You drop 'em over the side"

"Thanks, very much," said David, who had the lower bunk beneath Sammy.

"You'll get more than flea-bites if you don't get a move on," warned Philip, nodding his head in the direction of the figure who had appeared in the doorway.

We joined the line of men clad in overcoats, scarves, balaclavas and gloves, shuffling in their clogs to where "Ukraine Joe", the *Feldwebel* long steel rod in hand, stood waiting at the end of the hut. The sight of that silent, menacing figure was sufficient to get the laggards on their feet and hurrying towards the open door.

Five o'clock in the morning! The stars shone in a cold, cloudless sky. Lines of men trudged ant-like from each of the long wooden barracks, across the snow-covered compound, hands deep in pockets, and took up their positions, hut by hut, in ranks five deep. They stood in untidy lines, stamping their feet, beating their arms across their chests or pressing frozen fingers deep into armpits.

Two middle-aged Germans, tired and unenthusiastic, went slowly from group to group checking numbers. They were hampered partly by their apparent inability to count beyond ten and by the deliberate sabotage of the prisoners, who, despite the cold, couldn't resist exacting some small measure of amusement for themselves by shifting their position in the line.

The two Germans, harassed by the impatience of the *Feldwebel* and by the bloody-mindedness of the prisoners, arrived, with much recrimination, at a different total on each of the many counts.

We suffered too. There was the long cold wait in the snow without any hot drink or food to sustain us, and many had diarrhoea. I, myself, having recovered in Brussels with the help of the prison doctor's carbon tablets, was now prey to a second attack.

My group was, fortunately enough, stationed next to the "Forty Holer", and feeling a violent stab of pain in my stomach, I hurriedly made for the entrance, my absence yet one more unresolved statistic for the two Germans making their umpteenth count.

The large brick building had been erected over a huge cesspit with a sloping concrete floor. The excreta slid by gravity to the deepest part of the pit into an extraction well at the rear of the building.

Sammy and I, in our perambulation around the camp's perimeter, had seen an old horse enter the camp pulling a long, closed, barrel-like cart. It came to a stop behind the Forty Holer and stood patiently as the long process of pumping the excreta from the well into the cart proceeded.

Eventually the laden cart trundled slowly out of the camp. The sad old mare clip-clopped its way past the compounds, through the massive entrance gates, out into the freedom that lay beyond, to empty its rich load onto the surrounding fields.

Sammy, the farmer's boy from Lincolnshire, had eyed the load appreciatively. "They wouldn't let us do that," he complained. "All goes to waste down home, that does."

The Forty Holer had four rows of ten seats each, with no partition between them. I chose my favourite position, back to the wall. The idea of my own backside bared for all the world to see was not to my fancy. However, despite the lack of privacy, the building offered a retreat from the crowded prison hut, a quiet place to read, to think, to dream.

There was, it is true, the shortage of toilet paper, which became acute, especially now, when so many of us were suffering from diarrhoea. Fortunately there was a solution ready to hand, so to speak; a plentiful supply of Pelican books sent by the Red cross to satisfy the prisoners' cultural needs. The subjects were mostly scientific, abstruse or esoteric, and not all that well suited for young men of limited cultural aspirations.

I, however, avid for reading matter, would plough my way through such books as *The Bases of Modern Science* or *The Economics of Inheritance*, in much the same way as the French book and with similar difficulties with vocabulary. My main difficulty, however, was to balance the grosser needs of nature with my progress though the book, always taking care to have a few pages in reserve.

The Forty Holer, however, held a hidden terror, which, when I first learned of it in those early days of captivity, destroyed all my pleasure in this retreat. Beneath the well-scrubbed wooden seats, but above the cesspit and its fetid content, in a sort of "Middle World", were the rats, the concrete ledges supporting the seats their runways.

From time to time there were rat-hunts. Smoking rags were stuffed into air vents, and prisoners with sticks, spades or any weapon they could find would wait for the creatures to emerge. I took part in none of these sorties, not because of any scruple about killing but because rats were a secret terror of mine. Their rapid movement, their association with unnamed filth and disease, had, since childhood, filled me with horror.

There were gruesome tales told of scrotums or testicles being bitten or ripped off, so that during those first weeks of captivity I would never sit down properly, but maintained a painful crouch, protecting my private parts as best I could.

Night, however, held the most terror. Forced by diarrhoea to hurry along over trampled paths, in snow marked by the feet and faeces of other sufferers, I would enter the unlit building and kick the wooden side of the seat before venturing to sit down, but would still see, or imagine I could see, green eyes at vent holes. Yet time and habit gradually calmed my fears and left me able to enjoy the advantages of the Forty Holer, although never entirely free from nervous apprehension.

Elbows on knees, head propped on my joined hands, I gazed vacantly before me. Lassitude brought on by diarrhoea, by interrupted sleep, possessed me, drowning thought.

Several times each night that week I had been forced to climb down from the bunk, put on my overcoat, grope in the dark for my clogs, shuffle to the door and face the trudge in the biting cold, along the path of shadowed broken snow, too weary to bother about any trigger-happy German sentry on guard.

I now sat dreamily at peace. From time to time I could hear the high-pitched expostulations of the *Feldwebel*. Another recount? Seeking further comfort, as one might for a packet of cigarettes, my hand crept towards the left-hand breast pocket of my tunic. I unbuttoned the flap and felt for the thin folded sheet of paper and carefully drew out my mother's letter, read and re-read whenever I judged myself alone.

In the dim light it was impossible to see her schoolgirlish scrawl, but there was little need. My fingers, touching the thin, official letter-form, touched an unchanging world in which she had been the fixed centre. I knew whole phrases by heart and could see in my mind's eye the pattern of the paragraphs and the dark blue lines of the censor's pencil.

"My dear ... I cannot say how happy we all were ... we had waited so long for news ... I couldn't believe, God forbid, that anything had happened to you ... the neighbours are so very kind ... I went to a church service for prisoners ... I told them I was Jewish, but they said it didn't matter."

I carefully folded the letter and put it back in my tunic-pocket.

A trickle of prisoners began to enter the building. The parade must be over. I recognized Palmer's bird-like profile, who, seeing me, pointedly made his way, much to my relief, to the extreme end of the building.

When Philip came in, his solid silhouette unmistakeable, I waved. As he approached, I asked, "Did they notice?"

"Notice! No, they didn't notice."

We sat side by side for some time without exchanging a word. I was determinedly silent, having resolved that very morning to be more mature in the future, less talkative, more withdrawn. But my resolution quickly faded. "Phil," I said. "D'you think there's any chance of escaping?"

Philip seemed absorbed in his own thoughts and appeared not to hear. He had been, of late, subdued and depressed, although he was never what one might call outgoing. In fact it was his silence that I greatly admired. It gave him a kind of strength that I should have loved to emulate. Still, he was a married man and I suppose he had more to worry about than most of us.

"Sorry," he said, "What was that?"

"I was wondering if we could get away, a tunnel or something," I said.

"A tunnel!"

"I suppose you think I wouldn't be any good at it?"

"It's not that. You don't escape from a place like this through a tunnel. You don't need a tunnel. It's easier to change places with a soldier and get out on a small working party and escape from there."

"Well," I said. "A working-party, then? What d'you think?"

"You need to be a certain type."

"And I suppose you think I'm not," I replied.

"I'm certainly not," said Philip.

"I got away once. I was free for nearly eight days!"

"There's a difference between 'escape' and 'evasion'. What you did was evasion; very different from having to get away once you've been caught."

Thursday 10 December: The Fourth Panzer Army, with the aid of seven German divisions drawn from the Caucasus and Orel fronts begin an offensive to relieve the Germans trapped at Stalingrad.

The pattern of life had become established. It was almost as if the recent past had been blotted out. All that had become an irrelevant memory: the briefing of crews in the crowded room with target maps, coloured ribbons marking flight paths, the clipped tones of briefing officers. All was as if it had never been: air tests in the afternoon, the planes flying low over the familiar countryside; the forays into town, the pubs, the girls, the cinemas. and even operations, the reality, a faded memory: climbing into the plane at night, heavy and clumsy in full flying kit; the clinging smell of oil, of leather and petrol. And over the target itself the long agony of fear and suspense, no longer now even a subject of conversation. Nor do we now remember the weary relief of the safe return, coffee spiked with rum, sandwiches in debriefing, an early breakfast, ham and eggs, bed and exhausted sleep.

That life is now as if it had never been, and in its place other preoccupations; the next parcel, the next letter; dirt, hunger, discomfort and, over all, above all, the endless tedium; each day the same, with no sight of the end; the same faces, the same conversations, the same squalid routine.

But on parade that morning, there was something very different. There as usual Ukraine Joe, sternly impassive as ever; but in front of him was the portly Commandant of the Camp, gold-braided, cigar in hand. At his side stood the senior officer, RSM Taylor. Next to him was the gnome-like Palestine interpreter, and behind them all, behind the officials, a long line of SS guards, standing stiffly to attention.

The Commandant ceremoniously unfolded a paper and read the declaration in German. The interpreter stepped forward:

"By order of the Führer and the German people..."

Dieppe! The Canadians struggle ashore from landing barges under heavy fire from a shore battery. A column of smoke from an exploding ammunition dump spirals upwards as Commandos stumble across rocks and sand, crawl across exposed ground raked by machine-gun fire and snipers' bullets.

Shells from Allied mortars crump over the German battery. RAF planes dive, cannon firing. Men run for cover, lie still, stopped by a bullet or shell-splinter.

Prisoners are taken and hustled down to the beaches. Their hands tied, they lie huddled together, helpless, pressing their bodies into the sand, waiting for landing craft that will take them to the ships.

The Allied forces withdraw as best they can. Beneath the lacerating fire of German shells and bullets landing craft capsize as the evacuating troops struggle to get aboard.

The invading force disappears over the horizon, leaving behind the bodies of German and Allied dead. The German dead have their hands tied.

Hitler, "morally" outraged, orders a thousand prisoners to be tied up. Churchill declares he will tie up the same number. Hitler orders two thousand to be tied up. Churchill ... and so on. The ripples reach Stalag VIIIb, first engulfing only a few bewildered Canadians, but now all air-crew (non-workers) in the camp.

The formalities completed, the officials saluted each other. The Commandant did a smart right turn and marched out of the compound, followed by the RSM and the interpreter.

Ukraine Joe remained, as did the young SS troops. Lengths of string cut to size were loosely draped around their necks. The prisoners waited docilely in line; no tricks today, not with this lot! At a command the cream of Hitler's army advanced on the line of prisoners. We obediently held out our arms. The guards, fingers blue with cold, had difficulty tying knots in the string.

After the parade the usual tramp around the compound while we waited for the cleaning fatigue, Palmer and Graham, to finish their sweeping. They took their time, enjoying, no doubt, the sense of privilege and power – the rest of us kept outside in the cold until they should decide to let us in.

Round the dreary morning circuit, in our clumsy wooden clogs we went, solitary figures, heads down, immersed in our own thoughts, walking in small isolated groups; past the cookhouse, source of the daily ration of boiled potatoes and vile swede soup, standing in guarded isolation on the other side of the barbed wire fence; past the four long wooden huts which housed us; past the Forty Holer, crunching the dirty snow beneath our feet, slipping at times on patches of ice; and all the time now, our hands bound, and held before us as if in prayer.

At last, inside, out of the cold, first things first ... a brew up! We sat at our tables, a hot mug of tea or cocoa between cold, mittened fingers. A young SS guard patrolled up and down the length of the hut, automatic weapon in his hands, making sure we made no attempt to untie our hands.

He was small, dark hair, pale face, very similar in looks and build to David. He stopped from time to time, watching men playing cards, reading, or brewing up, and would pause at a table, frowning intently on the game being played, or, picking up a book, would look blankly at the print, turning over a page or two as if he hoped to find there something familiar.

When he reached our table, he looked at David, came to a halt and smiled. David grinned and raised his bound hands, indicating that he would like to take it off. The guard understood David's mime and nodded. When David stood up, the resemblance between the two men was remarkable. Placing his gun carefully on the table, he untied David's hands, helped him off with his coat, and once more tied his wrists together.

As he moved further down the hut, other men made similar requests, but he refused. As soon as he had passed through the door to the washroom wrists were untied, overcoats taken off and the string looped around wrists to look as if they were still secured.

Greater difficulty was encountered at the Forty Holer, where the Germans, with military thoroughness, had placed a guard. No prisoner was allowed to take off the string to attend to sanitary needs; but, adaptable and youthfully agile, we managed.

After the evening parade, our wrists officially unbound, the four of us – myself, Andy and David with our mentor, Philip, – would look forward to our evening game of bridge. It was a pleasure to which we were fanatically attached. After eating we would play until lights out, and even in our dreams would pursue an elusive grand slam or a cunning finesse.

We now had Palmer and Graham as immediate neighbours. The two had formed a close friendship. Physically dissimilar, Palmer built like a whippet, and Graham a powerful giant, they shared a vicious energy, a snarling discontent, bred in the slums of the East End and the Gorbals, a discontent which cemented their relationship.

From my point of view Palmer was, as I often confided to the others, a pain in the neck, an irritant, ever complaining of my alleged transgressions of his bedspace. Whenever the piece of cardboard he had put up to mark his territorial boundary fell down, as, I must admit, it frequently did, he accused me of deliberate provocation. There were vague threats from Palmer and weak, muttered ripostes from me.

Nevertheless, discontent rarely erupted into violence. There were taunts, jeers, arguments, but rarely blows.

There had been an obstinate insistence on the reprisal action on the part of the Führer, but the tying up of prisoners was being maintained at some cost. Young and active soldiers, badly needed now on the Russian front, were being used to patrol huts. The Führer, after some weeks, had, apparently, second thoughts.

His answer to the problem was the introduction of handcuffs and chains. In theory it was a solution. The steel chains were about eight inches in length and allowed considerable freedom of movement.

The handcuffs were hinged and clicked shut with a ratchet and spring. It took the guards only seconds to chain a man, and only a minute or two to release him; even so quite a long process. Once chained, we remained so, in theory, until released in the evening.

The SS guards were withdrawn from the camp and replaced by the usual elderly and middle-aged men. The new system should have worked.

That very first morning, however, using the corner of our metal prisoner-of-war identity tag, supplied, ironically enough by the Germans, it took only a few minutes experiment to learn how to release the catch.

It became routine every morning on entering the hut to remove the chains ourselves, take off our overcoats and put the chains back on again.

A guard patrolling the hut would see us sitting, or going about our usual activities free of overcoats, but still wearing chains. They appeared to notice nothing amiss, or perhaps had a tacit understanding with each other to ignore our Houdini-like act.

However, the chaining was more a source of irritation for them than for us. A guard would enter a hut in the evening and stand waiting, key in hand, while the long queue of chained prisoners inched slowly forward. Each prisoner, as he reached the head of the queue, would step forward and extend both hands. The guard would insert the key and screw down the spring, first of one handcuff and then the other. The released prisoner would pass behind the guard and put the chains on a table. The whole business could take the best part of an hour, but, if we were in playful mood, it could take much longer. Instead of placing the chains on the table we would, behind the German's back, fasten the handcuffs once more on our wrists and rejoin the end of the queue. The guard, wanting his supper, would mutter and curse as the prisoners moved around the hut in a seemingly never-ending circle.

Wednesday, 16 December, 1942: Berlin; Himmler orders that everyone of gypsy or mixed blood be sent to Auschwitz.
Thursday, 17 December, 1942: London; Anthony Eden, Foreign Secretary, condemns Nazi's systematic extermination of Europe's Jews and gives warning that those responsible will face retribution after the war.

Since our arrival at Lamsdorf we had adapted to the dirt, the crowded barracks and even to the tying of our hands. The one condition to which we were unable to adapt was the shortage of food.

The Germans supplied us with rations which, although minimal, were, in effect, sufficient to keep us alive: a ration of bread, swede soup, a few potatoes, an occasional piece of evil-smelling cheese or slice of sausage, and mint tea. Our dreams were not of girls, nor of home and family, but of food. Conversation centred on meals we had had, or meals we intended to have after the war.

We awaited with eager impatience the delivery of Red Cross parcels. Unfortunately our arrival at the camp in October was not propitious. The difficulties of transport in winter conditions in Europe at war made regular delivery a hazardous enterprise. As conditions deteriorated, so the number of parcels arriving became fewer and fewer. Instead of a whole parcel each, we often had to make do with one parcel between two, or even one parcel between four, and on one occasion one parcel between eight.

The parcels, when they did arrive, were a treasure trove; jam, tins of meat, cheese, tea, cocoa, tins of condensed milk. Condensed milk! In my family, as in most Jewish families, condensed milk bore the taint of being working class. I had always hated its sweet, oleaginous consistency. Yet now, if I were fortunate enough to have a tin of it, it became impossible for me to be moderate and sensible. As in that shameful incident when I had accepted the saliva-covered sweet from the young German, my body still craved sugar. Although I would attempt to ration myself, reason was again and again overcome by appetite. I could never apply restraint.

While sitting at our table, talking or playing bridge, my attention was fixed, not on the matter in hand, but on that tin of condensed milk on my shelf. One small spoonful; that was my intention, but inevitably I would take another and another, and, alas ... another.

Christmas, 1942: a whole parcel for each prisoner! A Christmas to remember. Even Graham and Palmer became, if not friendly, at least less pugnacious. The arrival of the parcels with their covers of printed red and green holly changed the atmosphere of poverty that had dominated the hut. There was now no need to bother with the rations the Germans gave us. The mint tea, being relatively hot, was now used as shaving water, the cheese was thrown away and the swede soup followed it.

Now that bellies were filled the conversation was no longer of food, of dream menus, but of women. The boastful talked, the timid and the more discreet listened. I, normally burdened with an irrepressible urge to confess all, drew the line on the subject of my virginity.

I remembered Anne, a Land Army girl, small, dark, as innocent and as inexperienced as I, alone together in the small cottage she shared with a friend. An idyll; toast, cheese and cocoa in front of the fire, and timid love-making. I was coaxing, persuasive, but when Anne falteringly agreed or at least made no resistance, I became hesitant, not knowing what to do with all those straps and buttons, and faced with that final intimacy...

"Do you really want me to? I'll not unless you want me to.," Anne, pensive, silent!

Jimmy Thomas explained to me the reasons for his success with women. It was, apparently, the little things that counted, opening doors, holding a woman's arm when crossing a road, and small details such as placing a warm towel over the sheet before getting into bed. I was surprised by this last detail and, although failing to see its significance, nodded my head in agreement.

At night men would call to each other as they climbed into their bunks;

"Who you having tonight?"

"Dorothy Lamour. What about you?"

"Me? I had her last night. I fancy a change. Marlene Dietrich, I think. Those legs!"

During the day lots of small fires would be lit, marking our prosperity. A grey cloud would form, hanging close to the ceiling.

Stews were heated and ambitious concoctions attempted, and because so much smoke was coming from the small individual fires it was decided to use the large tiled stove that dominated the centre of the hut.

Each man using the stove had to contribute one of his bed-boards, a process which, once established, meant that eventually few prisoners would have any bed-boards at all, mattresses being slung like hammocks from the four corner-posts of the bunks.

There had been of late reason for rejoicing other than food. We lived on war-rumours. No matter what we might be doing, some part of our mind seemed to be waiting for news. The sources were few and not that reliable. News was brought in by men coming in from the working camps attached to the main camp or from secret crystal sets scattered about the camp. These were weak, but sufficiently sensitive to pick up an "underground" transmitter, the "Drum", operating from nearby Poland.

The sets were never kept for long in one place, but shifted around the camp from hut to hut. It added spice to life to know that the thin aerial, strung from one end of the hut to the other, was only a few feet above the head of the German guard patrolling the hut.

And the news was good! Rommel was being chased out of Africa and it looked as if the tide of war in Russia was turning against the Germans.

Nevertheless, when the Christmas food was exhausted reality once more appeared in all its disagreeable detail. The crowded condition which forced men to live cheek by jowl soured and acerbated relations. The tension between Palmer and myself inevitably deepened. Our beds adjoined and the tables at which we ate and lived were adjacent. There was no way in which we could avoid each other. The point at issue was still the alleged invasion of Palmer's bed-space. I felt, however, that he saw me as one of nature's victims on whom he could, without fear, exercise his proclivity to dominate and bully.

Crisis point was reached when, one day, standing as usual on the middle bunks making up our beds, Palmer found that his precious cardboard barrier had once again been knocked to the ground.

"Look," he said, "I've 'ad enough." He sat on his bunk with an air of decision and turned towards me. I continued to make my bed. "I've given you every chance. It's no good. You'd better move. I bin thinkin'. There's an empty bunk at the end of the 'ut. You'd better go there."

I laughed. "I've got a better idea," I answered. "You move!"

"I ain't jokin', mate," Palmer said menacingly. "I'll give you till tonight."

Having finished making my bed, I turned and faced him. "And what happens if I don't move?" I asked.

"What 'appens? We settle it outside, that's what 'appens!"

This was no new threat. Palmer often invited me to "Settle it outside", an invitation I had until then ignored. The idea of a brawl behind the Forty Holer was not to my taste. Palmer looked vicious and tough despite his half-starved appearance. I fancied neither being hurt nor humiliated, especially by a man I despised. Much to my own surprise, I heard myself saying, "All right!" It was as if the words had been put into my mouth, an impulse outside my own volition.

Palmer, equally surprised, asked, "What d'you mean, all right'? You'll move?"

"No, I won't move. We'll settle it outside."

"Right!" he said, "If that's the way you want it," and dropped lightly to the ground. I watched this athletic display with foreboding.

It was apparent from the first few moments that neither of us had a clear idea of what we were doing. We stood facing each other in what we both supposed to be fighting stances, seemingly rooted to the spot, a practice which had the merit, as far as I was concerned, of keeping us at a safe distance from each other. However, urged to more violent action by the cries of the delighted onlookers, one of us would take a timorous step forward, whereupon the other would take a hurried step backwards, which, repeated several times in sequence, resembled nothing so much as an elaborate, avian mating ritual.

This bizarre dance could have continued for some time without harm to either of us had it not been that Palmer, backing up a little too far, found himself back to the wall with no more ground left for retreat.

Urged on by the hectoring crowd, bored by the lack of action, I advanced. Palmer stuck out a rigid left hand and hit me on the nose. Stung by the pain and forgetting 'technique' I advanced.

Palmer, having little weight to resist my heavy-footed attack, and even less skill in countering flailing arms, met a flurry of blows as I whirled my fists in panic. Without further ado Palmer slithered to the ground and, once there, despite exhortations from the crowd, refused to get up. I stretched out a helping hand in the best *Boys Own* tradition to help the prostrate man to his feet. Palmer refused my offer.

"'e kicked me! You saw 'im!" he appealed to the bystanders. He pulled a dirty handkerchief from his pocket and, wiping a trickle of blood from his ear, offered the bloodstained rag in evidence. "Look! 'e kicked me!"

Graham, who had vociferously urged Palmer on during the fight, berated him in defeat.

"Ye couldn'ae punch yer way oot a paper bag," he said.

I enjoyed my success, the grudging admiration of Graham and the surprised congratulations of friends.

Palmer approached me later." Great little scrap that, weren't it? I mean, didn't do any 'arm, did it. Cleared the air like." I nodded. "Course," Palmer continued, "I weren't meself like. Not in form. Know what I mean? We oughta 'ave another go sometime. Not a scrap like. I don't mean a scrap. Just a friendly match ... sparrin'! Know what I mean?"

That night he moved his bed to the other end of the hut and for some days I walked about with an exaggerated athletic bearing.

Friday, 22 January, 1943: General Paulus radios Hitler from Stalingrad: "Rations exhausted. Over 12,000 wounded unattended in the pocket." Hitler replies: "Surrender is out of the question." Saturday, 23 January, 1943: British forces enter Tripoli to receive the surrender of the city and the province.

I can't remember who first suggested the raid on the potato store. The idea had been in the air for some time now, provoked by boredom and encouraged by our ever-present hunger.

As we stood there in the winter sunshine looking through the barbed-wire fence at the closed green shutters, men passed on the usual morning constitutional.

The squat, white-washed, one-storey building which served as cookhouse stood on the other side of a single, eight-foot, barbed-wire fence, an invitation and constant provocation.

Each morning at about eleven o'clock two representatives from each of the huts would line up at the shuttered window to collect the day's rations. The green shutters would open and potatoes would be shovelled out into large wooden containers.

The idea originated from Giddens, a New Zealander, whose job it was to collect the rations for our hut. It was he who had pointed out how easy it would be – the window never locked and the shutter easily unhooked from outside.

The last of the men disappeared into the huts, leaving the four of us. Andy, David, Paddy and myself – Philip would have nothing to do with the scheme – standing at the wire looking through the fence. Behind those green shutters were several tons of potatoes, ours for the taking.

David scratched the end of his nose. "Nothing to it!" he said. "Organization, that's all, just organization." Then, although no one had contradicted or questioned him, he, no doubt taking our silence for opposition, said irritably.

"Look!" It's just a potato store, not the ruddy Bank of England."

The moon cast soft shadows on the sandy soil between the huts. A distant glow from the lights of a watch tower evidenced an ever-present vigilance over the huts and the sleeping prisoners within. Paddy and I, balaclavas pulled down, stepped furtively from the comparative safety of the enclosed entrance porch, and stood together, backs pressed against the wall of the hut.

"Got your box?" I whispered.

"Under my tunic," Paddy answered. "Are we supposed to wait here?"

"By the porch," I answered.

"You sure, Harry?" he asked.

"Yes, Paddy, I'm sure," I answered irritably. "They'll be along in a minute."

"Perhaps they meant the porch at the other end," Paddy suggested. He could well be right. The building consisted of two separate huts placed end to end, with a wash-room between them. Andy and David could have passed through the two huts and gone to the porch at the far end, and out of that door instead of following us. But I had no intention of losing any authority I thought I might have by admitting to Paddy that he might be right.

"What do we do if a Jerry comes?" Paddy asked.

"No Jerry's going to come. There aren't any Jerries in the compound."

"But supposing?" Paddy insisted.

"No supposing! We're going for a crap. We say we're going for a crap," I said firmly.

"For a crap?"

"Good grief! You know what German is for crap, don't you?"

"D'you speak German?" Paddy asked.

"A bit."

There was a further silence, the reason for our standing there now half-forgotten. We could have been waiting for a bus.

There was a movement in the shadows.

"What's that?" asked Paddy. "There, coming towards us."

A small figure, sidling along the side of the hut, detached itself from the shadows.

"We didn't say wait here. What you waiting here for?" David hissed indignantly.

"You said the porch. He said the porch, didn't he Paddy?"

"The other porch, you clot, the porch at the other end, not this one," David countered fiercely.

"I said..." Paddy mumbled.

"Come on! We've been waiting ruddy ages. You haven't forgotten the boxes, have you?" David asked; and when we got to the other end of the hut Andy hissed, "Where've you been, for crissakes?"

Feeling a little foolish, we advanced in little rushes from the shadow of one hut to the shadow of the next until we reached the site of the projected operation. We waited, huddled together in a group in the shadow of a hut.

"Hold the boxes till I get over the fences," David whispered to me. The two of us crossed the few yards of open space to the wire fence, the other two waiting in the safety of the shadows as I helped David climb the fence close to a supporting post.

As he reached the top and turned to get down the other side, the fence swayed under his weight. Silhouetted against the moonlight, he looked like a monstrous crow as he clung there, swaying perilously, one hand on the post, the other gripping a strand of wire.

When he had clambered down the other side, I reached up, tipped the empty Red Cross boxes over the fence and joined the other two in the shadows.

We watched as David retrieved the boxes and, bent double, ran like Groucho Marx across the open space to the shuttered window of the potato store. He seemed to us to take an age to unfasten the retaining stay and we heard with some alarm the dull sound of the metal hook strike against the wooden shutter.

His small figure stood facing the open window and then suddenly disappeared head first into the black void beyond. A moment later he reappeared, right side up, waving a cheeky and cheerful hand, and leaning out, pulled the shutter closed.

"Right, cocksuckers!" said Andy, a little breathlessly. "Come on, Paddy! Me next!" With Paddy's help he climbed the fence and, balancing on the top wire, with one hand on the post, jumped down and sprinted across the open space which lay between the fence and the cookhouse.

The shutter opened briefly and David handed over a full box of potatoes and closed the shutter. Andy turned and ran back, clutching the box close to his chest, Paddy and I running to the fence to meet him.

"Get cracking!" Andy whispered as he climbed back into the compound. "He's filled the other boxes."

"Andy!" said Paddy. "I think you've left the box of potatoes on the other side of the fence."

"You think!" said Andy. "Why didn't you say?"

"Never mind," I said. "I'll get them."

Awkward and less co-ordinated than Andy, I climbed the shaking fence, helped by his and Paddy's propelling hands beneath my thighs and bottom.

As I turned round at the top of the fence, it shook violently under my weight. Shifting my grip in a panicky effort to regain my balance, my thumb became impaled on a rusty barb. I stifled a cry of pain and clung desperately to the wobbling fence, the sleeve of my jacket now enmeshed on the wire and blood trickling from my injured thumb.

"*Halte! Halte!*" There was a shout from the distant shadows.

"Jesus! It's a kraut!" exclaimed Andy. "Under the huts Get under!"

Paddy and Andy ran for the cover of the nearest hut leaving me stranded on top of the fence with my thumb bleeding and my sleeve caught up in the wire.

From under the hut Andy hissed to me in an agonized whisper, "Stop messing about for Chrissakes!"

"I'm stuck!" I said.

"Get your ruddy leg over!" Andy hissed as he ran to the wire.

Calming down, I unhooked my sleeve from the wire and with his help climbed back over the fence and jumped down into Andy's supporting hands.

There was a second, closer cry of *"Halte!"* from the approaching guard, and the sharp crack of a rifle as the man ran towards us.

"Under here! Under here!" Paddy called, flat on his stomach under the hut.

The three of us lay peering out from under the hut. We could make out the dark shape of the German sentry as he ran towards us, rifle in hand. We saw him stop and again take aim in our direction. There was the sound of another shot.

The guard advanced slowly towards the fence.

"Mary, mother of God!" whispered Paddy. "He'll see the potatoes."

The guard stopped at the fence, the box of potatoes unseen at the foot of the post where Andy had left them. The man was now directly opposite us. He looked to his left, then to his right and finally turned and walked slowly towards the cookhouse where David lay in the dark interior. He stopped and turned to look once again at the fence.

We held our breath. Standing midway between the fence and the cookhouse, he seemed to hesitate. Finally he turned and walked away in the direction from which he had come.

"The potatoes!" I whispered. We emerged from our hiding place and, standing at the fence, looked towards the shuttered window.

We waited, watching for some sign of movement at the potato store. After what seemed an interminable time the shutter slowly opened and David put his head out of the window. We waved wildly, urging him to hurry. He climbed out of the window and scuttled towards us. Andy said to him as he drew near, "The potatoes! Get the potatoes!" "Bugger the potatoes!" said David as he climbed back into the compound.

To tell the truth, I had never seen Steve with his feet on the ground and there he was as usual, on his bunk, freshly shaved, tunic neatly buttoned up to the neck. He shook his head slowly from side to side, a patient smile on his long lugubrious face.

"I don't know. I don't know. Someone's looking after you," he said, and nodded vaguely towards the ceiling. I smiled sheepishly.

"All your mates were killed in that plane, weren't they? And you were the only one saved."

I nodded agreement, avoiding the directness of Steve's gaze.

"They could've shot you in that prison, or sent you to a concentration camp, couldn't they?" he continued.

There was a pause.

"And now this potato raid." He paused. "Someone is looking after you all right," he said. I opened my mouth to speak.

"Look," Steve continued, "you're young. Got all your life before you. The war'll end soon ... one year, two years; that's nothing, nothing at all. It may seem a lot to you, but a couple of years passes like a dream when you look back on it. When you're my age you'll know that. It seems to me, now, looking at you, that no time at all has passed since I was just like you. A couple o' years; what's that? Nothing at all. You don't want to take chances. It's not worth it. What for? Make the best of things! Settle down here! Stick it out!"

Although I made no reply, I could see from Steve's expression that he knew his words would have little effect on me.

"You're not still thinking of this escape idea are you? This swapping?"

"No," I said, "Not really."

Steve pursed his lips and shook his head slowly from side to side. The two of us sat in silence.

At length he asked, "What's your mattress like?"

"My mattress!" I exclaimed, startled.

"Is it comfortable? You get yourself comfortable and you won't want to keep on with these ideas of yours."

I smiled. I rather liked these little homilies of Steve's. They seemed to mirror that other world when, as a child, everything seemed so fixed, so certain.

"I'll get Ken to bring the mattress over. It's stuffed with real Red Cross packing paper. You can set yourself up, make yourself comfortable, forget about swaps and escapes.

"Where you going to get that from?" I asked.

"Never you mind." Steve smiled.

"That potato raid," he went on, "a really daft idea, if you ask me. If you'd wanted a few potatoes you only had to ask."

He again shook his head from side to side. "I don't know, I can't make you out, you RAF lot. Supposed to be clever, educated! You could've been shot, and all for a few ruddy potatoes."

Thursday, 6 May, 1943: Allied forces launch final offensive against Axis positions in Tunisia. Defences are breached by the British First Army, and two armoured divisions push on to Massicault, half-way to Tunis.
Saturday, 10 July: Sicily invaded: First elements of the U.S. Seventh and the British Eighth Armies begin landing at 2.45 a.m. on the south-east

coast of Sicily. The occupation of the island is regarded as a necessary prelude to an attack on Italy itself.

Tuesday, 31 August: General Castellano meets Allied officials in Sicily and tells them that the Badoglio government could not accept proposed surrender terms until guarantees were given on sufficient numbers of Anglo-American troops landing in Italy to protect the Italians from German reprisals.

Stalag VIIIb, in the middle of a vast and sandy plain distantly bordered by a forest of pine, was itself devoid of trees and vegetation. There was nothing within its arid confines, neither leaf, flower nor bird, to mark the changing season, but imperceptibly the growing heat of the sun, the deepening blue of the sky, the wisps of cirrus cloud proclaimed the advent of summer.

Blankets were taken outside into the warm air, and the accumulated winter's dust vigorously shaken from their flea-infested folds, a game for the prisoners, whose arms would shake and shake the blankets with zestful force.

Shirts, vests, pants and handkerchiefs, scrubbed clean in the stone troughs of the washhouse, were hung to dry in the sun on lengths of string stretched from hut to hut across the sandy space between.

We sat, backs against the wall of a hut, or stretched full length on the sandy soil, eyes closed, faces turned towards the sun, free at last of the confines of the overcrowded huts. We were content.

The sun warmed our limbs, tanned our faces, shone on naked torsos. Men smiled at each other, forgetful of the long winter's gloom.

As if awakening from a long unpleasant dream, I began to take a more active interest in the life of the camp. I had so far chosen to ignore all forms of organized activity, feeling, perhaps instinctively, that to take part would mark the permanence of prisoner-of-war life. This I refused to accept. It was temporary and, despite the assurance I had given to Steven, I was going to escape; not this week, not this month perhaps, but soon.

Nevertheless, despite intentions, despite myself, camp life began to have meaning, no longer merely a temporary stopping place where I stood ready for flight.

Hunger was no longer a constant nagging ache. The days were gone when I would stand, minutes on end, weighing my bread ration in my hand to see whether I was being cheated, or when, a food parcel just having been issued, I would gulp down spoonfuls of the once abhorred condensed milk. No longer did I feel the need to consume, in one day, a sugar ration that had to last a fortnight.

Life was easier too in other respects. The Germans had seemingly tired of their game with chains and handcuffs, for it had become a game. Rules were relaxed. The guards no longer bothered to put the chains on us, but issued them every morning, in bundles of ten. It had become, unofficially, our responsibility to put the handcuffs on our own wrists.

As the guards became more and more indifferent to the whole business, the bundles would be left in a tangled heap on the tops of cupboards until it was time for the evening unchaining.

Occasionally, when a visiting officer decided to inspect the huts, the guards would give us warning and there would be a panicky rush to the cupboards.

Unlike its inception, without ceremony, the long-drawn-out episode came to an end. One morning the chains were not brought into the huts. They were never seen again.

Free of hunger, free of chains, living in a world free from danger, I should have been content, but I found other reasons for complaint. Lying in the sun I became excessively conscious of my long skinny frame and envious of the strong, confident bodies all around me.

Clad in a pair of white shorts with blue stripes down the side, made from a towel and a blue handkerchief sent form home, I would follow Philip, a keep-fit enthusiast, to a quiet corner of the compound.

Following the then fashionable principle of dynamic tension, Philip and I tensed, relaxed and stretched muscles I had never known I possessed. I now walked hollow-backed with an athletic spring to my step and watched anxiously and optimistically for the first signs of the burgeoning new muscles promised by Philip.

When a set of Red Cross boxing gloves appeared in the hut, with a confidence engendered by my new athleticism, and the memory of my successful encounter with Palmer, I sought sparring partners. Andy and David looked the other way with a weary disgust, but I managed to persuade Sammy, who, too kind to think of hurting anyone, would lean his solid fourteen stone against my light frame, until, exhausted from supporting his weight, I would admit I'd had enough.

My new enthusiasm was of short duration. It finally evaporated altogether after a challenge from Bert, an Army man, a "swap" living in the hut, who confessed to knowing a bit about boxing. That bit, however, was far more than I could encompass. Benches and tables pushed aside to form a ring, he hit me persistently, monotonously, on my unprotected jaw. Drifting in a dream-like mist, I was judged technically knocked out, much to the disgust of my vociferous RAF supporters.

It gradually became too hot for boxing, too hot to think. Stretched under a persistent sun, perspiration streaked our foreheads and our bodies left damp patches on the blankets on which we lay.

In the centre of the camp was a fire precaution, a large static water tank. No question of diving in there! It was too crammed with bodies. Standing in its tepid waters, men would dream of other days; days spent bathing in sea or lake, of walks along a riverside path, of the rustling green dampness of trees and bushes.

Soon a greenish-white scum formed on the surface; yet the more obdurate or the more obtuse, I among them, despite repeated warnings from our own British doctor, returned time and again to splash in the evil-smelling water. Finally the Germans acted and placed an armed guard on the tank.

As the summer heat of 1943 merged into the pleasant warmth of autumn, maintaining my self-image of tough athleticism, I joined the hut's seven-a-side rugby team.

Reality was again more painful than I had imagined, whether having my shins hacked as hooker or my ears kneaded as back-row forward.

I eventually learnt, however, to ape the expected behaviour of a "rugby man" without doing anything too dangerous. I would rush down the field screaming, "Tackl'im! Tackl'im" while maintaining a sensible distance from the fleet-footed, heavy-handed, opposing backs, among whom, on occasion, were some enormous, bare-footed Maoris. I would, however, from time to time, with an apparently reckless courage, hurl myself carefully on to the heap of writhing bodies, which inevitably formed over the ball.

As with boxing, I soon tired of rugby. Little by little I put aside the athletic image. I became my more lethargic, and as I chose to think, my more intellectual, philosophic self, much, no doubt, to the relief of David and Andy, who found this concept easier to live with.

Wednesday, 13 October: Italy declares war on Germany. Premier Badoglio tells Eisenhower, "By this act all ties with the dreadful past are broken and my Government will be proud to be able to march with you on to the inevitable victory."
Berlin reports the surrender as treacherous and cowardly.

As winter approached and the supply of food became once more irregular, my thoughts turned from the frivolity of sport and the luxury of long hours spent lounging in the sun to the more immediate need of survival. I was beginning to acquire some understanding of the primitive society in which I was living.

The economy of the camp was based on cigarettes. Master-racketeers, cardboard boxes tucked under their arms, roamed the camp on mysterious errands. They lived in domestic splendour with armchairs made from Red Cross packing cases, and with subservient orderlies to do their cooking and wait upon their needs.

There were, of course, racketeers and racketeers. Men like Steve had contacts in all parts of the camp and friends in hundreds of working parties outside the camp. The really big men, however, were those who had direct dealings with the Germans and could obtain, so it was rumoured, anything they needed.

Such a man was the little Palestinian interpreter, who lived in style at the far end of our hut in what was virtually a small private room, the walls made from the sides of Red Cross crates. Beneath his bunk, so rumour had it, there were piles of Red Cross boxes packed tight with cigarettes.

He was small, thin and inoffensive, with bushy grey hair, a pointed elfin face, and small blue eyes – an RAF aircraftsman second-class captured in Crete. An Army man served him as batman. He lived his enigmatic life aloof from the rest of us. I never dared speak to or approach him, feeling all the awe the poor feel for the rich.

The camp was in many ways a microcosm of the world outside, and I learnt the truth of those political aphorisms to which I had been so much addicted as an argumentative seventeen-year-old. I saw with my own eyes how power corrupts, how fellow-prisoners critical of the "rackets", and impatient of "injustice", once elected to office, succumbed to temptation.

Such men, chosen as hut-representatives, and charged with the distribution of rations, would quickly forget principles they had once held dear. Within days the inevitable Red Cross packing-case walls would go up, cutting off the man and his cronies from prying eyes. I would knock timidly on the packing-case wall for admittance.

Aircrew, however, were, for the most part, not seriously involved. We lacked contacts, not being allowed out of the camp on working-parties, and having been prisoners a relatively short time.

The Army, on the other hand, mostly captured at Dunkirk, were well entrenched, holding positions in all the most advantageous areas of the camp.

Many soldiers, too, had a natural disposition for living by their wits. The "scrounger" was a respected role in the army, and the "rackets", as practised in the camp, a natural extension of that philosophy.

All prisoners, however, whether army or aircrew, were engaged in some kind of barter. The most common was the exchange of a cigarette ration by a non-smoker for some other desirable commodity. I regularly exchanged mine for an extra bread ration.

It was Steve, my mentor in all things appertaining to camp life, who first suggested to me the opportunities for exploiting one's fellow men, a practice implicit in the barter system. I entered these murky waters with a naive enthusiasm.

The Sikhs lived close to the RAF compound. These tall, dark-skinned, turbanned men lived their own mysterious lives, making no attempt to mix with other prisoners. They had of late been receiving English parcels, instead of the special Indian Red Cross parcels which catered for their particular culinary needs.

They eyed with horror the tin of pork and stuffing, dipped an exploring finger into the condensed milk, puzzled over the custard-powder and the rolled oats and welcomed tea, but the cocoa they firmly rejected.

There was the basis for exploitation. Englishmen preferred cocoa to tea; Sikhs preferred tea to cocoa. This was the theory to be tested. Steve pointed out the commercial strategy. With the English, I was to trade one 4oz tin of cocoa for two 2oz packets of tea. With the Indians I was to trade one 2oz packet of tea for one, or if the market would bear it, two tins of cocoa. I could thus expect to make at least 100% profit, possibly even 200%.

In need of moral support, I managed to persuade Paddy to become my business partner. Armed with four packets of tea, the two of us set out for the Sikh compound. Passing through the gates was like entering a foreign land. Handsome hooked-nosed men strolled about in pairs, their voices high-pitched. A few of the strolling couples held each other's hands. I turned to Paddy and raised a significant eyebrow, but Paddy explained, "It doesn't mean anything. They're just good friends."

As we entered the first of the barracks, the impression of being in a foreign land was more marked than ever. A tall Sikh stood before a piece of broken mirror patiently combing his long dark hair with sweeps of a thin muscular hand. Another, with an air of patient habit, braided and coiled his shining plaits.

The air was full of exotic scents. Men kneaded and flattened small balls of dough into thin pancakes, while their companions, kneeling over the ubiquitous tin stove, cooked chapattis on thin sheets of tin.

We threaded our way through the huts feeling as Alice must have felt when exploring wonderland. Although fascinated by all we saw, we were too timid to approach anyone. We could well have returned to our own hut still carrying the four packets of tea had it not been for one of the Sikhs, pock-marked and excessively ugly, who called, "Johnny! Johnny! Come here, Johnny!"

It was clear that "Johnny" was the sobriquet used for all English soldiers. Despite my avowed liberalism, I felt somewhat offended. As a socialist, I would have demurred had I been addressed as "sahib", but the use of "Johnny" I found a little too familiar.

As Steve had predicted, the Sikhs were only too eager to trade. "What you got there, Johnny? What you want, Johnny?" It needed no gifted salesmanship.

Delighted with the success of our mission, we returned to the hut carrying eight tins of cocoa, the equivalent of sixteen packets of tea, a profit between us of twelve packets of tea.

Unfortunately neither I nor Paddy had yet learnt the commercial discretion essential to all such enterprise. We couldn't resist boasting of our business exploit. Soon the Sikh compound was regularly dotted with eager vendors of tea.

A sequel to my venture into commerce was the friendship I formed with that very first customer, the ugly pock-marked Sikh.

Towards evening, while playing our usual game of bridge, the man would mysteriously appear from nowhere and stand silently behind me.

I hoped that the man would tire of waiting and go away, but David or Andy would say, "Your friend's here." I would ask Paddy to take over my hand and greet my "friend". The Indian spoke little English, apart from the phrases he had used in our trading session, and these were of little use in our new relationship. In an embarrassed silence, following the paths between the compounds, I would walk along at his side. When the Sikh took my hand I remembered Paddy's words, "It doesn't mean anything," but nevertheless pulled my hand away. The Sikh appeared not to be rebuffed and on his next visit brought with him a box of Indian sweets, from which, as we walked, he would select one and push it into my mouth.

I was beginning to have doubts about the accuracy of Paddy's analysis of Indian "friendship" and when he tried to kiss me on the cheeks I pushed him away.

Sunday, 28 November: Italy; Montgomery declares "the Road to Rome is open", as the Eighth Army launches a heavy attack across the River Sangro.

The onset of wintry weather had once more confined us to our huts, now the centre of all social activity. Each was filled with the noise and paraphernalia of living – a small village where the occasional visitor was eyed with suspicion or curiosity.

If the hut was the village, the tables were clearly the houses of which it was composed. Each had room for half a dozen men and were ranged down one side of the hut with only sufficient space between them to allow access. Each was "home" for the group of men who belonged there. Here we ate, read, played cards, bickered or philosophized. It was a home from which we rarely strayed, and where a visitor from another table would be treated as a guest and, in times of affluence, offered hospitality. Men, drawn together from choice or chance, became, with the passing of time, a tightly knit family, with its own family jokes, loyal to each family member and locked defensively together against outsiders.

These relationships had formed slowly over that first year and, once formed, the memberships of the groups rarely changed. Towards the end of September, however, this social pattern was disturbed.

In Italy, the Germans, retreating before the advancing Allied forces in Italy, were now transferring British Army prisoners of war from Italian POW camps to those in Germany.

Late one evening the door of our hut opened and a group of dirty and dishevelled soldiers straggled in. They were tired and hungry and in no mood to answer the excited questions of the men who gathered round them.

The first priority was to house them. Every bit of space in the already crowded hut had to be used. The bottom beds of the three-tier bunks, the most dust-laden and flea-ridden, were taken over by the weary men.

As they had arrived without rations, a meal was produced by contributions from all parts of the hut. The men, exhausted by their long train journey, gratefully accepted the hospitality and, having eaten, took to their beds.

Next day there was little room at the tables and many of the newly arrived prisoners had to squat on the edge of their bunks as they told their stories to an eager audience, avid as ever for news of the war.

In the Italian prisoner-of-war camps the news of the surrender had come as no surprise. The prisoners had already heard of the fall of Sicily and of the successful landings on the mainland.

When Rome radio gave official news of the surrender they expected the British or the Americans to arrive at any moment. Even so, it had been hard for them to believe that they would soon no longer be prisoners of war. The reality was brought home when they found that the guards had disappeared, leaving the camp gates wide open.

The senior British officer in each camp gathered everyone together and told them that he had received strict instructions from London: all prisoners were to stay put and leave the roads free for the movement of the Allied troops. He pointed out how dangerous it would be were they to leave the camp. Although the Italians had surrendered, the German troops were still fighting with their usual ferocity. They would shoot first and ask questions afterwards. There were, too, Republican Fascists around, still faithful to the deposed Mussolini.

The men reacted in different ways. Most were quite willing to do as they were told. They realized that in walking out of the camp they would be walking into a battlefield. The country around was mountainous, the terrain difficult and, possibly, full of excitable partisans and nervous villagers.

Some, however, had other ideas. A few had formed relationships with Italian girls while out on working parties and had decided to join them, living and working as Italians until the troops arrived.

Others, fewer in number, eager for adventure after their inactivity as prisoners, hoped to join up with a partisan group, or to try to contact the advancing Allies. Yet others, and these the most prolific, just wanted to get out of the camp for a few hours for the sheer pleasure of tasting freedom.

Those who stayed in the camp anxiously awaited the coming of their liberators, scanning the crests of nearby hills for the first glimpse of the jeeps and tanks of the advancing armies. However, when the troops did arrive with their lorries, staff cars and motor-cycles they were German.

Although a disaster for the prisoners transferred to Germany, from our point of view their arrival brought exciting news. The rumour that Italy had fallen had now been wonderfully confirmed. Italy had indeed surrendered. One big push was needed and there was little doubt in our minds that Germany would now be brought to its knees.

Nevertheless the hut was overcrowded and, men being what they are, the euphoria soon changed to grumbles and complaints on both the part of the newly transferred prisoners and their RAF hosts, the airmen complaining that the army men were insufficiently grateful, the army that the airmen were a soft lot who didn't really know what war was all about.

Fortunately for the comfort of all, the newly arrived prisoners were soon moved into army compounds and life in Lamsdorf settled down to its usual humdrum level.

We came to a piece of ground at the back of the Forty Holer, a small rectangle of earth marked off with string and a few stakes hammered into the ground. Sammy halted beside it, folded his arms, his expression exuding a dour satisfaction.

"What is it?" I asked.

"What is it!" replied Sammy. "It's a vegetable plot."

"Oh!" I said. "Yours?"

"Mine," said Sammy.

"How did you manage that?"

"I don't suppose you've ever done any diggin' before?" he suggested.

"Digging? What d'you mean, digging?" I asked, reluctant to admit ignorance on any subject. "What's so special about digging?"

Sammy smiled and shook his head.

"There's diggin' an' diggin'," he said. "Diggin's an art."

"What? Like ballet dancing?"

"There's the spade," said Sammy. "There's not many who knows how to hold a spade, let alone dig with it. There's some I wouldn't let get near a spade, let alone hold it. Low down you've got to hold it. No good holdin' it in the middle. Left hand low down, see, near the blade. Support the weight."

"I see," I said.

"And your foot," Sammy continued, "it's your foot that does the diggin', not your hand. That's the secret. Foot on the shoulder of the blade."

"Really!" I said.

"It's no good shovin' it in, like some of 'em," Sammy warned, "'an leverin' it out like a bag of coke. You make a cut, the full depth of the blade on all four sides, see. Then you lift it out gently, turn it over, and put it down exactly right, like a Christmas cake out of the oven, or a babe out of its cot. Each spadeful should be there, side by side, like squaddies on parade. What you..."

Feeling rather like the Wedding Guest held by the Ancient Mariner's glittering eye, I interrupted the flow.

"When you going to start?" I asked.

"Start!" Sammy seemed surprised at the question.

"The digging?" I insisted.

"Ah, well!" said Sammy, "I haven't got the spade yet. I'll start as soon as I get the spade."

This was the first of many visits to Sammy's vegetable plot. I would follow, while he walked around the still virgin plot of earth, like a squire walking his acres.

"Broccoli here; two rows of potatoes over there; onion, radishes and tomatoes by the wall; they'll get the warmth from the wall, see."

"What about a few flowers?" I suggested.

"Flowers!" Sammy's lips curled in contempt. "What's the good of flowers? You can't eat flowers."

Many of the men filled the dark days with painting, sketching or building models. There was such an evident array of talent that it had been decided to hold an exhibition of work in an empty hut. Andy had decided to contribute. He refused to say what his exhibit was, but, as he enjoyed drawing caricatures and sketching, it was assumed that his contribution would be along these lines.

He and I visited the hut chosen for the exhibition. In the centre, in pride of place, was a huge scale model of a black Wellington bomber, with working ailerons and rudder, clearly, in precision and detail, fashioned with great affection.

All around the walls were paintings and sketches, the subjects as various as the prisoners' moods, dreams, memories: shadows of home, of life in the prison camp, of remembered or imagined action in aerial battle.

Placed on tables stretched down one side of the hut, beneath the sketches and paintings, were models and objets d'art: exotic masks, vases, ingenious machines, jewellery.

All were made from the oddest assembly of materials: wood from bed-boards, papier-maché, tins from Red Cross parcels, bits of wire from barbed-wire fences, cardboard, straw and paper from packing materials, all the flotsam that might catch the eye and fancy of the ingenious prisoner, all fashioned by an artist's hand. There was no sign of Andy's work.

"Where's yours, then?" I asked. He nodded towards a dark corner of the hut. I crossed the floor and looked at his carefully framed exhibit, labelled in careful script –

Old toothbrush, made from a priceless jade Chinese chess-set

Christmas Day, 1943, was in fact merrier than we had hoped. Some Geordies had distilled a brew from potatoes, Red Biddy, a raw spirit with a foul taste, despite added sugar and raisins from Canadian Red Cross parcels. Offered half a cup, I gulped it down with a grimace and a shudder.

The extra Christmas ration recklessly spent, the air in the hut was tinted with spirals of cigarette smoke. Heavier vapours arose from cooking stoves where Christmas pudding bubbled in re-invented steamers, and slices of tinned ham spluttered in makeshift frying pans.

The atmosphere was warm and heavy with contentment. Men smiled at each other without reason and laughed immoderately at jokes they'd heard a hundred times. Warmth and conviviality intensified by the alcohol, the hut became a sergeants' mess or the smoky bar of a local pub. Life was simple, worry and hardships put side.

They were men among men, sharing a bonhomie, a comradeship, that asked for nothing but the present moment.

In the hut men lay asleep. There were grunts and snores. An urgent whisper arose out of the darkness from the side of the bunk.

"Harry! Harry! You awake?" Paddy's face floated upwards out of the shadows. I felt a hand gripping my shoulder.

"You awake?"

Turning sleepily towards him, I asked, "What's the matter?"

"Sorry! Harry! I had to tell someone. Listen..."

A voice came from the bunk underneath.

"Put a sock in it! What's the bloody idea! Get off my fucking bed." Paddy's face disappeared.

Now fully awake, I looked over the side of the bunk. Paddy was standing in the alleyway looking up at me, his overcoat over his pyjamas.

Leaning over towards him, I said in a whisper, "What is it? What do you want?"

"Will you shut it!" The voice from the bunk underneath had a menacing edge.

I pulled my overcoat from the covers and climbed down.

I found my clogs and pushed Paddy away from the danger zone. I followed him to the door of the hut. He grasped me by the sleeve and, pulling me clear of the corner of the hut, pointed to the far horizon.

The trees silhouetted against the moon stood like cardboard cutouts. I could see nothing.

Paddy whispered, "The gap in the trees!"

I looked again, my eyes gradually becoming aware of movement within the distant shadows, shadows shifting against the patterns of the trees – carts, horses, cannons, men, an endless chain, a slow funereal procession moving across the horizon.

"What is it?"

"Russian front!" Paddy answered. "Must be! Soldiers coming back. I've been watching for ages. Thousands of 'em! Thousands! No tanks, no lorries, just carts, horses and men."

Paddy and I watched and shivered in the cold night air. It began to snow. I looked around at the huts, the barbed wire, the watch-towers. Soon there would be nothing but snow, nothing to be seen of Sammy's vegetable plot except stakes and the string.

Wednesday, 15 March, 1944: Allied bombers again bomb Monte Cassino, dropping 1,200 tons on the German-held fortress.

Sunday, 2 April, 1944: Units of the Second Ukrainian Front cross into Rumania. Hitler continues to profess his belief in ultimate victory: "The Russians have exhausted and divided their forces."

This was the time known in the camp as the 'Airman's Spring Handicap', a lemming-like rush for freedom, engaging the minds of the adventurous or, according to my mentor Steve, the foolhardy. Inside the RAF compound, would-be escapers began to look for "Swaps".

Before leaving camp, soldiers selected for a working party were checked, documented and placed within huts in a specially guarded working party compound. The problem for the would-be escapee was to get inside that guarded compound and effect an exchange with the soldier with whom he was to swap identities.

I clung obstinately to my preoccupation with the idea of escape, despite the added danger of being Jewish. It was as if there was, within my otherwise timorous body, a macho hero struggling to break out.

Steve, with much tut-tutting and wagging of his head, pointed out the dangers. David and Andy listened po-faced to my plans. My tentative suggestion that we go together also met with a po-faced silence. I decided to go alone.

Only Bert, the Army man, the thick-necked giver of the boxing lesson, was enthusiastic. "You've really got guts, 'Arry lad."

He promised to look for a likely swap among his mates, and a few days later had found one, a Scot from Edinburgh.

"Like as two peas in a ruddy pod, straight up," Bert assured me, an assurance for which I felt grateful, but, one, which, had I been more seasoned in the ways of my fellow-men, I might have examined more closely.

The "Swap" proposed by Bert, a close friend of his, was dark and good-looking, as tall as I and of similar colouring, grey eyes and dark hair. I was flattered, but doubtful.

122

The man's hair was straight, mine was curly; his nose long like mine, but long and straight. He was at least ten years older, his accent markedly Scottish.

Nevertheless, there was little chance, so Bert said, of finding anyone more suitable and, according to Bert, the Jerries never checked.

The only problem remaining was to get into the locked and guarded compound in which the working party would be housed before leaving the camp, and Bert knew of a sure-fire plan.

In the days that followed we waited for the swap, Graham Anderson, to be placed on a working party. I tried to get information on his background, but only learnt his name, his number, and that his next of kin was a maiden aunt with whom he lived in a flat off the Royal Mile.

The man was irritatingly elusive and, when found, evasive, assuring me that there was "nae need for details ... the Jerries'll no check".

Now that there was a real possibility that I might have to put my escape plan into action I gradually became less enthusiastic. I began to suspect the fact, clear to others, that Bert's enthusiasm arose less from wanting to help me escape than in finding a safe haven for his pal, keen to avoid a working party. Having to rely only on Bert's suspect support, I felt abandoned and isolated.

A week passed without anything being seen of the elusive Anderson. I was beginning to think, with some relief, that the whole episode was not to be when Bert walked in one evening with a borrowed army uniform in a bundle under his arm. Anderson, he declared was in the working party compound and due to leave camp in a few days.

There now seemed no going back. The exchange was to take place the following morning, when Anderson, using Bert's sure-fire plan, would leave the working party compound with the bread detail for which he had volunteered, and I would take his place.

It was sunny. The roads through the camp were filled with sauntering, chattering men. I made my way through the throng to a small compound bounded by an eight-foot barbed-wire fence with heavy wooden gates guarded by a German armed with a rifle. It was here the working parties were checked, assembled and locked in, before being sent out of the camp the following day.

Small groups of army men were gathered outside the compound chatting to their friends on the other side of the wire. There was no sign of Anderson.

There wasn't going to be much time for me to go over those details which might help me pass scrutiny, should there be a check. I didn't even know the name of his regiment, nor where he had been captured.

There was a great deal of activity within the compound, but still no sign of Anderson. The opportunity of contacting him seemed to be slipping away when the door of one of the huts opened and a guard and four men, one of whom was Anderson, emerged, carrying the empty wooden bread container. The guard unlocked the gate and, the bread detail passed through. Locking the compound gates behind him, the guard shambled along a few yards ahead of the four men. The little group made its way through the stream of prisoners. I hurried my pace and, catching up with the bread detail, walked in step at Anderson's side.

"Look, we need to talk," I said in an urgent whisper. "I need to know more about you, more details."

"Dinna fash yourself. There's no need to worry. Plenty o'time."

"What about him?" I jerked my head in the direction of the guard walking ahead.

"No problem," said Anderson. "He'll no notice. Dim as shit!"

The guard, glancing frequently round, gave us little opportunity of effecting the change. When we reached the cookhouse I waited at the gates for the four men to come out. Some ten minutes later they appeared, each man having a shoulder under one of the carrying handles supporting the container. The guard followed. This time, however, prompted no doubt by Anderson, they walked on, not waiting for the elderly German to finish locking the gate.

Anderson, glancing over his shoulder at the guard still busy with padlock and key, said urgently, "Come on!" We changed places.

Having finished locking the gates of the cook-house, the guard turned round and, seeing the bread detail receding into the distance, ran after us.

As I passed through the gates into the working compound, I shouted hurriedly over my shoulder to Anderson, "See you at the wire! Wait at the wire!" but Anderson appeared not to have heard.

That night, in a strange bunk, I awoke from a half-remembered nightmarish dream. I sat up, my pyjama jacket clinging to my body and my forehead damp with sweat. I couldn't breathe. I tried to get air into my lungs, to get to the end of a full breath, but the more I tried the tighter my chest became, gripped as if by an iron band. I fought to control a rising feeling of panic.

Gradually, however, as I became used to the limited intake of breath, my body became more relaxed, my breathing easier. A wheezing sound escaped my lungs. I slowly lowered my head and dared to lie flat, drifting into sleep.

Next morning I awoke tired. I sat up, stretched my arms and drew in a deep breath. I dismissed the night's happenings. A cold in the head! That's what it was. Dressing hurriedly in my borrowed khaki, I could feel, facing the day's events, a mounting excitement.

As I queued for the ersatz coffee my neighbour in line asked, "You RAF?"

I looked down at the vaguely familiar figure and nodded.

"Thought so," the man murmured.

"You?" I asked. The little man nodded glumly.

"Did you do a swap?" I asked. He jerked his head. "Did I do a swap? I bloody did do a swap. Look," he said accusingly, "I don't know if you realize but there's half the bloody RAF in this compound!"

"What d'you mean, half the RAF? How'd they get in?"

The little man turned and faced me, "How'd they got in? I'll tell you how they got in. They got in over the bloody wire, under the bloody wire and through the bloody wire. That's how they bloody well got in!"

In a routine check it was found that there were eight too many prisoners in the hut. A round-faced, round-bodied officer arrived with an interpreter, a clerk carrying a folding desk and a box of record cards.

I eyed the preparations with dismay. Despite my attempts to get details from Anderson, I had never really believed I would be questioned. Getting out of the main camp should have been routine, a mere detail.

The clerk sat at the desk, the box of cards in front of him, the interpreter at his side, and the officer standing behind them. I hurried to my bunk and, rummaging among my effects, found a balaclava and pulled it on. It would at least hide my curly hair. I hadn't long to wait. Mine was one of the first names to be called.

"Anderson!" I stepped forward, balaclava pulled well down. The officer's round head pivoted on his fat neck, his eyes peering in my direction. The interpreter glanced at the list of questions.

"What is your number?"

I gulped. Oh God! The number! I knew the number! I had learnt it by heart; had repeated it a hundred times before going to sleep and again on waking. I couldn't remember it! I could *not* remember it!

"Your number," the interpreter repeated. "What is your number?"

A distorted, mangled, stream of vowels and syllables escaped from my throat in a strangled husky whisper; "Ee-se-of-si-vee-wa." The interpreter blushed, and glancing hurriedly over his shoulder at the officer, repeated the question.

"What is your number?"

"Ee-se-of-si-vee-wa," I said.

The interpreter turned towards the officer and shrugged his shoulder, explaining no doubt that the accent was impossible to understand.

The officer swivelled his body on its short legs and, arms akimbo, berated the luckless man who, licking dry lips, turned once more towards me.

"Who is your next of kin?" he asked.

Feeling that I was now on the right track, I gave vent to another strangulated explosion of sound, but, knowing the name of the maiden aunt, allowed a little more detail to come through.

"Mizbeth Anson," I said.

The interpreter smiled. He had actually recognized something that bore relationship to the information on the card. He nodded to the officer, who ordered him to continue.

"What," he said, "is your regiment?"

My heart sank. I hadn't the least idea what the bloody man's regiment might be. I supposed it might well have the word 'Scottish' or 'Highlander' or 'Fusilier' somewhere in the title.

"Sco-lan-seers," I said.

The interpreter again shook his head and despairingly shrugged his shoulders. The officer was not satisfied. Snatching the record card from the interpreter, he crossed to where I was standing.

He looked at the photograph, looked at me, then looked again at the photograph. He signed to me to take off my balaclava. Taking hold of my chin he turned my head to one side, studying my profile in greater detail.

The officer stood back, looking me up and down, then slowly walked around me, his podgy hand to his mouth, his head bent back on his fat neck.

"*Nein,*" he said, "*Das ist nicht Anderson. Du bist nicht Anderson. Nicht Soldaten ... Flieger ... nicht Soldaten. Was ist dein Name?*"

I stood in an office in the administration block, feet apart, hands clasped behind my back. With a mixture of obstinacy and mock-heroism I refused to give my name. Looking straight in front of me, with what I felt to be a steely gaze, I insisted that I was Anderson.

Two army men, in smart British uniforms, working there as clerks, belonged to an aristocracy among the prisoners. Their favoured positions, their ability to speak German, made of men like these a third force, certainly not Germans, but not quite prisoners. They looked on from the desks at which they were sitting with unchanging expression. I wondered where their sympathies lay.

A second officer was present, as fat as the first but with more gold braid. He, too, looked first at the photograph and then at me. There was a conversation between the two as they stood there belly to belly. I heard the word *Flieger* repeated several times.

They turned towards me and again asked my name.

"Anderson," I insisted, "Anderson." The two British clerks looked stolidly on.

The officer who had interrogated me earlier that day again took hold of my chin and turned my head to show my profile. He smiled, addressing his colleagues. "*Jude, nicht wahr, Jude?*" The two of them sniggered.

"*Komm!*" the *Feldwebel* said. I followed behind him and waited as he inserted a key in the lock and pushed open a door. The cell contained a double bunk, a sanitary bucket, a chair, a tap and a sink. There was a door with the usual spy-hole and a small barred window. Above the door a small window, opening on a stay, acted as a ventilator.

The walls and the door were of wood. I felt reassured. It was not really a prison, only a converted hut, a far cry from the massive stone walls, iron staircases and tiers of cells at St Gilles.

There was already a prisoner in the cell, a dark-haired young soldier of about my own age. He was sitting cross-legged on the top bed of the two-tier bunk with his back resting against the wall, his hands clasped behind his neck. He gave no acknowledgement of my presence.

The *Feldwebel* gestured for me to enter and said tersely, "No blankets! No food! You give me your name – blankets; food. *Verstehe?*" and, without waiting for an answer, stepped into the corridor. The key turned in the lock. My fellow prisoner continued to stare fixedly at the ceiling without speaking.

I sat down on the chair and despondently pondered the *Feldwebel*'s words. I'd made a mess of things. I should have planned it all more carefully. Should have taken no notice of Bert, should have insisted that Anderson...

I hadn't even a name now. What would happen to letters from home? I couldn't write, even if they were to give me a letter-form. They'd know from the address who I was. It wouldn't work. I'd have to give my name. Anyway, it was Anderson's fault. The idiot! With his "They won't check. They won't check." They checked all right.

Still, if I were to tell them my name, they'd be on to Anderson. It'd serve him right! It'd be giving in to the Germans though. Can't get away from that. What would they think, Andy, Phil, and the others? I looked up. My cell-mate was looking down at me, a smile on his face.

"It's not the end of the world, you know," he said.

"I suppose not," I answered ruefully, pleased that my hitherto silent companion now seemed to recognize my existence.

"Look at it like this," he continued, "if you're in here, you're not in a mine working your guts out."

"That's the point," I explained. "I wasn't in a mine. I'm in the RAF. They won't let us go out. I swapped, wanted to get on a working party."

The soldier shook his head. "One born every minute. I'm trying to get into the camp and you're trying to get out. You should've swapped places with me. You could have had a nice time working down that bloody mine."

"How long've you got?" I asked.

"Don't know. The longer the better."

"Get far?" I asked.

"Nah!" he answered. "Never do."

"You've done it before then?" I asked.

"Done it before!" the soldier grinned. "It's a way of life with me. What've I got to lose? They can only send me down a ruddy mine. As far as I'm concerned this is a kind of holiday. Every few months I go walk about. The Jerries arrest me, put me in solitary. I have a few weeks rest and then they send me back."

I stood up and walked over to the barred window. There was not much to be seen, just the corner of the administration block standing outside the wire of the main camp.

"What do they do when they catch you?" I asked.

"Depends. If it's some way off, they don't seem to mind so much. No skin off their nose I suppose. They get the credit for arresting you."

"D'you think he meant it?" I asked.

"Meant it?"

"You know! No food? No blanket?"

"Can't say. it's a bit of pressure."

"He wants my name," I explained. "They don't know my real name. I reckon I'll have to tell him," I said, hoping for some kind of sympathetic support, or at least, of establishing some kind of rapport.

"Up to you" he said.

"If I do," I continued, "They'll find Anderson, the chap I swapped with."

He made no comment ... clearly, I felt, a criticism on his part.

"He might take your blanket," I added. "D'you think he would?"

"I shouldn't think so. It doesn't matter if he does."

There was a long silence.

"I mean," I explained, "this chap, the one I swapped with, I could never get anything out of him. Not even his regiment. I hardly knew anything about him."

My companion looked away.

"I asked him. I kept on asking, but he wouldn't give me an answer. That's why they caught me. They wouldn've caught me if I'd had time to learn all the details. I didn't know what to say when they questioned me. He'd always put me off what to say when I asked. Wasn't worth the trouble, he reckoned. They never check, he kept on saying.,"

My explanation had become a monologue and my monologue had become a murmured complaint as I crossed the room and looked out of the window.

"Anyway," I continued, "It wouldn't be fair to you. I mean, they might take your blanket, in case you shared it with me."

"I shouldn't worry about the blanket. We'll not freeze to death. You want to spend a few days down that ruddy mine. You'd know what cold is."

"Still, it wouldn't be fair," and after a pause, "What about the food?"

"You've got a point there," said the soldier.

I crossed to my bunk and stretched myself on the mattress. There was silence in the cell. My tired brain was gradually cloaked by slumber.

I was woken by the sound of the *Feldwebel*'s key turning in the lock.

"Well?" the *Feldwebel* asked. There was a pause.

"Harry Levy," I mumbled.

A shabby orderly in odd bits of uniform and of uncertain nationality was now sweeping the corridor between the cells.

Seven days on bread and water! Still, it was a luxury to have a cell of my own, to be free of the crowded huts, the dirt and fleas, the morning *Fünf Appel*.

There appeared to be none of the irksome rules that regulated the prison régime at St Gilles. Here the *Feldwebel* locked the door and left you to it.

Towards lunchtime I was beginning to feel hungry. It wasn't going to be as easy as all that. A bit like fasting on Yom Kippur, only longer, and nothing else to think about except food.

I lay on the bed listening to faint sounds coming from the nearby compounds. They would be lining up for swede soup soon. The iniquitous swede soup, the half-boiled potatoes and the smelly cheese took on a new allure. Tomorrow the Red Cross parcel was due. They might get a full parcel. It'd be just my luck! I sat up and went over to the window. I stood looking vacantly at the distant fence.

There was a scratching sound. I glanced around. A hissing now accompanied the scratching. I crossed to the door. A voice whispered,

"Hey! Eengleesh!"

"Yes?" I asked.

The voice whispered, "Eat now! Queek!"

I heard a rustling from the ventilator above the door. I reached up and took down a piece of chocolate wrapped in torn silver paper.

"Thanks," I whispered. "Thanks very much."

"Eat queek!" the voice replied.

I ate in some haste, listening all the time for the *Feldwebel*'s footsteps. I'd hardly allowed the last square to melt in my mouth when there was the same scratching at the door and again the same whisper.

"Eengleesh!" I crossed to the door.

"Thanks for the chocolate, it was ..."

"Eat! Eat now!" The same voice!

Again I reached up to the ventilator, as if reaching into a bran tub to draw out a mystery prize – this time a slice of sausage.

"Are these your rations?" I asked in a whisper. "You really shouldn't."

"Eat! Eat!" the only reply.

The rest of that day and the days that followed a seemingly endless trickle of delicacies passed through the ventilator, followed by the same whispered injunction.

Every day of my seven-day sentence I ate a strange mixture: chocolate, sardines, sausages, slices of meat loaf, bits of cheese and these always followed by the same mysterious message from the same mysterious benefactor.

Nor was I able to find out anything about him, or where the food was coming from. The unseen's conversation, welcome as it was, was confined to those few phrases, "Hey Eengleesh! Eat! Eat now! Eat queek!"

My return to the hut was akin to that of a hero's. As I entered men gathered around and patted me on the back. Even Graham and Palmer added a relatively friendly greeting.

News had travelled fast. The clerks who had watched me being interrogated had given a highly dramatic account of my "stubborn resistance" to the German's questioning.

Phil said, "You don't have to talk about it if you don't want to."

"Try and stop him," murmured David, a murmur I chose to ignore.

"Nothing much to talk about," I replied, with self-effacing modesty.

"We heard all about it from a chap who works as a clerk in Admin," said Andy.

"Oh, him!" I said. "There were two of them. From the expression on their faces they seemed to think hanging was too good for me."

"This chap reckoned you gave the Jerries a right run-around," added David.

I put my mug on the table. "Well ..." I said, hesitating, as I tried to find the right blend of modest self-deprecation.

"He was the one who organized the food," said David.

"Oh! The food! I wondered where that came from. I nearly died of indigestion."

"You'll starve next time, you ungrateful bugger," said David.

"Next time! There'll be no next time. Not if I can help it?"

"Anyway", I added, "There wasn't much point to it. I didn't even get out of the camp gates, and in the end I had to give them my name."

"You gave them your name!" exclaimed Andy.

"Yes, I gave them my name. Do you want your chocolates and sardines back? What else was I supposed to do. Stay in solitary for the rest of the war? The man in the bloody iron mask. The prisoner without a name? And just to save Anderson's skin? If I can do seven days, so can he."

"All right! All right!" protested Andy. "Keep your hair on!"

"You know what Anderson was like," I went on indignantly. "I had to stand there like a dummy with those damned Germans breathing down my neck. Didn't even know his regiment." And without giving anyone time to say a word, I continued my indignant protest, "Couldn't write home, couldn't get any letters or parcels."

"Look," said Andy, "it's nothing to do with me what you did. It's your own business."

Far from finding Andy's remarks conciliatory, I felt as if he were accusing me of some cowardly act.

"Thank you," I replied angrily, "Thanks a bunch. That's really big of you. Torture wouldn't've made a chap like you speak, would it?"

We all sat in an awkward silence, until Phil, ever the calming influence in any dispute, said, "You're being silly, Harry. There wasn't anything else you could've done. Nobody's blaming you for anything."

The others, taking their lead from Phil, hurried to add consoling phrases; "Course not! What else could you've done," and so on.

Nevertheless, I felt that I had betrayed that heroic image of myself, long carried deep within me.

"Anyway," I said. "Where is Anderson?"

"I was going to tell you before you blew your top," said Andy. "We hardly ever see him. Sleeps in another hut, his old hut. Bert's there too."

"I'd better let him know what's happened," I said. "The Jerries are bound to be looking for him."

"Too true," said David, nodding towards the doorway of the hut in which the guard was framed.

I turned round. A small elderly German, rifle on shoulder and a slip of paper in his hand, was standing looking around him, a bewildered expression on his face. I stood up and walked over to the man, anxious to get to him before he had a chance to talk to anyone else. He had been sent to find Anderson, who the Germans thought they would find in my hut, using my name.

"*Was wollen sie?*" I asked, knowing very well what, or rather whom, he wanted. The German handed over a piece of paper. I looked at it and turned to the others.

"Anyone know anyone called Harry Levy?" The others grinned and shook their heads, but for one awful moment I saw Paddy open his mouth as if he were going to say something. I glared at him and he subsided back on to the form on which he had been sitting.

With an inward sigh of relief I turned back to the German, shrugged my shoulders, shook my head slowly and spread my hands in a gesture of regret.

"*Weiss nicht,*" I said. "*Weiss nicht,*" and gave the man back his piece of paper.

"*Danke schoen,*" said the German. He folded the paper and put it into his tunic pocket.

"*Bitte schoen,*" I answered politely as the guard made for the door.

My abortive attempt at escape was, a few days later, given a tragic and sinister postscript. Of seventy-nine airmen, from nearby Sagen, recaptured after escaping through a tunnel at Stalag Luft III, fifty had been shot dead, reportedly on Hitler's orders. The Germans are said to have warned PoWs that all areas within several miles of Sagen were now declared "death zones" – anybody entering these areas without authority would be shot on sight.

In Lamsdorf a special parade was called. The Senior British Officer made the announcement. The prisoners' reactions were strangely subdued. There was little vituperation, and that in whispers.

I tried to examine my own feelings. Fifty prisoners shot! A monstrous crime had been perpetrated, but I could feel nothing, neither anger nor sorrow. I looked at the others. Men were grave-faced, talking to each other as if at a funeral. What did the announcement of these deaths mean to them? They recognized the news of the men's deaths to be "shocking", yet they didn't appear shocked. They should have found the news frightening, realizing that they themselves were in the hands of the very same maniac who had ordered the slaughter, and yet they seemed, at least from outward appearance and manner, unaffected.

It was as if the murder of these men, which had taken place only a few miles from our own camp, had taken place on some other planet, as if the murderers and the men they had murdered were not human but fictional characters.

Tuesday, 6 June, 1994: Before dawn, Allied paratroopers and gliders begin landing behind German lines in Northern France. Bomber Command pound Normandy defences; Allies land along French coast from Cherbourg to Le Havre; by nightfall 156,000 troops landed. Hitler is convinced that landings are a diversionary attack.

Today Swiss representatives of the Red Cross were in the camp. It had something to do, so rumour had it, with the possible exchange of sick prisoners. We were not allowed to make personal representations to the visitors, and to prevent this happening the Germans had padlocked all the compound gates. Nevertheless, determined to make our presence felt we lined the wire and gave the "V" for Victory sign as the Swiss officers passed, surrounded by gold-braided Jerries.

Fearing some kind of demonstration, the Germans had a soldier, with an Alsatian on leash, patrol between the locked compounds. Spontaneously, to relieve our frustration and boredom, a new game arose. As the German and his dog passed the men would boo, jeer and miaow. Finally provoked, the guard would unchain the gate and release the dog. There would be a wild rush to get back into the huts, and a scramble to reach the top bunks. The dog, frightened and excited by the prisoners' yells and the banging of tins, would bound into a hut and leap up at the dangling feet. The more perverse would sprinkle pepper on the dog's muzzle.

The German guard would appear and drag the dog away, yelling over his shoulder as he left the hut, "*Verfluchte schweinerei!*"

I woke next morning with an excruciating pain in my right ear. Every muscle in my chest, arms and legs had stiffened in rigid resistance. I pressed my closed fist tight against the side of my head, my body rocking to and fro. I reached out blindly for my clothes, unable to think of anything but the pain. I found a scarf, tied it tightly around my head, and climbed down.

Philip, sitting at the table, looked up.

"What on earth!" he exclaimed.

"My ear," I moaned. "My bloody ear. A pain. I don't know what it is.,"

Philip stood up and unwound the scarf. "Let's have a look," he murmured, turning my face towards the window and peering into the ear.

"I can't see a thing," he said. "If it still hurts after parade, you'd better see the medic."

On parade, my head wrapped in the scarf, I waited in line. The ear was as painful as ever.

"What's with the scarf?" Andy asked. "Fancy dress?"

"My ear!" I muttered

"Come off it!" said David. "They'll never swallow it. They don't repatriate for earache."

I rocked my head in jerky movements, oblivious to all else but the pain.

Hardly had the word of dismissal been given than I ran like a hare for the gate of the compound, past the startled *Feldwebel*, Ukraine Joe, and along the road between the compounds leading to the main gate and the medical hut. As I neared the hut I could see a long queue of men waiting for treatment. The queue seemed miles long. I couldn't wait. As I ran past them, the men looked startled, then belligerent. "What's the idea!" "Who d'you think you are! Get in the fucking queue!"

I ran on, pushing past the men at the door, ignoring protests. Inside the hut men queued round the walls, waiting their turn to be admitted into the inner room. I hurried across to the door and, ignoring indignant cries, pushed it open. Inside, a medical orderly was bending over a patient seated on a chair. As I stood in the doorway he looked up in surprise and anger.

"What the hell d'you think you're..."

"My ear, my ear," I exclaimed.

"You can't rush in like that. Outside with you wait your..."

"I can't," I insisted. "The pain in my ear! I must see a doctor."

There could have been no mistaking the agony in my voice. The orderly gestured curtly for me to sit down.

"Take off the scarf!" he ordered. He peered into the ear and, shaking a thermometer, put it under my tongue. I became calmer. The orderly took the thermometer, glanced at it, and putting his head through a dividing curtain at the back of the room, said sharply,

"Come on, Aussie! Off your arse! See if you can find Harrison!"

Lying in bed, my head bandaged like a hero of the Crimean War, I awoke from a drugged sleep. The pain was now a dull throb; whatever they had given me seemed to have worked. I looked across the hut to the bed opposite. The orderly was leaning over a struggling patient. The man's voice was slurred as if he'd been drinking; his head rolled from side to side; his arms waved weakly in the air.

"Gerroff. What d'you think your doing!" the drunken voice complained indignantly.

The orderly looked across to my bed.

"Woken you up, has he? How you feeling?"

"Great!" I said "Much better!"

"It was perforated. A perforated eardrum," said the orderly.

"Perforated?" I asked.

The orderly crossed the hut and stood at the head of my bed.

"You probably had a bad head cold. The membrane got inflamed and infected. You've got a small hole in it. It'll probably heal."

Monday, 12 June, 1944: Normandy: Montgomery tells reporters, "We have won the battle of the beaches", as Allied Forces take Carentan.

"Sorry, Harry," said Paddy in the best hospital manner, as he sat down beside the bed, "couldn't get any grapes."

"How are things?" Phil asked.

"Soon be out, I should think," I answered.

"I shouldn't be in a hurry if I were you. Would you, Phil?"

"You've got it made," added Phil. "Cooked meals! Sheets!"

"What's the latest gen?" I asked.

"They're still stuck, apparently, in Normandy."

"Haven't seen anything of David or Andy," I remarked. "I suppose they're too busy planning the great escape."

"They've swapped," said Paddy. "Didn't you know? They're out on a working party."

Philip smiled. "You're better off here," he said. "They're mugs. The war'll soon be over. It's a race now between the Yanks and the Russkies to see who gets to Berlin first."

"Still," said Paddy, "it'd be great to make it on your own, wouldn't it?"

"That's what the poor buggers at Sagen thought," said Phil.

"If anyone can do it," Paddy insisted, "they can."

"Think so?" I said. "It's not as easy as you think."

Tuesday, 11 July: Washington: Roosevelt agrees to recognize De Gaulle's provisional government as the legitimate administration of liberated France.

Captain Harrison, the medical officer, said almost apologetically that he'd have to discharge me in a few days.

"The ear seems fine. You aren't having any pain, are you?" I assured him that I was feeling well.

That night, however, I awoke suddenly with the same feeing of suffocation that I had experienced that night in the working-party compound. I was again forced to sit up, again forced to fight for breath. I sat bolt upright, my forehead wet with sweat. Johnson, the medical orderly, was out of the ward on his rounds. I sat for what seemed hours leaning forward unable to draw a deep breath. Some time later Johnson put his head round the door intending to take a quick look and then carry on to the next ward. He came over to the end of the bed and watched for a few seconds without saying a word.

"Have you had an asthma attack before?" he asked. I shook my head.

"Hold on a bit," he said. "I'll get you something." In a matter of minutes he returned with Captain Harrison.

"Hallo, old chap! What's all this?" the doctor asked. "Bit of bother with the old breathing? You're playing a nice tune on the old wheeze-box. Ever had an attack before?"

"I think I have," I said, each word an effort. "I hadn't realized it was asthma."

Captain Harrison nodded and, turning to the orderly, said, "Roll up his sleeve, dear boy!"

The injection worked with wonderful speed. My heart began to beat more and more rapidly. Soon, my breathing became easier. I put my head back on the pillow and lay back, weak and grateful.

Monday, 17 July, 1944: Russian forces sweep into Poland, crossing the River Bug. German units ordered not to yield.
Friday, 28 July, 1994: Normandy: US troops capture Coutances.
Sunday, 31 July, 1944: Russian troops reach positions within ten miles of Warsaw as street fighting develops within the city.
Wednesday, 9 August, 1944: Eisenhower moves his headquarters from England to France.

My attacks of asthma were becoming more frequent and often quite severe. Aussie reckoned it was a pity I hadn't started having them sooner. I could've gone before the Repatriation Board. There had been an exchange of sick prisoners in May.

"You'd have been bloody 'ome by now," said Rod Steel, the Australian orderly who ran our ward, dropping his ash on my coverlet. "Still, the rate you're ruddy going, you'll be right for the next one."

I wanted the attacks to continue, at least until the next Board. I knew only too well that the attacks were genuine, but I couldn't help feeling a bit of a fraud stuck there in the hospital, and my feelings of guilt weren't helped by Rod giving me hints on how to exaggerate the symptoms.

"You got to push hard with your stomach muscles as you breathe out. You'll wheeze like a ruddy clapped-out cart-horse if you do it right."

Sunday, 12 August 1944

Andy and David were back in camp. They hadn't been to visit me yet, but, according to Paddy, they had managed to get as far as Stettin.

The attacks seemed to be getting worse. Aussie sat hunched on the bed next to mine, cigarette drooping from his lower lip.

"What d'you mean, I'm too late?"

"The Board, mate, the Board! If you'd gone before the Board, you'd be home by now."

"There'll be another. You said so yourself."

"Could be! Could be! If the ruddy war's not over."

When we first had news of the Second Front we all imagined the war would be over in weeks. Now it looked as if it could drag on indefinitely.

More and more repatriation began to play a part in my daydreams. In fact, I began to do more than dream. I set my heart on being repatriated.

I deliberately started to take less care of myself. I would get out of bed in the middle of the night and stand by the open window, my pyjama jacket undone. During an attack, I would practise the exaggerated wheezing Aussie had recommended, until, at length, I didn't know myself how much the attacks were real, how much pretence.

Phil turned up on Friday evening with Andy and David. They looked none the worse for their experience, though David's face was even paler than usual.

"You nearly made it then?" I said.

"We had a lot of luck really," said Andy.

The camp escape committee had advised them to scrape together as many cigarettes as they could and had supplied them with a forged *ausweis* (identity card) showing them to be French workers.

They had no trouble getting through the gates of the factory, just joining the stream of foreign workers. They hadn't even had to show their papers or gate-passes. With the cigarettes, they had been able to buy raincoats and berets and bribe a French lorry driver to give them a lift to Stettin.

The lorry driver had suggested they might make contact in Stettin with a Scandinavian seaman at a brothel he knew, designed for the use of foreign workers. He dropped them at the top of a narrow street leading to the brothel and they waited across the road for a likely sailor to emerge.

After letting several men go by without attempting to contact them, they finally saw a young merchant seaman come out, stand in the doorway and light a cigarette.

David, the "linguist", went up to him and, speaking in what he felt to be French, asked for a light. The young Swede laughed, and said, "You're English, aren't you?"

The three of them went to a café frequented by foreign sailors, where he bought them a meal. They drank a lot of beer and, more than a little tipsy, followed their new friend out of the café and down a street leading to the docks.

There was a guard at the dock gate and they decided to put on a bit of an act, to make it look as if the young Swede was bringing a couple of drunken shipmates back on board.

The Swede spoke to the guard who asked for his pass, while David and Andy made a drunken show of looking for theirs. The German waved them on. They staggered along behind the sailor, following him up the gangplank of the ship which was due to leave the next day for Sweden.

Once aboard, they climbed down a ladder into an empty hold, and it was there a German boarding party, making a routine check before the ship left, found them, still sleeping off the effects of the previous night's indulgence. They were pushed around a bit by the Jerries, and when they got back to the factory from which they had escaped, they were made to stand under a cold shower with their clothes on.

"Just as well I didn't go with you," I remarked.

My visitors looked at each other.

Andy said, "We would have liked you to come with us, but it's hard to explain."

"Explain? You don't have to explain."

"We thought ... you might b ... you know ... put out, or not confiding in you when we first thought of going.

"It was this Jewish business." David looked at me for the first time.

"It could've been dangerous," Andy explained.

"For me or for you?" I asked

"For all three of us."

"Anyway, I couldn't have gone, could I, what with my ear and now this asthma?"

"Phil was saying you might try for the next Repatriation Board," Andy said.

"He's been getting a bit of coaching," said Phil.

My visitors looked at each other, probably wondering whether I was putting on an act just to get home or trying to impress them with my astuteness.

Aussie tossed an official-looking letter on to my bed., A letter of any kind was a rare event. I first thought that it might have something to do with repatriation. Perhaps they'd decided to put my name on the list without me having to go before a repatriation board. I could be on the next exchange, be home in a matter of weeks.

The address was typewritten. They'd made a mistake, put my rank as warrant officer instead of flight-sergeant. That was it! I was due for promotion. It was automatic for aircrew. All you had to do to earn it was to keep alive. Even prisoners of war were promoted. I opened the enveloped and drew out the thin official letter.

"Good news, 'Arry?" Aussie asked.

"Not so much of the Harry, lance-corporal. You are now addressing, Warrant Officer 1st Class Harry Levy, RAFVR."

I could hardly wait to give Phil and the others news of my promotion, but they'd all had similar letters, which rather took the gilt off the gingerbread.

"Where's David?" I asked. "Haven't seen anything of him lately."

"Haven't you heard?" asked Paddy.

"Haven't I heard what?" I asked.

"He's being repatriated," said Andy.

"David is?! What d'you mean repatriated?" My reaction was one of shocked disbelief. I was the one to be repatriated, not David.

"He's been ill for ages; coughing badly ever since we got back from Stettin," Andy explained.

"Spitting blood," added Paddy.

"What is it?" I asked. "Not TB?"

"Could be," said Andy.

"That's terrible," I said, feeling, nevertheless, that David was a lucky bugger. We all sat in silence for a moment.

"It'll be funny if David and I go home together," I said.

"What d'you mean?" asked Andy.

"Well, there's a good chance, Aussie says, that I could be on the next exchange if I get past the Board."

Andy and Philip looked at each other but said nothing. Seeing their silent exchange, I asked, "Why, what is it?"

"Nothing!" said Andy, hurriedly. "Nothing!"

"I think the list's closed," said Phil.

"At least, that's what David said. He reckoned that the list had been officially closed. They've already got the full number, but as his case was serious they were making an exception. Of course he might have got it all wrong."

Sunday, 3 September: Brussels liberated by British 21st Army Group.
Monday, 4 September: British Forces enter Antwerp, U.S. units in South are 40 miles beyond Lyon.
Tuesday, 5 September: Moscow broadcasts call on Poles in Warsaw to stage an uprising: "Fight the Germans. No doubt Warsaw already hears the guns of the battle which is soon to bring her liberation ... join battle with the Germans ... this time for the decisive action."

We had lived as if all reality were encompassed within the bounds of the camp. Reduced to rumour and speculation, news of bombed cities, of the clash of armies, the death and suffering of thousands only faintly touched us. It was as if our barbed-wire enclave existed on a different planet. With the advent of D-Day, however, our perception of reality had changed. Events in that other world beyond the wire began to have greater significance. The sense of euphoria grew as news of the landings on the Normandy beaches spread.

We expected the impossible. The Allied Forces would sweep through France, through Belgium, through the Lowlands, into Germany itself. Hitler's blitzkrieg in reverse! In a matter of weeks, months perhaps, we would be home.

But gradually the reality became clear. There was to be no easy victory. The Allies would have to fight for each key point, for each river crossing, establishing beachheads, fighting to maintain them against violent counter-attacks. Excited expectations, raised by the successful landings in June and by the liberation of Paris and Brussels, faded.

Wednesday, 20 September: The British First Airborne Division suffers heavy casualties at Arnhem. Three hundred of its wounded surrender to the Germans.

Bored with life in the hospital ward, I was not sorry to be discharged. Now that the asthma attacks seemed to have stopped and hopes of repatriation faded, I looked forward to the comparative freedom of life outside in the camp.

"Should you have an attack," Captain Harrison told me, "we'll get the German doctor to have a look at you. You could get on the next exchange, if there is a next exchange."

I quickly fitted back into the life of the crowded hut. Soon it was as if my long stay in the quiet and cleanliness of the hospital ward had never been; but as autumn gave way to winter, and snow began to fall, the hut became once more full of smoke from the little tin stoves and the asthma attacks began again. Having suffered a particularly bad night, I decided to see Captain Harrison. As I put my head round the door, Aussie hurriedly rose from the bed on which he'd been resting and put out his cigarette. "Jesus!" he said. "It's you. I thought it was the bullshit brigade."

I explained the reason for my visit. He put his hands on his hips and looked hard at the floor of the ward, obviously thinking. At length he raised his head and eyed me up and down.

"Now," he said, "if you're going to see the Jerry doctor, we'll need to work on you a bit. You look about as crook as a ruddy rugby forward."

Aussie folded his arms. "Right," he said with an air of decision. "How good are you at the old gymnastics?"

"What you on about?" I asked.

"I'm not joking, chum. If you want to get back to Blighty, you not only have to be 'krank', you have to look ruddy 'krank'. Right! We'll start off with a bit of 'keep-fit', You know, feet together, feet apart and all that malarkey."

"Look...," I began to protest.

"Now, come on! Get ruddy moving! D'you want to go home or don't you? In! Out! In! Out! You know the drill."

141

Sheepishly I began to jump, feet together, feet apart, my hands and arms flapping up and down like an ungainly bird.

Aussie resumed his recumbent position on the bed. "That's the ticket. In! Out! In! Out!" He waved a languid arm in time to my movements. "In! Out! In! Out! One! Two! One! Two! he intoned as my breathing became laboured, my face red.

"Come on, you lazy sod?" said Aussie encouragingly as, gasping for breath, I came to a stop. "Get running! Go on! Up and down the ruddy ward. I'll go and get old Harrison."

As soon as he had left the ward, I stopped running and tried to catch my breath. I started breathing as Aussie had taught me, forcing air out of the lungs instead of the instinctive attempt of an asthmatic to breathe in, allowing the body's instinctive muscular reaction to suck in air. My wheezing could be heard from one end of the ward to the other.

Captain Harrison came in with Johnson, the chief orderly, and Aussie. Harrison looked at me, felt my pulse and smiled.

"First rate! First rate! Just the ticket!" He turned to Johnson and added in a confidential aside, "I'll get the *Oberst*. Get him running around ... jumping up and down ... you know the sort of thing."

By the time the German doctor arrived I was in the middle of an attack over which I had no control. Little need for counterfeit! The German doctor patted my shoulder sympathetically; "You will soon he home. January, February, perhaps," he said.

When the German, Captain Harrison and Johnson had left the ward, Aussie said, as he leant over the back of the chair, where, still wheezing, I was sitting, "All right, you can stop now. They've gone."

Friday, 12 January, 1945: Russian forces under Zhukov and Marshal Ivan S. Konev launch, from Poland and East Prussia, their greatest offensive of the war.

Although our camp, now renamed Stalag 344, lay directly in the path of the advancing Russian Army, life pursued the same peaceful tenor.

"You heard?" Paddy asked as he sat down at the table and peered into his Red Cross food parcel.

Andy moved his knight, threatening Philip's queen.

"There's a woman in the camp."

Andy raised his head momentarily from his study of the board. "Yes," he said, "I've seen them, typists, office-staff."

"Not German," Paddy continued, "Russian!" We all turned and looked at him.

"A Russian soldier, infantry, wounded, and taken prisoner near Warsaw. I've seen her," Paddy insisted.

"Where?" Philip asked.

"In the hospital compound. There's a crowd at the wire, all trying to get a look."

"What does she look like?" I asked. "Marlene Dietrich?"

"Well," said Paddy, "not exactly. More like Sammy, as a matter of fact. Could be his sister: round face, red cheeks, five foot high and about five foot wide."

"Watch it!" warned Sammy.

"Nice big bum, though! Lovely round tits!" Paddy added.

"Definitely Sammy's double," said Andy, turning back to the chess board.

Wednesday, 17 January, 1945: Warsaw is taken by Marshal Zhukov and the forces of the First White Russian Front.
Thursday, 18 January: Russian forces advance rapidly towards Upper Silesia. The German High Command begin evacuating civilians from the eastern fringes of the German Reich.

The Russians were now advancing towards the camp. All we had to do was wait. They might send us home from Stettin or one of the Russian ports, but some prisoners were not so enamoured by the thought of being in Russian hands.

"I'm no waiting," Jock Graham proclaimed. "I'll take my chances with Jerry."

"Why?" I asked.

"I'd no trust a Russkie as far as I could throw 'im," the Scotsman affirmed.

"And how many Russians d'you know?" I asked.

"Never mind how many Russians I know," said the Scot. "They're all fuckin' Communists!"

"What's that got to do with it?" I asked.

"Russians!" Graham, grinned, delighted to have provoked me, "They're just a lot of ignorant peasants."

"Takes one to know one," I murmured, living dangerously.

Men stood talking earnestly to each other, clustering in groups, converging on each new rumour. Guns had been heard, planes had been seen, or at least someone knew someone else who had heard guns or seen planes. The Russians were reported as being fifty, forty, or as close as ten miles from the camp.

One worrying rumour more persistent than the rest concerned the evacuation of the whole area by the Germans. They had, it was said, no intention of leaving prisoners behind. Everyone would be taken on foot, or by train, towards the west, away from the advancing Russians. We viewed the prospect with a mixture of excitement and apprehension.

The elderly guards made no reply to the taunts of prisoners. Some would shake their heads and mutter that everything now was ... done for.

"*Fertig! Alles fertig! Alles kaput!*"

Friday, 19 January, 1945: Krakow, Lodz and Tarnow in Poland now occupied by the Russians. Germans are in full retreat along a 500-mile front.

The Russians were at Jagensdorf, about ten miles from the camp. We would stand at the outer perimeter wire looking eastwards across the flat sandy plain, towards the dark green belt of trees. There were no planes, no sound of guns, no tanks, no armoured cars. Silence hung across the snow-covered ground.

We were told to be prepared to move at a moment's notice. Ten thousand men or thereabouts in the camp! It would take days to evacuate all of us. We hurriedly sought to prepare, as best we could, for a journey on foot or train, duration unknown, destination unknown. Each prisoner had to carry his own food and spare clothing. Some chose to make packs or kit-bags, others sleds to drag behind them through the snow. Resigned to the fact that there would be no exchange of sick prisoners, no pleasant journey home, I was cobbling together with string a rucksack made from the canvas cover of a palliasse. I would have to take my chances with the rest and hope I would stay free of asthma attacks.

From my top bunk where I was sitting, tailor-fashion, cross-legged, needle in hand, I saw Paddy burst into the hut. He stopped at our table and, out of breath from running, asked Phil and Andy where I was. Phil looked and gestured towards my bunk.

As I emerged Paddy turned to meet me, and said.

"You're wanted. The hospital compound. You've to report there with all your things."

My heart started hammering away as if injected with one of Captain Harrison's shots of adrenalin. I hurriedly put together food and clothing in one large untidy bundle, my blankets in another, and struggled over to the table.

They were all there: Andy, Philip, Sammy and Paddy. Their faces were turned towards me. Ours had been a family relationship, linked by chance as much as choice. Belonging to the group had been important for me. It had replaced my sense of identity.

"Lucky bugger!" said Andy, "you'll be home tucking into bacon and eggs before you know where you are."

"Against my religion," I said.

All doubts were dismissed. This was it! Why else should they send for me? They must be grouping together all the sick in one compound. We might even leave today. They'd have to get us out quickly with the Russians so close. We'd probably be taken by train or lorry to Stettin, then by boat to Sweden or Denmark.

Nobody questioned me or asked my name as I passed unchecked through the unguarded gates of the hospital compound. Men stood idly around, their belongings at their feet, looking lost and cold. My attempts to find out where I should report met with blank stares or a shrug of the shoulder.

A medical orderly stood looking about him. I approached him, but as I opened my mouth to speak the man said, "Just find yourself a bed somewhere," and turned away.

"Excuse me," I said, "can you tell me what's happening? When are we leaving?"

"Leaving? Haven't a clue. We leave when the others leave."

"What others?" I asked.

"We'll be in the last group. They're trying to keep all the sick together."

I realized with a dreadful certainty that my hopes of repatriation were an illusion. We weren't going to be repatriated. The Russians were only ten miles away. How could I have been so stupid? How could I have hoped that, in such circumstances, there could be an exchange of prisoners?

I opened the door of the nearest hut and made my way down the central aisle. Men stumped about on artificial legs held on by a complicated harness of leather cup and straps.

On either side of the ward men sat or lay on the beds, the pale wasted stump of a leg or arm exposed to view. The loose skin, folded and neatly tucked in, like the ends of a brown-paper parcel, was drawn tightly over the end of the severed bone.

I put down my bundles on an empty bed at the far end of the hut and sat down, miserably speculating as I gazed dejectedly into space. What was the point of my being here if there was to be no repatriation? I should have stayed with my friends. Still, they must have had something in mind in grouping the sick together. There was, too, the chance that if we were the last to leave the Russians might get here before we were evacuated. They were only ten miles from the camp.

"Hi, Mister! What you doing here? You sick or something?"

My head jerked up at the sound of the heavy German accent. The man, large and fleshy, broad-shouldered, his unbuttoned khaki shirt revealing a thick mat of ginger hair, lay comfortably ensconced on the bed opposite. His small brown eyes peered out at me from beneath thick bushy eyebrows. He stood up, crossed the room and sat at my side. Yitzac, a German Jew, had left his native land in the thirties to settle in Palestine. When war broke out he went to England where he joined the Pioneer Corps. Captured in Crete in 1941, he had been in Lamsdorf ever since. He was, he told me, interpreter for the hospital compound. Having volunteered these details concerning his own life, he began to question me about mine, with a Gestapo-like thoroughness.

"You live in Ilford? Ilford I know. A very good neighbourhood. Your father, he owns a house or rents? You have a girlfriend? You sleep with her? What does her father do?"

He extracted details of my education, sex life and war experience. I enjoyed the self-indulgent pleasure of confession, but later often regretted it, when Yitzac passed on these confidences in the most casual way to all and sundry, often embellishing details to satisfy a kind of vicarious vanity. To satisfy this vanity he promoted me from warrant officer to pilot officer and upgraded my position as wireless operator to that of pilot. I would hear him say, his syntax and intonation coloured by his sojourn in London's East End. "How many times he's been bombing? You crazy? Don't ask!"

I would stand by, embarrassed, but enjoying the undeserved respect these distortions drew from listeners. I did, however, object, albeit weakly, when Yitzac hinted darkly at my aristocratic connections, at the wealth of my parents' at the riotous life, presumably carried on in Ilford, into which I had promised to induct him.

When I remonstrated he defended himself stoutly. "So! I shouldn't exaggerate a little? That's bad? Men here have so much to live for I shouldn't be trying to cheer them up?"

Yitzac's powerful personality was such that people with whom he came into contact were attacked or repelled by his lack of those English virtues, modesty and understatement. He charged through life like an uncontrolled tank, tending to crush the quiet and timid beneath his tracks. You could admire his force and energy but be repelled by his egocentric behaviour and his failure to recognize the rules of conversation – I speak/You speak. Nevertheless, his circle of acquaintances was wide. He had, however, two friends to whom he was particularly attached. The older of the two, Finlay Greer, was a middle-aged Scots guardsman, white-haired and pink-faced, captured with Yitzac in Crete, as quiet and inoffensive as Yitzac was loud and abrasive. These two were in some respects like an old married couple. They had their set routines, took their daily walks together, brewed up at set times, cooked and ate together, played a nightly, noisy – at least on the part of Yitzac – game of draughts.

The other, Richard Craven, was a young, six-foot-three paratrooper, a medic captured the previous September. He had had a bad time at Arnhem and Finlay and Yitzac had more or less adopted him, his nerves still badly shaken by his experiences. He had been with the 1st Airborne Division when they were dropped behind the German line.

"A wash-out from the start," he said. "You've never seen anything like it. The gliders were coming down all over the place. A lot of the chaps were dead before they landed; others never got out of the wreckage alive.

"The Jerries were there, waiting. It was like a clay-pigeon shoot. There were so many casualties, some hurt in the crash, others shot up by the Jerries as the gliders landed, that we medics had hardly time to get a few minutes' kip.

"Two days they said! We only had to hold out for two days until the Second Army tanks got through. Two days! We were there for ten bloody days – bullets, shells, bayonets, the lot. In the end the Jerry tanks were round us in a tight circle and most of the lads were dead or wounded."

The three friends, Yitzac, Richard and Finlay, on hearing the camp was to be evacuated, decided that they would be more likely to survive by escaping from the column than risking a possible forced march through Germany, with the dangers that entailed: wintry weather, German bullet, Allied bomb. They would try to get to the Russian lines at Jagensdorf or hole up somewhere and wait for the Russians to find them.

They had little difficulty in persuading me to join them, but mindful of my own failure in planning my escape I insisted we make a detailed plan.

Yitzac gave me a withering glance. "Plan! Shman!" he said. "What you mean plan? You crazy or something? I got plenty plan, up here." He tapped his forehead. Nevertheless, yielding to my arguments, he drew a sketch map. It showed the road leading from the camp gates to the line of trees which, for me, behind the wire, had symbolized freedom. The road led due south into the woods and then changed direction westwards towards the little railway halt where, nearly three years earlier, the train had brought us to Lamsdorf. At the bend in the road Yitzac had marked a logging track leading eastwards through the trees towards a cemetery where we could spend the night. To get into the cemetery we would first have to cross a metalled road and then climb a wall or find a gate.

"What about the guards?" I asked.

"We've got that sorted out," said Richard.

Yitzac nodded approvingly and added, "Guards! That should be the last of our worries!"

Richard explained, "We'll be the last to leave, but there'll still be more than a thousand of us left and only a few old codgers to guard us. They'll be forced to space them out. All we have to do is to choose a place in the column midway between each of them."

Yitzac looked on with paternal pride as Richard outlined the plan. "We bide our time as the column makes its way through the wood towards the station. When we reach the bend in the road, we'll be out of sight of both the guard in front and the guard behind, and it's then we make a run for it."

Still playing my role of hardened escaper, I nodded my head sagely and asked, "What about papers?"

"Papers?" Richard turned to Yitzac.

"We'll need papers," I insisted. "We may be stopped. We'll need an *Ausweis* or some kind of identity card."

"Look," said Yitzac patiently, "You think the Germans are worrying their heads about us? They'll be too busy running the other way."

Finlay smiled and shook his head and added, "They'll no be worrying about papers."

"The idea," said Richard, "is for us to keep our heads down until we hear the train leave. They won't keep the train waiting for four prisoners."

"I suppose not," I said, and Finlay added the final word, "They'll no be askin' for papers."

Sunday, 21 January, 1945: The First Ukrainian Front troops cross into Upper Silesia. Several towns fall as Russian units reach points ten miles from the River Oder

A barbed-wire gate swung and creaked on its hinges as I entered my old compound, deserted now that the airmen had gone. I followed the snow-covered path past the cookhouse and saw the brick-built Forty Holer, retreat and home of reverie. My footsteps instinctively took the path leading to the hut. I pushed the door open and stepped inside. Dirty and desolate, the long narrow space between the bunks on the one side and the tables and benches on the other was littered with empty tins and cardboard boxes. The tiers of wooden bunks stretched one behind the other like a gloomy depopulated forest.

I walked towards the centre of the hut and looked down on our table, like every other table, but special to us.

David must have reached home by now ... and the others?

I walked to the far end of the hut where the little Palestinian interpreter had contrived a small room for himself and his batman, a small private room, complete with bunks and Red Cross armchair. The empty armchair, symbol of brief privilege, stood there still.

When I got back I found everyone in a great state of excitement.

"Come on, Harry lad!" Finley urged. "Shake a leg! We're on the move."

Playing, a little self-consciously, a new role of imperturbability that I was far from feeling, I asked, "What's the hurry? Where's Yitzac?"

"Had to go to the office," Richard answered. "The Hauptmann wanted him. Got to be outside with kit at 1100 hours."

"1100 hours! Well, Well!" I said. "What do we do now, synchronize watches?"

"You'd better synchronize something," Richard answered. "The SS are coming in to clear the camp of stragglers, or anyone who might feel like staying behind to wait for the Russians."

A few moment later Yitzac came in followed by a German officer, and made directly for my bed-space where I was packing my kit.

"Look," said Yitzac jerking his head in the direction of the German standing at the door. "They're having trouble clearing one of the compounds. They want we should go and explain."

"What d'you mean, we?" I asked.

"They said I must bring the senior officer."

"The senior officer! What on earth are you talking about? I'm not the senior officer."

"By me," said Yitzac, pulling at my sleeve, "you;'re the senior officer."

Rancorous and morose, the Geordies sat on home-made kitbags or squatted with their bundles in the snow. I stood hesitantly before them feeling myself the focus of their frustration and anger.

"Can I help?" I asked. Their replies were difficult to understand because of the accent but the message was unequivocal.

"Who the hell are you?"

"Bugger off!"

I glanced at Yitzac, who nodded encouragingly. I tried again. "Look, we've all got to get out. They say they're bringing in the SS to make sure we do."

"Fucking get out then," shouted one foxy-faced, man. "You get out! We're staying."

I turned away, leaving Yitzac to explain to the bewildered German that the men had no intention of leaving. Yitzac and
I left the German facing the obstinate hatred of the soldiers.

6

ESCAPE FROM COLUMN

Prisoners of war filled the road from one end of the camp to the other. The sea of men stretched from the main gates to the distant perimeter wire, spilling into several of the compounds where others waited patiently to join the main column. Their uniforms, or in some cases, the remnants of uniforms, could only hint at the diversity of the men's origins. They reflected a myriad nations, cultures, religions and a variety of tongues and accents. Few had been regular soldiers. War had given the butcher, the baker and the candlestick maker a new trade.

In the long khaki-clad stream were infantrymen taken at Dunkirk, Crete and Greece; Commandos captured at Dieppe; Montgomery's Desert Rats made prisoner in North Africa and Italy, and paratroopers like Richard, recently captured at Arnhem. They were all prisoners of war now, stripped of those qualities which had made them distinctive. They stood in line, kitbags, rucksacks, boxes and bundles at their feet. There were few signs of erstwhile regimental spruceness; many hadn't shaved for several days.

Balaclavas were the favoured headgear, often surmounted by a khaki or coloured forage cap, a beret or knitted bonnet. The general effect was of a defeated army, a horde of refugees.

Richard and I stood together in the hospital compound waiting to join the ragged array. It was midday and the snow had been falling since morning. The sun was shining and the air cold, a crisp, dry cold.

The mood of the men was half excited, half apprehensive. They were content that the long monotonous misery of prisoner-of-war life seemed at an end, yet anxious as to what experiences might yet await them.

Apart from Richard, I knew none of the men who now stood around me. Yitzac and Finlay had managed to get out of the medical compound and were now somewhere near the head of the column. We had split up, deciding that each pair should take its chance.

It seemed hours before the column finally started to move. We began to wonder if there had been a change of plan. Perhaps the Russians were too close. There was a slight agitation among the crowd, a movement which grew from an inching forward to a slow stumbling progress over the hard-packed snow.

Richard and I elbowed our way out through the gates of the medical compound, I with my haversack and Richard carrying a kitbag. There was some good-humoured shouting and a few curses as heavily-laden men struggled to reach friends through the tight press of bodies.

As the head of the column passed through the main gates spaces between the ragged ranks eased and the long khaki column moved steadily forward leaving the enclosure that had so long contained us.

It was with a feeling compounded of excitement and emotion that I found myself in the forecourt of the camp, that same forecourt where, on a moonlit night two years and six months previously, I had begun my education as a prisoner of war.

The column wound its way towards the distant trees. As we entered the woods the transition from sunshine to shadow was sharp and cheerless. I turned to get a view of the guard. He was some distance away, stumbling along, rifle slung from his shoulder, chin buried in the collar of his overcoat. I looked up at Richard and winked.

"Piece of cake," I mouthed silently, holding up finger and thumb joined together. Richard nodded a grudging agreement. We walked along, stumbling and slipping on the trampled snow.

Richard, with the advantage of height, was the first to see the bend in the road. He gripped my sleeve. "There it is!" he said. I peered ahead and then looked back over my shoulder. The guard had moved closer but was still some distance away. I dropped back to the rank behind, walking at the side of the man at the end of the row, who looked at me blankly, almost with hostility.

"We're making a break for it when we reach the bend," I told him. "Can you cover for us? ... the Jerry behind ... spread across the road a bit." The man's expression was unchanged. Without waiting for reassurance, I rejoined Richard.

The road curved sharply to the right. Glancing frequently over our shoulder, we waited until the curve hid us from the guard's line of sight. The men behind had spread out to the very edge of the road, making a hedge behind which we could slip away into the trees.

"Right!" said Richard, giving me a push. We ran into the woods, twisting and turning through the trees. I followed behind Richard, my rucksack thumping against my back. Gasping for breath, I was at last forced to stop. I bent over double, hands on knees, my breath wheezing painfully through restricted air-passages. My fear was that I might have an asthma attack here in the woods with no possible chance of help. After a few minutes my breathing became easier. I straightened up as I saw Richard running through the trees, retracing his steps towards me.

"Take your time," he said reassuringly. "There's no need to rush. We're well away from the road."

"I'm fine," I said, "just a bit puffed. I'll be all right."

"There's a dip in the ground a bit further on," Richard said. "We can rest up there for a bit."

The hollow, under its canopy of trees, was free of snow. I eased my arms out of the straps of the rucksack and lowered it to the ground. We sat on Richard's kitbag, our backs resting against the stump of a felled tree.

Suddenly it came to us that we were free. We gripped each other's hands and shook them vigorously. Free! No guards! No crowds of men! No barbed wire! We were alone! We were, amazingly, gloriously, free!

We decided to eat. Anxious to conserve what food we had, we had had nothing that morning apart from a piece of bread and a brew of tea. It was now, we reckoned, about one o'clock. Over the last few days we had saved as much food as we could and had supplemented it by a judicious bartering of our cigarette ration.

Bread and meat-loaf eaten in freedom under the pine trees tasted like ambrosia, and as a special treat a cream cracker spread with cheese and honey. It would give us stamina for whatever lay ahead. We should have liked a hot drink, but the difficulties – the melting down of snow, the lighting of a fire – were too great, not worth the bother.

"How long d'you think it'll be before it leaves?" I asked.

Richard shrugged his shoulders. "It'll be waiting for them; cattle-trucks, Yitzac reckons. They'll not keep a crowd like that waiting long."

Richard added, "Wonder if they've made it!"

"Yitzac's probably organized a taxi by now, all the way to Jagensdorf," I said.

"To Moscow, I shouldn't wonder," said Richard.

"Do you think we'll hear the train from here?" I asked.

"Bound to," said Richard. "The station's only a bit down the road; bound to hear it as it pulls out."

"When the train goes," I said, "all we have to do is to find our way to Jagensdorf."

"Yeah," said Richard, "that's all we have to do."

"What d'you mean?" I asked, detecting a note of doubt."

"Nothing!" said Richard thoughtfully. "Only I was wondering how they'll know we're not Jerries. They could shoot first and ask questions afterwards.

"Our uniforms," I said, "they'll see our uniforms."

Richard stood up and stretched his long frame. "Let's hope they know the difference."

"Of course they will," I said, trying to reassure myself as much as wishing to reassure Richard. "They must be coming across hundreds, thousands of POWs," and added as I too stood up, "Let's get moving. I'm cold."

Richard helped me on with my rucksack and, shouldering his kitbag, muttered, "See if we can find this logging track of Yitzac's."

As we trudged along the rutted track, avoiding patches of mud and ice, we could hear nothing but the crunch of our boots, an occasional fall of snow from a branch and the soft soughing of the wind through the trees.

After the initial excitement of our new-found freedom I was feeling depressed. Reality began to replace euphoria. Ahead lay the prospect of a night in the open in the cold of a January winter. I thought of the safety and warmth of the crowded prison hut.

Some distance ahead we could see what appeared to be a clearing, but as we reached it we realized that the path forked. We paused, not knowing whether to turn left or right.

"This can't be it. It's supposed to lead directly to the cemetery," said Richard, lowering his kitbag to the ground. "Keep an eye on my stuff! I'll try this way," he said, taking the left-hand fork.

As I waited, looking down at his kitbag, I found it amusing that Richard should be worrying about his stuff. Who'd he think was going to pinch it? The rabbits?

Within minutes he returned. It was obvious he'd found the cemetery from the expression of relief on his face. "Come on! It's just over there through the trees." Picking up his kitbag he was off.

I found him standing looking down a precipitous bank which fell steeply to the tarmac road below. Across from where we were standing was the high wall of the cemetery. It was all I could do to stop myself whooping with joy. "I told you," I said gleefully, "a piece of cake. Let's get the stuff and get across."

"We said we'd wait till dark."

"Yes, but the road's empty. There's no one."

"We said we'd wait." I was surprised at the determined note in Richard's voice. We walked back to where we'd left the rucksack and kitbag and sat down.

"I should've thought we'd have met up with Yitzac and Finlay by now," murmured Richard.

"They might be waiting for us in the cemetery," I said.

There was a faint clanking of metal on metal, then a chuff-chuffing noise, a rapid explosion of steam followed by a series of thin, sharp whistles.

"That's it," I said, "They've gone!" We sat without talking. The sound of the train's departure had marked an irrevocable step.

"I expect Yitzac and Finlay changed their mind," I said.

"Changed their mind?"

"Decided not to wait till dark, I mean."

Richard made no answer.

"It's going to be hard to find our way in the dark without a torch," I continued. "I expect you're right about waiting. We don't want to take chances. Still, now the train's gone."

Richard got to his feet. "All right," he said, "Let's go."

We stood looking down the snow-covered surface of the road. It ran in a gentle curve, skirting the wood, preventing us from getting a clear view either to left or right. It would mean taking a chance. Once we had climbed down we would be exposed to the view of any chance passer-by; it wouldn't be possible to dodge back into the wood.

There was a long pause as we considered the next step. Clearly we had to make the choice as to who should go first, but, feeling responsible for having persuaded Richard, I felt that it was up to me to volunteer.

"I'll go first, shall I?" I suggested. "If it's clear I'll give you a signal."

Richard looked doubtful. "I don't know...," he began, but I had already started to scramble down the bank.

I stood on the road looking up at Richard. "I'll cross and see if it's clear," I said.

I crossed the road. There was nothing to be seen in either direction, a smooth empty ribbon of white. I turned and looked at the cemetery wall. It was high, with a coping of thick white snow; it was going to be difficult. Still, I thought, the two of us should be able to manage.

I walked a little further on looking for a break in the wall, or possibly a gate. I stopped. A little way ahead there was a heavy covering of ivy cloaking the wall. That would do, I thought, and turned, intending to retrace my steps and call to Richard; but as I did so, I saw a man cycling towards me.

I felt the same tight knotting of stomach muscles as in the bombing trips over Germany. I knelt down, pretending to be fastening my laces.

I glanced up and saw with relief that the man was a civilian. As he cycled past he turned his head. I heard him say something, possibly a greeting. I lifted a hand in a deliberate attempt at a casual reply. Waiting a moment, I got to my feet and watched as he rode past. Some way off, however, he stopped, first sitting on his cycle and looking over his shoulder, then dismounting and turning his cycle round to face in my direction.

A large man, pear-shaped, narrow shoulders and large stomach, he stood by his cycle, waiting. However, he seemed to be looking beyond me rather than at me. I turned my head and looked backwards along the road in the direction from which he had first appeared.

A soldier, rifle slung across his back, was slowly pedalling his heavy cycle towards me. He glanced as he cycled past, but when he reached the waiting civilian he stopped. They talked together, frequently glancing in my direction. The German soldier got off his cycle and lifted it laboriously around so that he too faced me. The civilian held both cycles while the soldier unslung his rifle and held it threateningly pointed at me.

"Jesus!" I murmured.

Now that their suspicions were clearly aroused I had little choice. I could neither attempt to climb the wall nor turn and walk in the other direction. I walked slowly towards them.

"*Papieren!*" The German prodded me in the chest with the rifle.

"*Nix papieren,*" I answered, my face flushed, my heart beating fast. "*Ich bin Arbeiter, Französich,*" I added hopefully; there was little chance of my being mistaken for a French soldier, having neither the right uniform nor the right accent.

The soldier smiled and turned to the other German.

"*Flieger,*" he said, tugging open my khaki overcoat and revealing the blue battledress beneath, and repeated, turning to the civilian, smiling and nodding his head in confirmation, "*Jah Jah! Ein Flieger.*"

"Nein, nein," I insisted, more for form's sake than with any hope of being believed.

The soldier laughed and took his cycle from the civilian, who suddenly, having glimpsed a movement, jerked up his head, pointed towards the wood and muttered something. The soldier turned to me;

"*Du hast ein Kamerad, nicht wahr?*"

"*Nein, nein*" I protested, "*kein Kamerad.*" The soldier shrugged his shoulders and jerked his head in the direction he wished me to follow. I walked dejectedly down the centre of the road, the German following, rifle slung from his shoulder.

We passed the spot where I had clambered down the bank. I glanced up at the trees, but there was no sign of Richard, not that I expected to see him. I wondered what he would do now.

When we reached the end of the cemetery wall I turned to look over my shoulder. Fifty yards or so behind the German a tall khaki-clad figure wearing a red beret was plodding along down the centre of the road, kitbag on his shoulder.

We stood in front of a German officer in the forecourt which we had left that very morning. A few soldiers were carrying boxes and files from one building to another. I faced the German in my usual civilian posture, arms dangling loosely at my side and a placatory smile on my face, Richard, on the other hand, was standing rigidly to attention, every inch a paratrooper, his gaze fixed several inches above the head of the ranting German, as if he were back home in front of a bullying corporal.

The man was very angry. I had seen him about the camp before, but only at a distance; never had I had that face inches from my own. We stood defenceless before him with no interpreter to act as intermediary.

The ranting voice stopped and the German's hand went to his belt, fingering the strap of the holster. Instinctively I took a step back, interposing Richard's bulk between the German and myself. Richard remained stiffly at attention as the cold, blue eyes stared up into his face. There was a sharp slap as the German's hand struck Richard's cheek. Richard continued to stare straight in front of him.

Our presence in the camp was without doubt a problem. What could be done with us? The camp was now empty of prisoners; the few remaining German soldiers could not be spared for escort duty. It said something for the man, vicious though he appeared, that he hadn't chosen the easy solution. Not that I expected to be shot; I felt more like a guilty schoolboy than an escaped prisoner.

I found myself once more in the prison block where I had served my seven days on bread and water. Richard was in the cell next to mine, but this time there was no camp outside teeming with prisoners, no friends to surreptitiously send in food. We were cold, hungry, without blankets and sleeping on damp and dirty palliasses.

Talking to each other through the thin dividing wall, I tried to be cheerful. "I didn't really fancy spending a night in a cemetery," I said.

"No, but I didn't exactly have this place in mind either," Richard replied.

"By the way," I asked, "why didn't you stay in the woods?"

"You had the food, remember?"

"We're not exactly story-book heroes, are we?" I said. "We should've knocked Scarface out, pinched his gun and shot the rest of 'em."

"Heroes, Schmeroes," said Richard in an unexpectedly good imitation of Yitzac. "As long as you've got your health and strength."

"Do you reckon they've made it?" I asked.

"I expect so. Unless they're in one of the other cells."

"We'd have heard Yitzac before now," I said. "They must have got away."

But soon the cold and the surrounding silence became too oppressive and conversation lapsed. We each lay huddled on our bunks, coat-collars up, gloved hands thrust into pockets. Warmed by the heat of our own bodies, we finally slept.

Some time later the faint intermittent drone of an aircraft woke me. It grew louder as the plane passed overhead. There was the crump of an explosion and the hut shook. I climbed down the side of the bunk and lay face down on the floor, scared, yet at the same time overjoyed; the Russians had at last given evidence of their existence. There was a second explosion. Like a crab I scrambled sideways under the bunk and waited tensely for the next explosion, but there was nothing, nothing but the sound of the aircraft's engines receding into the distance.

"You all right?" I shouted.

"Yes, I'm under the bunk. Where are you?"

"Under the bunk," I replied.

Silence once more enveloped the camp. Tired from our exertions and the emotions of the day we sought in fitful sleep refuge from cold, hunger and anxiety.

We were hustled from the cells out into the forecourt. A white ambulance stood in the middle of the square, its driver somnolent, his arms folded across his chest, his head drooping forward.

The viperish officer of the day before, now seemingly in better humour, pointed without a word to a spot next to the ambulance where we were to stand. Its chance arrival, too late to evacuate the disabled, had solved the problem of what to do with us.

The driver stirred, wound down his window and put his head through the opening.

"*Vous êtes quoi, vous?*" he asked Richard, who turned nervously towards me.

"English ... *Anglais*," I said.

"*Moi, Français*," he replied and added, pointing an explanatory thumb towards the ambulance, "*Elle aussi*." He paused and took from his breast pocket a packet of cigarettes. "*Une cigarette?*" he said and proferred me the packet.

"*Merci, non,*" I answered, feeling rather proud of my fluency.

Richard poked me in the back. "Ask him where he's taking us."

Such a question made more demands on my linguistic skills than I could easily encompass, but, ever adventurous, I pointed to the ambulance, then to myself and Richard, spread out my hands and, shrugging my shoulders, asked, "*Ou?*"

The Frenchman answered with a flow of musical sound, utterly defeating my attempt to understand.

"What did he say?" asked Richard.

"I couldn't quite understand," I said. "He's got a terrible accent."

The driver, seeing our confusion, held up a finger and said, "*Moment!*" and, withdrawing into the cab, produced a piece of paper, wrote a few lines and passed it to me through the window.

Richard and I peered together at the scribbled words.

"Well?" said Richard. "What's it say?"

"We're going to Prague," I said.

At this point the driver passed us another piece of paper. He'd drawn a simple sketch-map of the route: Lamsdorf, Prague, Weiden/Bavière *près de* Nuremberg. We were going via Prague to a place called Weiden which was in Bavaria and near the town of Nuremberg.

Seated in the ambulance I looked at our escort, two elderly German guards on the bench opposite. For greater comfort they had pushed their rifles under the seat.

"Look at those two," I muttered in Richard's ear. "I had to give one of them a hand to get up the step into the ambulance. It's an insult, really."

Richard raised an eyebrow.

"I mean," I said, "they can't think we're very dangerous ... two old age pensioners to guard us."

"You could complain to the management," said Richard. "We could hit them over the head, get the Froggie to drive us to Jagensdorf and hand them over to the Russians. They'd give us a medal."

I eyed the two old men. "They're probably tougher than they look."

I settled in my seat. Things were fine! There'd be no forced marches along German roads strafed by Allied fighters, no living off turnips pinched from farmers' fields, no sleeping in barns or ditches in a countryside gripped by winter snow and frost. We were on our way west towards the advancing Allies.

All that morning the ambulance wound its way slowly upwards through the Sudeten mountain passes and down serpentine curves to the wooded hills and fields of the Bohemian countryside. We made slow progress, the French driver appearing in no great hurry to arrive, and, as for us, we enjoyed feeling like tourists, able to forget for a while prison-of-war life.

By midday we had reached the industrialized suburbs of Prague and, passing between factory buildings and dull rows of workers' houses, we eventually glimpsed in the distance the spires and buildings of the city. As we drew near the centre of the town we crossed a broad river spanned by an ancient stone bridge, and found ourselves in the heart of the city.

Nearing the station we experienced all the excitement engendered by our long exclusion from urban life.

As we waited for the train, the curious gathered around us, disregarding the feeble efforts of our elderly guards to deter them. Richard's size, his military bearing, his red beret, all drew their attention. They wanted to know what news he had of the war, where and when he had been made prisoner.

Insignificant, and looking strange in army greatcoat and woollen balaclava, I stood by his side, ignored and resentful. They know I'm Jewish, I thought bitterly. They're probably as anti-semitic as the Germans.

Richard turned and said, "This chap wants me to go with him. Reckons he can hide me until the Americans get here."

I noted that it was "him" and not "us" who was wanted, and looked at the little man at Richard's side.

"What d'you think?" Richard asked.

"Please yourself." I said, "Don't ask me."

"We could both go, not just me," said Richard. "He'd take both of us."

"Thanks," I said, "I don't think I'll bother."

"Bother!" said Richard. "What do you mean bother?"

The little Czech at Richard's side looked from one to the other, only half-understanding what was being said. Richard stood looking at me, at a loss for words, unable to see the reason for my resentment. Perceiving betrayal on his part, I remained obstinately silent, transferring the animosity I felt for the supposed anti-semitism of the people of Prague to Richard.

"I suppose you're right," he said. "We'd better stick together."

"Stand more chance, together," he said.

I looked obstinately away.

"It's not worth it, is it?" said Richard. "I mean, staying here; the further west the better really."

I maintained a sulky silence.

Richard, without really understanding what he had done or said, felt guilty.

My mood didn't last long. Excitement at the prospect of a new camp set in the path of the advancing Allied armies swept away my resentment. By the time we had reached Weiden I had recovered my good humour.

The camp, which had held only French prisoners of war, now had to take the flow of prisoners transferred from camps in the East, as the Germans retreated before the advancing Russians.

Hardly had I entered the hut when my hand was seized and shaken in Yitzac's bone-crushing grip.

"So, you too they catch! We had bad luck. What d'you think? Such bad luck you can't imagine. We had to walk slap and bang into a German unit."

"What did you say?" Richard asked.

"What you think I say? I tell them we're sick. We get left behind."

"And they believed you?"

"Course they believe me. You crazy of something? What for they shouldn't believe me?"

Yitzac quickly organized four bunks together and we settled down once more to prisoner-of-war life.

This time, however, we all knew, prisoners and guards, that the war was virtually over. Everything pointed to the fact; the guards who were eager to explain that they were not really German but Austrian, or Czech, or Polish; the news bulletins over the loud speakers, which, although retaining much of the former bombastic claims and distortions, were unable to conceal that on both the Eastern and Western fronts the Germans were in full retreat.

The Russians, in enormous strength, were now well into Germany itself and pushing towards Berlin. On the Western Front the Allied forces were once more moving forward to the Rhine, the final barrier.

7

WEIDEN

*Auschwitz–Birkenau, Saturday, 27 January, 1945: Red Army stumble
upon the Nazis' biggest extermination-camp. As the noise of Russian
artillery came nearer, the Nazis had attempted to conceal all traces of their
hideous mass-murder.*
*Monday, 29 January, 1945: Allied thrust into Rhineland continues with
the capture of Oberhausen, ten miles north of Duisburg.*

With Germany itself fast becoming a battlefield and roads and
communications constantly bombed and strafed. Red Cross supplies of
food and clothing were no longer getting through to the camps. The
prisoners' irritation turned on the small group who had managed to get
control of "distribution". They were a set apart, smartly dressed, well
fed and spaciously housed in a hut of their own. Mutterings and
protests grew as suspicions mounted. Who were these people running
the camp? By what right?

It was decided to elect a new camp leader by ballot excluding the
French, who had their own organization. Rather liking the sound of my
own voice, I was not slow in putting forward my views. We weren't, I
declared, looking for a leader. Surely, we'd had enough of leaders.
Look, I said, at the hut representatives we'd elected in the past, who, as
soon as elected, withdrew with their cronies into comfortable little
cubby-holes, cutting themselves off from the rest of us.

Who knew, I asked, what went on behind the walls of those special
retreats. We needed, as far as I could see, not a leader, but an
organizer, someone accountable to the rest of the prisoners for the food
and clothing that passed through their hands, someone who shared the
same hardships as everyone else, and who didn't use their position as a
means of securing special privileges for themselves and their friends.
Without too much persuasion, I allowed my own name to be put

forward for the position of camp leader and was elected by an overwhelming majority.

At first I enjoyed my new position, but gradually I became aware of the disadvantages.

As camp leader I had to organize the checking and distribution of supplies, deal with queries and lengthy, often unreasonable, complaints, be judge and jury in disputes between prisoners and act as go-between with the German administration. This had to be done in the midst of a crowded and noisy hut. In refusing the perquisites of office, a quiet hut and others to help, I had, effectively, been hoist with my own petard.

I had had no experience of such work and was too immature to accept criticism whether direct or oblique. Yitzac, who had appointed himself interpreter and aide de camp, persistently pointed out the need for an office. Finally persuaded of the justice of the suggestion, I approached the former ruling clique, who, having kept the advantages of office, although stripped of their function, claimed that the hut, commandeered for their own use, could not possibly be shared with me, as the "authorities" would not allow it. Lacking age and experience I retreated before the apparent reasonableness of their tone.

A further difficulty was that in my new, closer relationship with the Germans, I felt in their presence all the unease engendered by past experience, whilst the reaction of the German officers, seeing a youth of twenty-three put forward as camp leader, was one of amused surprise.

I saw in their smiles confirmation of my own feelings of inadequacy and writhed inwardly with embarrassment. Yitzac, however, regaled the Germans with his own inventive account of my heroic war record, giving in detail lists of towns which, according to him, I had practically destroyed single-handed. The Germans, not unlike Queen Victoria, were not amused, but nevertheless looked at me with increased interest.

One of the duties which I liked least was to take charge of daily parades. I had to call the men to attention when the German officer appeared and, after the count, dismiss them.

As a parade-ground sergeant-major I was painfully inadequate. I lacked the bearing and never looked anything other than a civilian in battledress. My voice was incapable of producing the kind of sounds that would make the men "jump to it". The soldiers, many of them experienced campaigners, would tolerate my lack of expertise with hardly a smile.

On one occasion, however, even their tolerance was strained. On that particular day, with the men in line before me, I was watching the office door, waiting for the German officer to emerge. He came out and stood in the doorway. I called the men to attention. The wretched man turned on his heels and walked back into the office. I waited a few moments, then stood the men at ease. A few moments later the German re-emerged and took a step forward into the courtyard. I called "Attention!" The German turned around and walked back into the office. I ordered the men to stand at ease. The third time the German emerged, I waited. He turned towards the office, then, settling his cap straight on his head, took a step forward. I again called, "Attention!" The swine of a man turned round and went back into the office. Sweating with embarrassment, I had to face what seemed like imminent rebellion, sure that the German was deliberately trying to make me look an idiot – and succeeding.

This experience convinced me that I was not the man for the job. Despite Yitzac's protestations, I resigned, handing over to an army staff-sergeant, far more fitted for the role. The man took over an empty hut, staffed it with his friends and restored the status quo.

Wednesday, 7 March, 1945: The US Ninth Armored Division makes surprise dash across an undestroyed bride at Remagen, ten minutes before the Germans were to blow it up; crucial bridgehead established on east bank.

Thursday, 8 March: Hitler decrees: "Anyone captured without being wounded or without having fought to the limit of his power has forfeited his honour. He is expelled from the fellowship of decent and brave soldiers. His dependants will be held responsible."

Friday, 9 March: The main body of the US Third Army reaches the Rhine.

The three of us, Finlay, Richard and myself, watched as Yitzac walked slowly down the length of the hut and stretched himself full length on the bed, but said nothing.

"Well?" I asked.

"Is it true?" asked Richard.

Yitzac, pursed his lips and nodded affirmatively.

"When?" asked Finlay.

"Tomorrow. That's when. All British prisoners they take as hostages into the Bavarian mountains."

"Tomorrow!"

"Tomorrow morning," Yitzac confirmed, and smiled as he looked up at our anxious expressions." You shouldn't worry! I arrange everything."

"Yeah!" muttered Richard. "You arranged everything last time."

"I'm no going under any wire," said Finlay, "and that's a fact."

"Under, over!" said Yitzac. "You crazy altogether? Who's going under any wire? We stay here. They want us to leave? Good! We stay!"

"You mean, hide in the camp?" I asked.

"Hide in the camp," he confirmed.

"The French huts," Richard suggested. "They'd hide us."

"No huts!" said Yitzac, "They search the whole camp, French, British, everywhere. Half an hour to collect our things. They count. If any missing they search."

"But you've found a place for us to hide," I said, reading Yitzac's self-satisfied expression. he grinned and tapped the side of his nose.

"I need cigarettes," declares Yitzac.

"How many?" asked Finlay. "I hav'nae got many."

"You got plenty cigarettes. I know you. All cigarettes I'm needing!" said Yitzac firmly.

Finlay opened his kitbag and, fumbling around inside, took out four packets and put them on the bed.

"What about those?" Yitzac asked, pointing to a packet in Jock's battledress pocket.

"I'm smokin' these. You cannae have these." Yitzac, a look of patient resignation on his face, held out his hand for the packet.

"All packets," he repeated.

Jock mumbled plaintively. "That's all I've got."

Richard and I handed over the cigarettes we'd saved and Yitzac stored them away with the rest.

"How do we get out of the compound?" Richard asked. "They've locked the gates."

"Get out? You want we should get out? Whose getting out?" Yitzac asked.

"All right, Yitzac," I said. "Where are we going?"

"Where we go? You follow me. That's where we go!" It was clear that Yitzac was intent on dragging every ounce of mystery he could out of the affair.

Outside on the square men were lining up with their bits and pieces. Yitzac led us, skirting the end of the huts and making his way towards the lavatory block. He continued on and, rounding the building, led us

165

towards a huge boiler supported on two low brick walls. At one end there was a large round metal door like the entrance to the conning tower of a submarine.

"Jesus!" said Richard, "it's where they delouse clothes!"

As we approached, a German carrying a rifle appeared from behind the grey bulk of the disinfectant chamber.

"All right! All right! Don't worry!" Yitzac reassured us. The guard opened the door and gestured us to hurry.

"*Schnell*! *Schnell*!"

One after the other we squeezed through the opening. Yitzac, the last to get in, took a packet of cigarettes from his battledress blouse and gave it to the guard.

The four of us squatted opposite each other, our backs against the curved sides of the metal casement.

"It's still hot!" I exclaimed indignantly.

"You want I should ask for an electric fan?" Yitzac asked. The guard, understanding our fears, pushed the door to, but left a small gap, allowing us to breathe.

"How long do we stay in here?" Jock asked. "It's as hot as an oven!"

"It is a ruddy oven!" said Richard.

"Stop talking, already!" ordered Yitzac. "You think I got cigarettes for the whole German Army."

Warm and drowsy, we sat crouched together. From time to time there was the distant sound of footsteps outside. The footsteps passed. No one approached our hiding place; nevertheless we sat in silence, hardly daring to breathe.

Time seemed to drag slowly past without our hearing a sound except our own sneezes or stifled coughs. Then once again there was the sound of footsteps, but this time they seemed to be coming directly towards us.

The door was still slightly open. We dare not pull it shut lest the movement be seen, or a sound be made. We heard the sharp click of the guard's heels as he came to attention, then the sound of voices. The door was pushed to and clamped shut. We now sat in complete darkness without the sparse light that had filtered through the narrow gap. We waited, straining to hear what was happening. We could hear nothing, the oven appearing not only air-tight but sound-proof. We felt anxious. What had seemed a bit of a lark now seemed threatening.

"The bastard's locked it!" whispered Jock, voicing all our fears. "He's locked it!"

"Why should he lock it?" exclaimed Yitzac. "Of course he hasn't locked it."

"Push it a bit and see," I suggested.

"If I push it," objected Yitzac, "and there's an officer outside, he'll see."

"He won't notice if you push it a bit," I insisted.

Yitzac put his hand against the door and pushed. There was no movement. He pushed a little harder. The door remained firmly closed.

"It must be locked," Yitzac admitted.

"Push harder!" Richard whispered.

"It's no good. it won't budge."

"Let me try!" Richard felt in the darkness for the rim of the door, pushing gently at first and then with all the strength he could muster.

'You're wastin' your time," said Jock. "did you nae hear? They've locked it."

Fear gripped us. Perhaps the guard had been ordered to lock the door or perhaps it was deliberate, a macabre joke. Who knew what these bastards were capable of? We could be left to suffocate in this airless prison. There was a metallic clanking as the clamp was released. The door swung open and the guard peered into the dark interior. Everything was all right, he told Yitzac. The *Feldwebel* suspected nothing. We would have to wait a little longer; the men were lining up at the main gate; no one had noticed our absence. Once again the guard pushed the door to, leaving the gap for us to breathe. The light from the narrow opening was our only connection with the world outside. We could see or hear nothing except for the occasional sound of gravel beneath the guard's feet. From time to time we would exchange a whispered remark, but for the most part we sat in silence.

Nearly an hour had passed when once again we heard the sound of approaching footsteps. The door was still slightly ajar, but we dare not close it;' the sound of footsteps was too close.

Outside there was again a brief exchange between the guard and the *Feldwebel*. We heard the sound of his footsteps turning to go and then stopping.

He said something to the guard. The door was once again pushed shut. There was a torrent of words from the *Feldwebel* punctuated by a series of "*Jawohl!*" from the frightened guard.

The door was pulled open and the figure of the *Feldwebel* was silhouetted against the open door. He peered in and then yelled something at the guard, who said nothing.

Yitzac beckoned to the *Feldwebel* and, as the man leaned forward, whispered in his ear. Yitzac's hand moved to the opening in his battle-dress blouse. The *Feldwebel* nodded and the cigarettes passed from one hand to the other. The *Feldwebel*, turning to the guard, said a few words in German. The guard saluted and sprung again to attention with the usual, "*Jawohl!*"

We asked Yitzac what the man had said. It was, apparently, "Keep your mouth shut, you understand! You have seen nothing."

The adventure had been a success, but, as it happened, quite pointless. The men who had been marched out of the camp that morning returned later that evening. The roads had been impassable, full of men and military traffic. The camp guards escorting the prisoners had been ordered by exasperated field commanders to get the prisoners back into the camp.

Sunday, 25 March, 1945: US Third Army units begin attack across the Rhine after preliminary bombardment by 1,250 guns. 6th Armoured Division breaks through and starts driving along Autobahn towards Frankfurt. Remagen bridgehead expanded to a thirty-mile front, ten miles deep. All organised resistance west of the Rhine ended.

A sunny spring-like day and in the camp an air of expectancy; they would come at any moment. Yitzac had been told by his friend the *Feldwebel,* who had it from the Commandant himself, that when we heard the sirens sound five times it would mean that the tanks had broken through.

Inside the camp there was an air of stillness. Men were going about their daily affairs abstractedly, living in a transitory world which had neither depth nor real existence. I shared this feeling of unreality, but within me there was a premonition that something would stop me from getting home.

I walked about the camp mostly alone. Sometimes I would go to the French compound, attempting a few French phrases. I met a Chasseur Alpin dressed in black cape and large floppy black beret. We exchanged badges. This, however, was not the time for forming friendships. Relations were temporary, everything was impermanent. Waiting was a tedious business.

I was too far away to see what it was that was engaging the attention of the men at the wire. As I drew closer I could see that all eyes were gazing skywards. Closer still, I could see Richard, head and shoulders above the rest.

"What d'you think? One of ours?" Richard asked, pointing to a glint of wings above the trees.

I shaded my eyes against the glare of the sun. "Can't tell. Too far away."

"It's attacking something," Richard explained. "Keeps on diving down."

By the time I'd arrived the plane was too high for even the sound of the engine to reach us.

"Must be one of ours," I said. "Yitzac reckons the Jerries haven't any petrol."

The sound of the train came faintly to our ears as it slowly appeared, a black caterpillar edging out from under the cover of the trees., Smoke was billowing from its funnel as it emerged into the clearing opposite to where we were all standing, a toy train pulling along a line of toy waggons.

Now as the plane dived we could hear the thrust of its engine, the tap-tapping of its cannon, and see the line of tracer shells visible against the blackness of the trees. It climbed again, the note of its engine changing as it climbed, banked, turned and dived again. The train slowed and stopped in the middle of the clearing.

As we watched and waited the cloudless blue of the sky above us appeared empty of threat. suddenly from another direction the plane soared above the horizon and, diving down, swooped along the length of the train, its cannons firing as it disappeared over the trees.

Excited men, silent during the action, now began cheering:

"Come on, you bastards!"

The train stood quietly in the clearing. We waited for the plane to return but nothing happened and the shouting died down. The train stood motionless in the clearing. We watched in silence hoping to see a further attack. When nothing appeared to be happening men began to drift back to their huts.

There was a murmur from those nearest the wire and men who were leaving returned to see what it was. Richard and I edged our way to the front. A few wisps of smoke were coming from one of the waggons. We watched and waited and then realized that the engine had been uncoupled and was moving away. We stood watching at the wire for quite a time. Eventually I said to Richard, "I've had enough. I'm going back; have a bit of a sleep. You coming?"

"In a minute," he said.

I sat up in bed. The shock of the explosion had woken me. The floor of the hut was strewn with glass and debris. Yitzac was sitting on his bed opposite mine. He, too, had been taking an afternoon nap.

"What is it?" he asked.

Others in the hut were making for the door, some cut by flying glass, and, as Yitzac and I stepped outside, we could see men running towards the wire where Richard and I had stood watching the attack on the train.

The ground was covered with bits of wood and twisted metal and as we neared the fence we could see two men supporting a third, his head drooping forward on his chest, his arms around their necks. He was wearing a red shirt, startling red in the afternoon sunshine. As they passed I realized that the man's tunic was soaked in blood. Those nearest ran to help. Carrying him between them they moved slowly away, making for the medical hut.

Yitzac, Jock and I walked towards the perimeter fence. A wide gap had been blasted in the wire. Beyond, in the clearing where the train had been, there was no sign of the waggons. Debris, baulks of wood, twisted metal girders filled the intervening space between where the train had once stood and the fence.

Tuesday, 17 April, 1945: The American Seventh Army begins to close in on Nuremberg, fifty-five miles from Weiden.
Friday, 20 April: US Seventh Army takes Nuremberg.

The violent aftermath of the attack on the train had served to exacerbate for me the atmosphere of threat. My mind dismissed the vague worrying fear as irrational, but my body seemed to have developed a web of nerve endings sensitive to my own seemingly pre-ordained death, ready to flinch at any sudden noise or alarm.

The camp still preserved an air of frozen tranquillity despite more and more frequent signs of the approaching armies. Fighter planes had been seen on the horizon and recently there had been a spotter plane.

Every day we expected the sirens to announce the break-through of the Allied tanks, but it was eventually sounded, not by sirens, but by the heavy whirr of shells, passing so slowly overhead as to appear almost visible. The target seemed to be the town of Weiden. The gun trajectories appeared to lie over the camp and, with a touching faith in Allied artillery, we followed the passage of the shells with academic interest. The chance of one exploding short of the target appeared to occur to nobody.

Despite the signs of battle, men went about their familiar routines. Red cross provisions were no longer able to get through, but supplies within the camp were sufficient.

The end, when it came, was not at all as I had imagined. It was a warm afternoon and, as had become increasingly my habit, I was asleep in the hut. When I awoke and looked around the place seemed deserted.

It was unusual to say the least. If there was one facet of prisoner-of-war life that remained constant, it was the lack of privacy. A prisoner was rarely alone, whether in the lavatory, whether eating, whether sleeping, he was never alone.

I climbed down from the upper berth and looked around to see if there was anyone sleeping on any of the other beds. There was no one. I looked at the washroom but that, too, was empty.

I walked to the door and looked out. It was a bright sunny afternoon but there was nobody about. Nor could I hear voices or any other sign of human life.

I crossed to the neighbouring hut and, mounting the wooden step, put my head in at the open door. There a similar scene of abandonment – tin mugs, tins of food left out on the table. I knew then what had happened.

I began to walk towards the distant perimeter wire. My walk changed to a run. I passed disinfectant oven and came out into the open space beyond.

There they all were, hundreds of prisoners, backs turned towards me, standing at the wire as if on the touchline at a football match. Above their heads was the grey metal turret of an American tank. It stood outside the wire in the middle of a narrow lane that ran between the perimeter fence and the high brick wall of the barracks housing the guards.

The tank was far bigger than I had imagined. My eye was drawn to the white star painted on its side. Behind the tank were half a dozen GIs chewing gum, their faces white with dust and streaked with sweat; the prisoners this side of the fence looked on as if at a theatre.

A ragged line of German prison guards were standing in the middle of the lane threatened by the Sten guns of the Americans. As I watched, a German helmet appeared above the wall of the barrack. An American soldier swivelled on his heel, bracketing the gun to cover the man's head as it slowly rose above the wall. The watching prisoners remained silent, as if what was happening had nothing to do with them. The man scrambled over the wall and, joining the others in the road, he too put his hands behind his head.

There was a burst of firing from a distant wood. We suddenly realized that we were not merely spectators but in grave danger of being numbered among the dead or wounded.

As the guns from the wood continued to fire, the tank swivelled its gun round on its target; the bullets from the wood whining above our heads, we threw ourselves flat on the ground.

The tank's shells sped towards the SS men making a last desperate stand among the sheltering trees. Smoke began to spiral upwards from their hidden position. The firing from the wood stopped. There was silence. Slowly, one after another, we rose slowly to our feet, no longer prisoners of war but free men.

8

FREEDOM

13 April, 1945: The Nazis have forced Allied POWs to march up to 500 miles across Europe on starvation rations, according to reports published today in British newspapers. The reports allege that of 6,000 Russians, Britons and Americans who set out in January only 553 are still alive. [The Russians came from camps in Poland and the British and Americans from Stalag VIII(b), near Breslau. In January both groups marched to Gorlitz, in Silesia. In February they set out again. Most of them died of starvation, exhaustion or dysentery, and a few from the random cruelty of the guards.

The British liaison officer attached to Patton's Third Army arrived in an American jeep.

"Know you chaps want to get back to Blighty. Have to be patient. Hang on a bit longer. Soon get you home."

Many of the "chaps" were not willing to "hang on a bit longer", preferring to chance their luck and hitch-hike to Brussels. The French prisoners, too, disappeared overnight.

Yitzac, however, decided to stay, reckoning that the roads would be full of tanks armoured cars and lorries, all of them heading in the wrong direction. I rather suspected, though, that he was eager to explore the town. Being Yitzac, he was soon able to persuade us to follow his lead.

"You are so big travellers, you don't want to see how other peoples live?" he said.

The streets appeared untouched by war, the solid houses undamaged, and its sedate citizens well-dressed and well-fed. The shells passing over the prisoner-of-war camp had clearly not been aimed at Weiden.

Yitzac, although Palestinian, was in fact a native-born German. This town, which for Jock and myself was strange and hostile, was for Yitzac, despite a Nazi philosophy expressing the contrary, his cultural home ground.

In British uniform, he homed into the little town like a bee into its hive. With his ability to speak the language he had little difficulty in making friends. He was eager for Jock and myself to meet them.

Walking in Yitzac's wake, it was, as far as I was concerned, sufficient to be free. After years of living in a barbed-wire compound, walking along a street was in itself a delight to be savoured.

Frau Erchlinger, whose husband had been killed fighting on the Russian front, lived by herself in a small block of flats. I was vague as to the reasons for our visiting her, but Yitzac insisted we go with him.

The lady seemed surprised that he had brought along two uninvited guests. The room was small and over-furnished and it was difficult to move without knocking into small tables laden with family photos and bric-a-brac. Jock and I sat side by side on stiff-backed chairs, ill at ease.

It seemed strangely immoral, that I, a Jew, should be sitting there. Yet I found it difficult, looking at this woman, to feel animosity towards her.

Seeing her in her own home, seeing the small tables covered with family portraits, and sensing the pain she had suffered from the loss of her husband, I was too conscious of her human qualities to be able to attribute to her the barbarous horrors her country had inflicted on defenceless minorities.

Although an Englishman by birth, by language, by education and culture, I was tied by ancestry to the long, proud history of the Jewish people, and deeply resentful of the anti-semitism which found its iniquitous depths in the rise of Hitler. However, glimpses I had had of the once civilised nation that lay beneath the evil machinery of Hitlerian philosophy, had tempered, to some degree, my hatred and outrage for all things German.

Yitzac, also Jewish and driven by the Nazis from his home, reacted differently, appearing to share few of my feelings. On the contrary, he treated the flat and its owner as if both belonged to him. He pointed with pride to the curtains, the carpet and trinkets and asked us to make a guess as to their value, a request we both hastily declined.

Having helped the lady to serve the coffee and cakes, he perched heavily on the arm of her chair. For the first time I saw Yitzac in a new light as he listened quietly to her story with what seemed genuine sympathy.

The visit over, I asked him why he had felt it necessary for us to accompany him. Unabashed, but a little defensively I thought, Yitzac smiled. "What's the hurry!" he said. "You going somewhere? I introduce you to nice lady, not to Adolf Hitler. Germans, you know, are not all bad peoples."

The next day I stood in the middle of the empty street chatting to a young American soldier of about my age. Frau Erchlinger came along the pavement opposite carrying two heavy shopping bags. Recognizing me, she stopped, put down her shopping and waved with friendly enthusiasm. I crossed to where she was standing.

"*Guten Tag.*" I said politely.

"*Guten Tag,*" she replied.

The conversation lapsed. I knew no German phrases that would cover the situation. I could have asked her for a cigarette or a light, or at a pinch for some potatoes, but these phrases seemed hardly suitable.

She, on the other hand, made her intentions quite clear, indicating with a gentle movement of her head and a friendly smile the bag she had put down on the pavement. Being normally of an amiable disposition, I should have been pleased to carry her bag. However, fraternization in front of a witness when a lady is inviting you home to bed was one thing, but when it was merely a question of getting you to carry her shopping, that was asking too much.

Frau Erchlinger seemed surprised, shrugged her shoulders, blushed and, clearly offended, picked up her bag and without a word walked off.

The young American looked on enviously. Noting his expression, and although inwardly ashamed of my behaviour, I tried to make it appear as if it were an everyday occurrence for young women to stop me in the street and plead with me to take them home.

"Gee!" said the American. "I sure wish I could speak the lingo!"

"Oh, I don't know," I said modestly. "I'm not really fluent."

"You sure knew how to chat that baby up! What she after?"

Veracity being defeated by my desire to seem a man of the world, I said, "She wanted me to go home with her, I suppose," and added, "but you can have too much of that kind of thing, can't you?"

"Gee!" said the American hesitantly, "I guess!"

Wednesday, 15 April, 1945: Berlin completely surrounded by Russians.

Once in a moment of reckless disclosure I had confessed under Yitzac's relentless probing that, although I had had many girl friends, I had never, "gone all the way".

Some days later, with some trepidation, Jock and I followed Yitzac into a seemingly deserted building. Passing through what must have been the reception area we saw in the far corner of the room a grilled gate leading to the cells.

"Come on!" he said. "Through here!" Yitzac surged through the gate and along the dark passage followed meekly by the two of us. The cell doors were all unlocked and the girls, having as yet nowhere to stay, were using the prison, their erstwhile home, as a hotel.

We three were not the only visitors. In one of the first cells we passed, chatting sedately with some of the former girl-prisoners, I recognized a group of the "elite" from the camp, those whose authority I had usurped as the elected camp-leader. There was no exchange of greetings as they looked up; both groups eyed each other with distaste and suspicion.

As we passed down the long corridor there were some cells whose ambience was less sedate, girls giggling together as they passed round bottles of beer and schnapps, presents from visitors. The air was thick with cigarette smoke.

As we neared the end of the passage we could hear, above the general babble of conversation and explosions of laughter, the thin soprano voice of a girl singing in English;

"You make me happy, ven skies are grey,
I only know dear, how much I luff you,
Pliss don't take mein sunshine av . . . ay."

The singer was a blond, curvaceous girl in her twenties, who, when Yitzac appeared, jumped up and threw her arms around his neck and drew him by the hand to take a seat beside her on the bed. With much formality, he introduced us to her and her two friends.

I sat down next to one of the girls, dark, with a slight moustache and a bad complexion. My attention, however, was turned entirely towards Yitzac's girlfriend. I cast envious glances at her ample bosom, pretty round face and rosebud lips. She was a vivacious young lady and well aware of the admiration she had aroused.

The girl next to Jock looked thin and ill, her hair in lacklustre disarray around her head; her fingers to her mouth, she bit her nails with a nervous intensity. As Jock sat down beside her, she shrank away and, springing to her feet, fled with a torrent of German to the blond girl's side, pushing between her and Yitzac.

"What's wrong with her?" Jock asked.

"Don't worry," said Yitzac, "she's a little *meshugge*. She thinks everyone wants to rape her."

"She should be so lucky," murmured Jock.

The girls, so they claimed, had been imprisoned by the Germans for fraternizing with English prisoners of war. Magda, Yitzac's girlfriend, explained in a mixture of English and German, the indignities they had suffered. My attention was fixed on the palpitating bosom and the rosebud mouth.

The dark girl sitting next to me, sensing where my interest lay, began to exchange meaningful glances with Jock, who was not slow to respond.

"You pilot?" Magda cooed, putting her hand on my knee. I nodded, not feeling capable linguistically of entering into distinctions between the different kinds of aircrew, and content to assume, under the circumstances, the glamour of pilot rather than the more humdrum rôle of wireless-operator.

"You are brave man," Magda continued. I shrugged my shoulders modestly, now more and more enamoured.

"We find you nice girl," she said.

Jock by this time had a friendly arm around the dark girl who, unnoticed by me, had changed places and was now sitting at Jock's side. The third girl, seemingly distraught, was still biting her finger-nails and from time to time flinging her arms around Magda's neck.

Yitzac smiled benevolently on the scene, encouraging Magda in her advances.

"She likes you," he assured me. "What am I telling you?" Pink in the face, I nodded, my glances conveying to Magda more than any trite phrase my feelings towards her. She had become the epitome of all desire.

"When are we seeing them again?" I asked.

"This afternoon. They are moving to a hotel. They wait for us," Yitzac promised.

The hotel was in fact a large boarding house. That afternoon Magda and the dark girl were waiting for us in a musty sitting-room. The two girls had managed to find new dresses. A faint perfume filled the air.

I had eyes only for Magda, and certainly no thought for Yitzac, thinking of him only as a provider of delight rather than a rival suitor. As she stood up and leant against the piano her blouse clung closely to the full outline of her breasts. She opened the piano and fingered the notes.

"Play, Magda, play!" commanded Yitzac. She sat at the piano and, accompanying herself, she sang;

"You are my sunshine, mein only sunshine,
You make me 'appy, ven skies are grey
I only know dear, 'ow much I luf you.
Pliss don' take mein sunshine a . . . vey."

She rose from the piano, crossed the room and sat on the arm of my chair. I was conscious of nothing but the heavenly creature poised beside me. I could smell her perfume, and, as I turned my head, my cheek brushed the firm silky cloth at her breast. I looked at Yitzac.

"What happens now?" I asked.

Yitzac came over and whispered in Magda's ear. She turned to me and stroked the back of my neck.

"I find nice girl for you," she whispered.

"What does she mean?" I asked.

"Her friend is coming soon. She wants to meet you. She is crazy about Englishman," Yitzac explained. I frowned.

"I thought I was going with ..." My voice faltered.

"No, 'Arry," said Magda, "I too old for young man. You like better this girl. She very pretty, young, like you."

I was filled with jealousy, disappointment and confusion. I stood up and walked away, my face burning, trying hard to appear unmoved.

Magda rose and walked over to me and began to sing her song in a whisper, specially for me;

"You are my sunshine, mein only sunshine ..."

I knew that pride demanded I walk away, but I remained where I was.

"You like this girl, 'Arry. I choose her for you myself," she whispered.

There was for me a long miserable silence. Magda crossed the room and had a whispered conversation with Yitzac.

There was the sound of a door opening and shutting and footsteps. She stood in the doorway, her dark hair plaited in coils around her head, her eyes almond-shaped, high cheek-bones, delicate nose. Surely they couldn't mean this girl! She was a goddess! A girl like that couldn't possibly want me.

Magda crossed the room and, taking my hand, led me towards the girl who stood composedly in the centre of the room.

"This is 'Arry. He is pilot. English pilot."

The goddess smiled and, taking my hand in a bone-crushing grip, shook it vigorously.

"How do you do?" she said. "I am pleased to be meeting with you." She turned to Magda and began a long involved explanation.

I stood in the centre of the room, uncomprehending, by their side. I was sure she was making some excuse. Now she had seen me she was crying off. Words were ready on the tip of my tongue, words in defence. I didn't like her, didn't want her, didn't care. Magda turned to Yitzac, explaining at some length. He turned towards me.

"You mustn't be upset," he began. My heart sank. "The girl is very young ..."

I quickly interrupted. "Look, this was your idea. I didn't want ..."

"No!" said Yitzac. "You don't understand. The girl she want you very much, but she has old lady who is looking after her. She cannot come straight away. She says you must go to her bedroom and wait. She will come later, when the old lady goes to bed."

I smiled, turned to the girl and nodding vigorously, said,

"*Verstehe. Ich verstehe.*"

I lay in bed, naked, waiting for the girl. My body seemed to float in the warm enveloping softness of sheets, pillows and heavy quilted eiderdown.

Through the thin walls I could hear every movement in the room next door where Magda and Yitzac were together. I could hear the girl's light laughter, the low vibration of his voice and the creaking of the bed beneath their weight. I imagined Magda's round softness.

For years in the dark loneliness of my prisoner-of-war bed my imagination had conjured up companions to bring consolation and delight. I had at my command the power to evoke any woman I desired. My hands caressing my own body would feel the firm flesh of the dream-creature summoned for my pleasure. She could in turn be capricious, timid, passionate, and I, cruel, tenderly loving.

My mind would invent a face, words, cries. My body would respond, reach a climax, thrusting against the hard unyielding mattress of canvas and straw. The bursting rush of semen would bring peace, but a peace tempered with feelings of guilt.

My mind could now engage a real flesh and blood creature. I could see the German girl's face, her eyes, her hair, her breasts. I imagined her as she entered the room, undressing, getting into bed, the first contact of our bodies.

The habit of those years took over. My body refused to wait; my mind inventing sights and moans, I thrust again and again against soft imagined flesh. Too late! I felt my manhood burst from me, leaving nothing but the panicky realization that all desire had gone and the girl had yet to come to bed.

Next morning after a sleepless night of impotence and frustration on my part, and kindly, uncomplaining tolerance on that of the girl, hand in hand we descended the staircase together.

Yitzac and Magda stood below smiling sentimentally up at us, like proud parents. We acted out our rôle, I put my arm around the girl's waist; she leant her head against my shoulder.

EPILOGUE

An American lorry, packed with released prisoners-of-war, trundled along narrow roads heading for Nuremberg. Crowded together in the jolting vehicle, the men had difficulty in maintaining balance as the lorry navigated a road surface scarred and broken by the metal tracks of heavy tanks. I stood precariously at the tail-gate, gripping the metal frame of the canvas roof, my eyes and nose filled with dust and exhaust fumes.

As we entered the city, we followed a road cleared through the ruins of the town. The broken skeletons of isolated buildings stood dotted here and there in the devastated landscape. The rubble – brick, stone, twisted girders – had been bulldozed back to form on either side of the road, orderly, continuous embankments, pierced at regular intervals by dark square holes dug by the rescue squads.

The excitement and joy of this first stage on the journey home momentarily abated.

The Dakota flew low beneath heavy rain clouds, dropping and bucking disconcertingly. Sitting on the floor of the plane, the only airman among a crowd of soldiers, I felt sick and scared, more conscious, perhaps, than most, of the thin fragile floor beneath me.

It was difficult to block from my mind our last flight, the burning engine, my dead crew.

"All right for you," my companions commented, "you're used to it."

I tried desperately to control the waves of nausea which possessed me.

In Brussels, the final staging-post, I obtained permission from the officer commanding the unit to stay a few days before returning home.

I visited the flat at Woluwé St Lambert where I had been arrested. I stood before the door on the metal landing of the gallery where, more than two years earlier, I had been brought by Monsieur Walters.

I remembered the dark eyes of Monsieur Kauffmann suspiciously eyeing us through the narrow gap of the partially opened door, and next morning, the nervus rictus on his wife's face as she looked over the German's shoulder, as, his pistol levelled, I stood before him, my hands raised above my head.

I could get no reply, but I learnt from neighbours that they had not yet returned from the concentration camps to which they had been sent, she to Ravensbrück, he to Dachau.

Two years later I returned to Brussels and lived with them in their flat for six months.

I was more fortunate in seeking out Monsieur and Madame Walters, the young couple who had sheltered me that first night when I arrived from the Belgian countryside with my young guide, Gérard.

They had both survived unharmed, having had a narrow escape. The very morning of my arrest Monsieur Walters was on his way to the Kauffmans' flat to bring me the white, air-crew sweater which I had left behind.

On turning the corner he saw the black saloon car of the German *Feldpolizei* parked outside and, a few seconds later, he saw me, pistol held to my back, being led to the car by two Germans.

He returned to his wife and the two of them left immediately for Vichy France, where they lived safely before returning at the liberation of Brussels.

He learnt later that the chief of his organization, a Belgian, had been in the pay of the Germans and had informed on both the Walters and the Kauffmanns. It was this man who had given them each half of the torn playing card.

I now needed to find out what had happened to Dr and Madame Vekeman, who had sheltered me for nearly a week in the attic of their villa in Limburg, where I had been shot down.

The Belgian railway system was not functioning nor was there any other means of transport. I was, however, fortunate to meet with a young American officer. Over a beer we became good friends and I told him something of my story. I explained that I was eager to see the family who had hidden me, but that it seemed an impossible task, as roads were in a terrible condition and there seemed to be no means of getting there.

The next day we set out for the Vekemans' house in a jeep the American had commandeered. The road had been chewed up by tanks, as had most of the roads at that time, and we jolted along most of the way, the jeep at an acute angle to the ground.

We found the Vekemans safe and sound, and they greeted both of us with great excitement. Madame whispered to me that she thought the young American "vairy 'ansom," which rather put my nose out of joint.

However, Mérèse, now a young lady of about seventeen, soon soothed my ruffled feelings. She now spoke English fluently, but with an American accent.

We escaped as quickly as we could from the table where the family had fêted the American and myself, and, hand in hand, made for the field into which, on the 1st of August nearly three years previously, I had landed.

We talked, looked into each other's eyes, and spoke of the English lessons I had given her and of the night I had fled from the house.

They had, she said, listened night after night to the B.B.C. hoping to hear the message, "The blue bird has escaped from its cage". As the days passed without hearing anything they began to fear that I had been captured and that the Gestapo might arrive at any time.

Dr Vekeman looked with a somewhat jaundiced eye when Mérèse and I returned to the house, and I realized that he was not impressed with the idea of this ragged youth, not an officer and Jewish to boot, forming any relationship with his daughter.

Some years later when I was living at the Kauffmanns' flat in Brussels, I received a letter from Mérèse, but I, perhaps out of pique, didn't reply.

The plane with its cargo of ex-prisoners-of-war landed on an air-strip in the South of England. The multi-coloured triangular flags strung above the hangar where we were to be debriefed drooped miserably in the soft English rain. I was home.

APPENDICES

1. Telegram to Harry's parents saying that he is missing.

2. A letter from his Squadron Commander enlarging on the telegram.

3. Lady Ampthill, of the Red Cross, writes to a friend of Harry's parents.

4. The last page from the author's log-book.

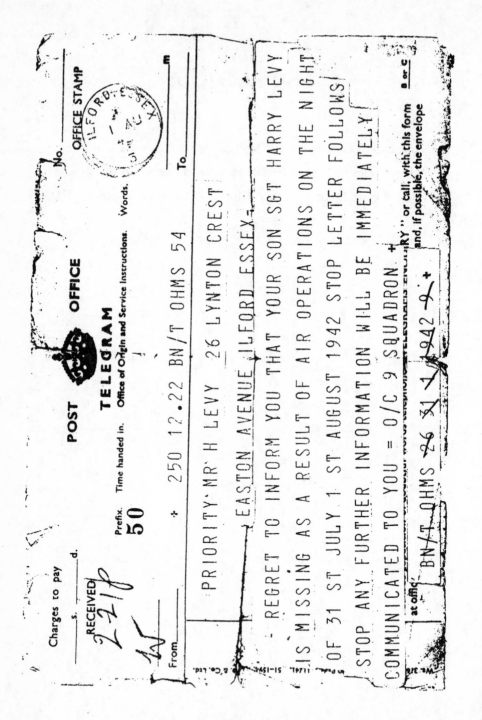

POST OFFICE

TELEGRAM

Charges to pay

s.   d.

RECEIVED

Prefix. 50

Time handed in.

Office of Origin and Service Instructions.   Words.

No.

OFFICE STAMP

ILFORD ESSEX

To.

From

◆ 250 12.22 BN/T OHMS 54

PRIORITY·MR· H LEVY 26 LYNTON CREST

EASTON AVENUE ILFORD ESSEX=

REGRET TO INFORM YOU THAT YOUR SON SGT HARRY LEVY

IS MISSING AS A RESULT OF AIR OPERATIONS ON THE NIGHT

OF 31 ST JULY 1 ST AUGUST 1942 STOP LETTER FOLLOWS

STOP ANY FURTHER INFORMATION WILL BE IMMEDIATELY

COMMUNICATED TO YOU = O/C 9 SQUADRON +

at offic·   BN/T OHMS 26 31 1 1942 9 +

B or C

·············RY·· or call. with this form
and, if possible, the envelope

No. 9 Squadron,
Royal Air Force,
Honington, Suffolk.
3rd August, 1942.

Dear *Mr Levy*,

It is with deep regret that I have to confirm the news that your son, Sergeant Harry Levy, is missing as a result of air operations on the night of 31st July/1st August, 1942.

I know you would wish to have all possible information, but unfortunately there is little I can tell you. Your son was the Wireless Operator of an aircraft engaged on a bombing raid against a target in Germany and nothing was heard of the aircraft after take-off. All we can do is hope that he and the crew are prisoners of war. It will be anything from 3 to 5 weeks before we can expect to hear any news through the Red Cross. I realise what a terribly anxious time this will be for you, and you have all the sympathy of myself, the officers and men of the Squadron.

Your son was a very efficient Wireless Operator, and his loss is a great blow to us. He was very popular with everyone in the Squadron. The captain of the aircraft was a very able pilot and I have great hopes of his being able to save the crew.

Please let me know at once if there is anything I can do for you. You will, of course, be informed immediately of any further news.

Yours *sincerely*,

J m Smith. W.C.

WING COMMANDER, COMMANDING
NO. 9 SQUADRON, HONINGTON.

Mr. J. Levy,
25, Lynton Crest,
Eastern Avenue,
Ilford, Essex.

President:
HER MAJESTY THE QUEEN.

Grand Prior:
H.R.H. THE DUKE OF GLOUCESTER, K.G.

WOUNDED, MISSING AND RELATIVES DEPARTMENT

Chairman:
THE DOWAGER LADY AMPTHILL, C.I., G.B.E.

TELEPHONE NO.:
SLOANE 9666

TELEGRAPHIC ADDRESS:
"WOMIREL, KNIGHTS, LONDON"

In replying please quote reference: FM
RAF/C. 3769

7 BELGRAVE SQUARE
LONDON, S.W.1

22nd October, 1942.

Dear Mr. Barbarasch,

With reference to the enquiry which you made here in our Interviewing Room yesterday for Sergeant H. Levy, 1270422, on behalf of his parents, we very much regret to tell you that we have so far received no news of him.

We are writing to you, however, to send you some news, which has reached us from the International Red Cross Committee at Geneva, concerning the aircraft crew of which Sergeant Levy was a member, and while we feel we should not be justified in withholding it from his parents, it is, we fear, of a very grave nature.

A cable sent by the International Red Cross Committee at Geneva, quoting official German information, states that Sergeant Miller, Sergeant Martin, Sergeant Hall and one unknown airman lost their lives.

As a result of this information, the Air Ministry have posted the above three men, whose names are given, as missing, believed killed in action, but as the other man mentioned is unidentified and the remaining member of the crew is unaccounted for, they must both be regarded as still missing until some further information is received.

We realise that this letter must only add to Mr. and Mrs. Levy's grave anxiety for their son and can only ask you to assure them that if any news reaches us in reply to the further enquiries being made, we will not fail to let them know.

We would also like to convey to them our most sincere sympathy at this anxious and distressing time.

Yours sincerely,

Margaret Ampthill
pp ew

Chairman.

B. Barbarasch, Esq.,
102, Forburg Road,
Upper Clapton, N.16.

SQUADRON

Time carried forward :— | 110·10 | 94·30

REMARKS (including results of bombing, gunnery, exercises, etc.)	Flying Times	
	Day	Night
TR CROSS COUNTRY	1·45	
AIR TEST	·35	
OPERATIONS TO HAMBURG 1 x 4000		6:15
AIR TEST	·40	
OPERATIONS TO HAMBURG 1 x 4000		6·00
AIR TEST	·25	
Missing on operation		
Total times	114·35	106·45

[signature] Fl/S/LDR

O/c "B" FLT.

TOTAL TIME ...		